"[Butler] . . . synthesizes and carries forward the work of analysts including Albert Ellis and Eric Berne, and presents a workable method for improving how we talk to ourselves." — *Vogue*

"*Talking to Yourself* shows us how to communicate with ourselves honestly, build self-esteem, relieve stress, and generally create success in every area of life. The author very accurately states, 'There is a person with whom you spend more time than any other. . . . This ever-present companion is your own self.'" — *Yoga Journal*

"One of the best books I know of for teaching clients about monitoring what they say to themselves."
— Steven Zlutnick, Ph.D., Department of Counseling Psychology, University of San Francisco

"*Talking to Yourself* is a clearly written, popular version of a theoretical approach that explains the effects of 'voices' that hurt people and seriously limit their lives."
— Robert W. Firestone, Ph. D., author of *The Fantasy Bond* and *Voice Therapy*

"Dr. Butler's book is a major contribution to the field of being human. She teaches us how to diagnose and change our internal conversations so each one of us can become who we really are."
— Ruth McClendon, M.S.W., psychotherapist

"A must for every self-development library. As usual, Dr. Butler offers easy-to-follow, mer
— Maria Arapakis, aut
How to Speak Up, Set Li
Losing Your Lover, Your

"*Talking to Yourself* shows you how to become aware of your on-going inner dialogue — the conversations we all have with ourselves that can make our lives constricted and painful, or expansive and joyous. This is a no-nonsense book with a wealth of important, practical applications."
> —Martin L. Rossman, M.D., author of
> *Healing Yourself: A Step-By-Step Program for Better Health Through Imagery*

"Dr. Butler has developed a program to help people become aware of their negative thinking and talk and change it into positive self-talk to their own advantage. It's a great book that all people with a problem of self-talk should read and digest."
> —Arthur B. Hardy, M.D., author of *Agoraphobia: Symptoms, Courses, and Treatment*

"*Talking to Yourself* is the one book I recommend to all my clients. They consistently report that this book explains and demonstrates the influence of their internal self-talk on their behavior. I have observed many individuals begin to understand why they have been stalled for years despite making great efforts to change their behavior patterns."
> —Michael J. Corley, Ph.D., author of *Goal Achievement Training*

"Butler's methods for transforming inner voices from negative to positive are simple, elegant, and profoundly effective. If you are ready to exchange your relentless internal critic for a patient, encouraging guide, read this book."
> —Kay Leigh Hagan, author of *Internal Affairs: A Journalkeeping Workbook for Self-Intimacy*

Talking to
Yourself

ALSO BY PAMELA E. BUTLER

Self-Assertion for Women

Talking to Yourself

Learning the Language of Self-Affirmation

Revised Edition

PAMELA E. BUTLER

HarperSanFrancisco

A Division of HarperCollins*Publishers*

While each case history is true, some are composites, and all names and identifying information have been altered to protect individual privacy. The significant inner (self-talk) process has been carefully preserved.

Library of Congress Cataloging-in-Publication Data

Butler, Pamela.
    Talking to yourself : learning the language of self-affirmation / Pamela E. Butler. — Rev. ed.
        p.   cm.
    Includes bibliographical references and index.
    ISBN 0–06–250119–4
    1. Self-talk.   I. Title.
BF697.5.S47B88   1991
158'.1 — dc20
                                              90–55809
                                                CIP

91 92 93 94 95 M-V 10 9 8 7 6 5 4 3 2 1

This edition is printed on acid-free paper that meets the American National Standards Institute Z39.48 Standard.

To my clients,

*who taught me about the
judgmental structure
and showed me the sunshine
underneath*

Because people who "talk to themselves" are thought to be crazy, nearly everyone has an injunction against listening to the voices in his head. This is a faculty which can be quickly recovered, however, if the proper permission is given. Then almost anyone can listen in on his own internal dialogues.

Eric Berne, *What Do You Say After You Say Hello?*

■■■■■■
Contents

1

The Self-Dialogue   3

The Cognitive-Behavioral Approach, Internal vs.
External Reality, The Self-Talk Factor, The Intrinsic Self
vs. The Imposed Self

2

The Self 2 Judge   13

The Judgmental Structure, Drivers, Stoppers,
Confusers, From Judge to Guide, So What Does This
Mean to Me?

3

Drivers   22

Be Perfect, Hurry Up, Be Strong, Please Others, Try
Hard, Driver-Related Costs, Your Driver Profile

9

Obstacles to Self-Support   146

A Negative Belief System, The Second Line of
Defense, Driver Interference, False Pride, Practicing
Your New Language

10

Talking Yourself into Anger   158

Driver-Generated Anger, Anger-Generated Stoppers,
Anger-Generating Confusers, A Final Word

11

Self-Talk and the Rescue Process   178

The Chrysalis and the Butterfly, Rescuing Defined,
The Drama Triangle, The Price You Pay, The Price They
Pay, True Victims, The Rescue Beliefs, Anti-Rescue
Self-Talk, The Recovery: Facing the Void, The
Necessity of Grief, Self-Renewal

12

Sex and Self-Talk   208

Sex and *Shoulds*, Sex and Stoppers

13

Male Self-Talk–Female Self-Talk   226

Sex-Role Messages, Sex-Role Costs, Breaking Out

■■■■■■■
Preface to the Revised Edition

In the almost ten years since *Talking to Yourself* was first published, two phenomenal revolutions have occurred. The first of these has been in health care, where the new branch of medicine referred to as psychoneuroimmunology has documented at the biochemical and cellular level the interactions between the brain (thoughts and emotions) and the endocrine and immune system. Not only has it demonstrated that negative thoughts and emotions produce negative changes in the body but also that there is a relationship between overcoming depression and regaining health. Patients who decreased depression and despair showed significant increases in cancer-fighting immune cells. We now more clearly than ever have information that self-talk influences our living or dying.

In a second revolution, the Adult Children of Alcoholics (ACA) and other 12-Step programs have advanced like wildfire, vastly increasing the numbers of people who are actively involved in changing and healing themselves. John Bradshaw's program *The Family* televised on the Public Broadcasting Network gave millions of people a chance to acquaint themselves with the new psychological developments of the past decade.

I feel that *Talking to Yourself* has had a positive impact on both of these revolutions, presenting a simple, straightforward message of how to change your self-talk and thereby change your life. Upon rereading my book recently for the second edition update, I was impressed at how timely and clear-cut its message still is. Personal feedback from readers — about *Talking to Yourself* being one of the most important books they have ever read — took on a deeper reality as I stepped back and listened to my ten-year-ago self.

Because of this, I have changed very little of the original text. However, in constructing the second edition, I have made what I consider to be several important additions. The first is a chapter on the Rescue Process. This pervasive process, and the self-talk through which it is maintained, is surely one of the most pernicious and crippling syndromes experienced in our society. What's more, a vast majority of individuals operate from this destructive belief system.

A second major addition is a chapter called "The Development of Negative Self-Talk." For those people interested in how one's toxic inner companion comes into existence, I believe that this chapter will surprise you, and lead you both to understand and to appreciate the early development of what I have called the Judge.

In chapter 7, "The Language of Self-Support," four additional Permissions are outlined and discussed. The chapter previously entitled "Committing to Yourself" has been changed and expanded under the title "Listening to Yourself" (chapter 15). Here is new and exciting information on how to communicate with your Intrinsic or Real Self through the understanding of dreams, images, and symptoms.

Finally, I have included several additional visual diagrams. In my own consulting room, I always have a chalkboard on which to draw out illustrations of various concepts. I hope the ones added in the new edition will clarify the ideas in this book and increase your understanding of them.

■ ■ ■ ■ ■ ■ ■
Preface

WE live in a time of escape — through drugs, alcohol, smoking, overwork — escapes that often cause as many problems in the long run as they ameliorate in the short. The physical and psychological damage caused by these ill-fated attempts at feeling good, or at least not so bad, costs us billions of dollars and untold suffering. And what are we escaping from when we tranquilize ourselves with painkillers and mood-altering drugs, consume too many drinks, and work murderous fifteen-hour days in the corporate climb?

You may be surprised by the answer. Most frequently, we seek to escape from ourselves, or more specifically, from the part of us that pushes, nags, criticizes, judges, punishes, and in most respects, makes our lives miserable. This is Self 2, the Imposed Self. For many of us, it is the self that dominates. To forego the tranquilizer or the 6 o'clock martini would require us to confront the consequences of running our lives in accordance with the messages of this imposed self. We would have to confront the very genuine pain, sadness, and rage that occur when we act against our real feelings and needs. We would, in short, become aware of another self, one whom we have tried to subdue. This self truly reflects our inner being, and unbeknownst to most of us, it is our dearest friend and best ally. The emergence of this Intrinsic Self, Self 1, is the focus of this book.

Learning to listen to and honor the Intrinsic Self is not easy. Strong rules and prohibitions stand in opposition. These rules and prohibitions create a judgmental structure that directs us in hundreds of subtle ways, pushing us from aliveness into despair. This structure affects our feelings, our behaviors, and our self-esteem, exerting its control on a day-to-day, moment-by-moment basis, through the mechanism of our self-talk. Self-talk, the constant internal dialogue, is the prop by which the judgmental structure is upheld.

One of my clients describes the process well: "I used to criticize myself constantly. There were no periods, no semi-colons, no pauses whatsoever." In other words, her critical Self 2 was all-pervasive. "I wonder now, how I made it through all of those years."

Her question is well taken, because many people kill themselves as a result of their rigid structures, not only through suicide, but also by the slower process of overstressing that ultimately results in life-threatening illness. The well-known book, Friedman and Rosenman's *Type A Behavior and Your Heart,* describes how self-induced pressure, which is the end result of certain judgmental attitudes and beliefs, can lead to heart disease. And in *Getting Well Again,* Carl and Stephanie Simonton, along with James Creighton, note that the development of cancer has often been preceded by life stresses with which an individual believes he or she cannot deal. The Simontons note that this inability to cope occurs because a person "sees no way of changing the rules about how he or she must act and so feels helpless to resolve the problem." These rules usually include intense pressures to succeed through work and strong prohibitions against expressing emotions and taking care of oneself.

Life-threatening illness gives some people the permission to alter these rules. Pushed to the wall, the judgmental structure begins to crack. It is my belief that such positive changes in beliefs and attitudes can also occur without such catastrophes, that the experience of milder forms of self-warnings, if one learns to listen, is sufficient. Many of us will be able to revise the rules by which we live our lives simply by taking seriously the inner messages of Self 1—messages given us through our feelings, our intuitions, our images, and our dreams.

It is also my belief that such changes will do more than prevent dread physical disease or psychological despair. Altering our internal structures by changing our day-to-day self-talk will lead to optimal levels of well-being. We can become what Carl Simonton speaks of as "weller than well." A good illustration of this phenomenon comes again from my client, whom I have quoted before. When she had broken the back of her judgmental structure and had eliminated her negative self-talk, she reported, "I feel like someone who has just had a brick taken off her head. I feel so light. I can't believe that this feeling is natural, but I know that it is. I've spent thirty-five years with a brick on my head, holding me down, and now I'm free."

Without the weight of our Self 2 demands and warnings, we *are* free to function in a way that many of us have never anticipated—free to have fun, free to enjoy our lives, and free to connect with people who share our energy and vitality. *Talking to Yourself* gives you a method for change, a means of shifting the balance between Self 1 and Self 2 and of evaluating and discarding those Self 2 messages that work against your own life force and life direction. Let me now encourage you to examine your self-talk. It is the key to discovering what is hindering your development and what you must do to support and nurture your real self.

Acknowledgments

To the investigators and therapists who recognized the importance of what we tell ourselves in determining what we feel and what we do, I acknowledge my debt. Foremost among the cognitive pioneers who influenced this book are Karen Horney, Albert Ellis, Eric Berne, Aaron Beck, R. S. Lazarus, Donald Meichenbaum, Bob Goulding, and Mary Goulding. I would especially like to thank Shirley Luthman for her willingness to share her insights about the judgmental position and the emergence from it, and Dr. Karen Mashkin for her comments about internalization and externalization.

To my clients, those women and men with whom I have worked in individual therapy and in assertiveness and "Talking to Yourself" workshops; you have taught me more than anyone about self-talk and the influence that it has.

To Dr. Geri Alpert, Mary Hidalgo, and Nancy Wolfberg, thanks for your ideas and suggestions.

To Tom Grady, my editor at Harper San Francisco, thanks for your helpful input and your enthusiasm for creating this second edition. Thanks also to Kevin Bentley for your involvement in the numerous details this revision entailed.

Finally, to Clayton Smith, my husband, I want to express my gratitude for your tireless help in preparing the new manuscript, your profound insights into the workings of the inner self, and particularly for your special support for me.

Introduction

THERE is a person with whom you spend more time than any other, a person who has more influence over you, and more ability to interfere with or to support your growth than anyone else. This ever-present companion is your own self. As the creator of your internal environment, this self guides you or criticizes you, gives or withholds permission to you, belittles or supports you.

This internal figure has many names: superego, conscience, inner custodian, top dog, parent-part, witch-mother, value system. But whatever the name, you experience this inner self as a distinct person speaking to you. You engage with this person in an ever-constant dialogue, a dialogue that has extreme significance. It is through this internal dialogue that you make decisions, set goals for yourself, feel pleased and satisfied, dejected or despondent. In short, your behavior, your feelings, your sense of self-esteem, and even your level of stress are influenced by your inner speech. It is this dialogue, this talk with yourself, that this book is all about.

1
The Self-Dialogue

WE all talk to ourselves. What we say determines the direction and quality of our lives. Our self-talk can make the difference between happiness and despair, between self-confidence and self-doubt. Altering your self-talk may be the most important undertaking you will ever begin.

James is s 32-year-old junior college instructor. He is married and has two children. James basically enjoys his life, particularly in the summer, when his school load is light and he has time to pursue the activities he most enjoys — golf and tennis. This summer, however, James has reluctantly decided not to teach. He has instead committed himself to completing his dissertation. Several of James's friends have teasingly berated him for having too much of the good life — a three-month vacation — but James has shrugged off these comments instead of enjoying them as he ordinarily would. The fact is that James is experiencing an all-too-familiar dread as his "free" summer approaches.

James has tried to complete his dissertation before. He has often pulled out his research only to sit looking at the papers before him until sufficiently depressed to throw them back into his filing cabinet and avoid the entire topic for another month.

If we were able to listen to James's thoughts as he sits staring at his papers, we would probably hear something like this:

"You've got to get going on this."

"I know, I know, but I'll never get this stuff organized."

"You're not going to get anywhere if you don't. Think of Martha and the kids."

"I don't know how to sort this out. I've forgotten half of it."

"You're just being lazy."

"I'm tired."

"What are you going to tell everyone — that you don't have it in you? Some model you are as a teacher."

"I don't care. It's too hard." *(Putting his data aside.)* "I can't do it."

Although James doesn't realize it, his main problem is not with his dissertation material. It is not with the mass of figures he just can't seem to sort out. James's problem lies within himself. His self-dialogue — his inner conversation — is immobilizing him. As one part of his self commands, "You've got to get going on this. You're lazy," another part argues, "I'm tired. I just can't do it." James is at an impasse, a fight with himself that makes any productive work on his dissertation impossible.

A dialogue different in form, but similar in effect, is going on with Carole. Carole sees herself as an attractive, intelligent, articulate woman — at work, with friends, in almost all situations, in fact, except those involving her husband Charles. With Charles, Carole doesn't like herself very much. Although she tries to be a model wife, constantly pushing herself to please her husband, she ends up feeling hurt and angry. Carole doesn't really like the way Charles treats her. Yet her few attempts at discussing her negative feelings with him have been met with counterattacks — "You're just being selfish" or "That's absurd" — which Carole finds no way of contradicting. So most of the time she gives in, subordinating her own inclinations to those of Charles.

Interestingly, Carole's inner speech, her dialogue with herself, sounds something like her communication with Charles. What begins as the registering of complaints usually ends in severe self-reproach. It usually goes something like this:

"Charles is really putting me down tonight. According to him, I don't do anything right. I'm tired of his criticism. I don't deserve it."

"Oh, stop being so sensitive. Charles is tired. He's been working hard."

"Well, maybe so, but I work hard too."

"Come on, now, you're just being a martyr. You're lucky to have someone like Charles. He's going to get tired of you if you're not careful."

"I guess so."

"Why don't you take him a cup of coffee. Maybe if you were a more considerate wife, he'd be a better husband."

Carole's inner conversation, like James's described before, spins her around in an ever-enlarging spiral of negative feelings. The more resentful she feels, the more she criticizes herself. The more she criticizes herself, the more she tries to please Charles. Carole's self-dialogue pushes her to act in ways that contradict her feelings. Charles gets the message "Everything is okay" and makes no attempt to change his behavior.

James and Carole have one thing in common. They have an inner dialogue that is both influential and destructive. Influential, in that their self-talk has a major effect on the direction of their lives. Destructive, because their inner speech is leading to alienation, apathy, anxiety, and depression.

James and Carole are not textbook cases. They are people just like you and me, people who talk to themselves.

Philosophers have long told us that the events in our lives, in and of themselves, have less importance than what we tell ourselves about these events. To quote the Stoic philosopher Epictetus, "Man is troubled not by things, but by the view he takes of them." Whether you realize it or not, this simple observation can give you great control over your life, from the moment-to-moment shifts in your feelings to the decisions that form your very existence.

Today, this last hour even, what have you been telling yourself? Have you pushed yourself to hurry up, or scolded yourself for making a mistake? Have you worried about the future, or nagged yourself about the past? Have you praised or supported yourself?

If you don't remember what you have said to yourself today, rest assured that you are not alone. Your inner dialogue may have gone underground long ago. It may now operate automatically and unnoticeably.

If you *are* aware that you talk to yourself, you are, in fact, one step ahead of the game. But is your self-talk positive or is it negative? Does your body react to your inner speech with tension and anxiety or by relaxing and letting go? Does your self-talk allow you to be more or less responsive to your own feelings?

These are important questions, ones not easily answered or dismissed. Listen to the answers of one typical "Talking to Yourself" class. Each person was just beginning to examine his or her own inner voice.

A 45-YEAR-OLD ENGINEER: A lot of what I tell myself is negative. To give you an example, several years ago when I moved into management and had to take over some technical correspondence, I'd spend three or four hours writing one business letter. I was critical to the point of paralysis with every word. I wanted it to be just right.

A 38-YEAR-OLD REENTRY STUDENT: I'm always pushing myself to move on to something else. If I'm sitting and talking to someone, I'm going over in my mind what I have to do next and feeling guilty that I'm taking time to relax. Then, when I start to work, I regret that I'm not still visiting with my friend.

A 30-YEAR-OLD RESEARCH ASSISTANT: I took on a project to please my boss. I kept pushing myself to get it finished. I worked nights and weekends until I finally burned out. I did in three months what should have taken two years. I finally got sick and quit. Then I felt like a failure.

A 50-YEAR-OLD NURSE: Whenever someone else has a problem, I'm there. But for me, it's always, "My thing can wait." It took me eleven years to bring up something with my sister that took all of ten minutes to resolve.

A 24-YEAR-OLD GRADUATE STUDENT: In sports, if I can't do it well, I simply won't do it. I get so depressed if I'm not what I consider good, that it's not worth trying.

A 35-YEAR-OLD HOMEMAKER: I'm always afraid that if I don't spend all my energy pleasing my friends, I'll be left out in the cold. There are a lot of times when I do things I don't want to do just because I'm afraid to say no.

When self-talk is negative, like the preceding examples, you are creating a toxic environment for yourself. What's more, you will carry this internal environment with you, regardless of your physical location. It is simply not possible to escape from your own self, try as you may through alcohol or drugs or constant work. Though you may temporarily turn off your negative inner voice, invariably it will resurface with its companions of depression, confusion, and anxiety.

A positive, supportive way of talking to yourself also establishes an inner environment, one that can cushion you from the negative events in your life. Unfortunately, all too few people have developed this kind of self-talk.

The Cognitive-Behavioral Approach

Recognizing that what you tell yourself can have a negative impact on your life, important though this awareness is, does not tell you what to do about it. "Think positive!" the experts say. Unfortunately, they rarely get around to telling us how — how to stop punishing ourselves, how to gain self-confidence, how to reward and motivate ourselves.

Until now we have lacked, quite simply, a method — a bridge over which to move from an habitual negative self-dialogue to a new supportive language. Such a method is presented in this book. Here you will find a systematic, workable means of transcending what you have learned in the past, of discarding what is no longer helpful to you, and of developing a new communication with yourself. It will be the most important communication that you will ever learn.

You will not find any sugar-coated palliatives here, no overly optimistic phrases like "Everyday, in every way, I'm getting better." This is not an approach that calls on you to suspend reality. If you are a person afraid of public speaking, you will not, for instance, be asked to go against your gut feelings and declare, "I'm a wonderful speaker; I have nothing to fear; I'll be great!" Why not? Simply because such bravado will soon dissolve, leaving you with the reality "I am afraid" as soon as you face your task. Likewise, the pronouncement "I'm a wonderful speaker" will shatter against what may not be overwhelmingly positive audience feedback.

You will find an active behavioral process that can be applied to virtually any situation that causes you distress. You will learn a process that frees your own resources to work for you. Based on a growing body of psychological information relative to the development and consequences of a person's own internal dialogue, and drawing from the work of investigators like Aaron Beck, Albert Ellis, Donald Meichenbaum, Michael Mahoney, and R. S. Lazarus, this method rests on a firm scientific base. Like the assertiveness techniques of past years, the alteration of your self-talk can solve seemingly unsolvable dilemmas.

During my twenty years as a practicing therapist, I have had the opportunity to build upon the developing cognitive-behavioral procedures and to develop techniques of my own. From my initial focus on the importance of basic assertiveness skills came my book *Self-Assertion for Women.* The procedures presented in *Self-Assertion* helped people to untangle communication difficulties with their families, their friends, and their colleagues.

As I became more immersed within the assertive focus, it struck me that there was at least an equal need for the development of similar skills in dealing with the inner companion who is our own self. This realization led to the development of the method used in this book.

Internal vs. External Reality

It may never have occurred to you to examine critically your own inner speech. You may have just accepted your inner state as a given, something that could not be questioned or changed—like the perpetual cloud over Joe Btfsplk's head in the comic strip "Li'l Abner."

In contrast to this dim awareness of inner events, you may have overemphasized the importance of external situations in your life. "If only my job were different, if only my spouse would change, if only I had more money or more time," you may think to yourself. And, of course, there is some degree of truth in these "if onlys." External events are important, so much so that investigators are currently attempting to measure the cumulative environmental stress to which a person is subjected and the consequences of that stress.

As important as external stressors are, however, there is mounting evidence that any individual's stress score, in and of itself, doesn't actually say that much. How a person reacts to a particular stress is very much related to that person's own self-talk. To the exact same circumstance, one person will react with depression ("It's hopeless, I'll never succeed"), another with anger ("It's all their fault"), and a third with optimism ("You can't win them all. I'll do better next time"). As stress researcher R. S. Lazarus tells us, "Psychological stress resides neither in the situation nor in the person; it depends on a transaction between the two. It arises from how the person appraises an event and adapts to it." Hans Selye, who originated the stress syndrome concept in his book *The Stress of Life*, agrees when he says, "In our life events, the stressors' effects depend not so much upon what we do or what happens to us but on the way we take it." How we construe a situation and how we take it brings us back, of course, to our own self-talk, to what we say to ourselves about a critical incident.

The Self-Talk Factor

To test out this self-talk factor in my own work, I often ask people to rate a situation in terms of its realistic consequences (its external stress value) and in terms of its self-evaluative consequences (its internal stress value). See the diagram on the next page. For example, the realistic consequences of a divorce might entail financial difficulties; or involve a grief reaction that must be worked through; or result in a loss of contact with one's children. On the other side, the self-evaluative consequences might include the self-punishment "You're a failure; you can't do anything right; you'll never have a good relationship; it's hopeless; you harmed your children; etc." Depending on the degree to which these inner messages are accepted as true, the self-evaluative consequences may have as debilitating an effect as the realistic ones, sometimes even more so.

One of my clients was feeling depressed and overwhelmed about calling her attorney. She wanted to instruct him not to continue with certain actions relative to her divorce proceedings. It was important to make this assertion, yet she felt unable to complete the call.

When we separated the realistic consequences from the self-evaluative ones, her difficulty became clear. She was telling herself that her attorney wouldn't listen to what she had to say, that her assertion would result in an unpleasant inter-

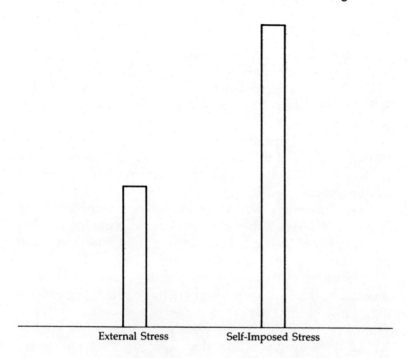

External Stress   Self-Imposed Stress

action, that she would end up having to get another attorney, and that she would probably have the same problem again. In short, she was scaring herself. When she realized that her stress was internally generated, based on what she was telling herself, and that the only realistic consequence facing her now was the minor inconvenience of a phone call, she went ahead and telephoned. Not too surprisingly, one clear communication solved her problem.

Likewise, for each of us, the recognition that we *do* talk to ourselves and that this self-talk has an immediate and significant impact is a crucial prerequisite to any decision to alter what we tell ourselves. The realization that this inner dialogue involves a confrontation between two basic aspects of each of us — the Intrinsic versus the Imposed — is equally important.

The Intrinsic Self vs. the Imposed Self

Self 1, the Intrinsic Self, is our basic core of aliveness. It is a register, moment to moment, of what we feel, what we want, what we need. If unhindered in its development, the Intrinsic Self allows for the full expression of our feelings, our abilities, our uniqueness.

We would all operate from the pulse of the Intrinsic Self, responding to and trusting our own feelings, if we were not constantly inhibited by our fears or driven by our images of what we should become.

These inferences, when they occur, come from Self 2, the Imposed Self. This is the self formed through our interactions with the world. Self 2 tells us what is right and wrong and what should and should not be.

Because our first and strongest feedback about what should be is given to us by our parents or parent substitutes, their views become important ingredients of Self 2. And even as we were evaluated by these early mentors, so we learn to evaluate ourselves. Self 2 develops as a punishing and severe critic or as a positive support. Self 2 becomes either a Judge or a Guide.

If you were fortunate enough to have had mainly supportive individuals in your life, your Self 2 may function in such a way as to allow the growth and development of your Intrinsic Self. On the other hand, if you learned to see yourself through judgmental mentors, you most likely employ many destructive, damaging messages in your habitual self-talk. The next chapter will introduce you to the custodian of these messages — the Self 2 Judge.

2
. . . .
The Self 2 Judge

ARE you frequently unable to meet your self-imposed deadlines?

Do you hold yourself back out of fear of intruding upon other people?

Do you believe that what you do is never enough?

Do you need a drink or a tranquilizer in order to relax?

Are you more forgiving of other people than you are of yourself?

Do other people frequently disappoint you?

Are you unable to do "nothing" and feel okay about it?

Are you considered to be a perfectionist?

Do you generally lack confidence in yourself?

Are you anxious, depressed, or angry more often than you would like?

If your answer to any of these questions is yes, it is likely that you have incorporated a Self 2 who is critical, faultfinding, and blaming, a self-monitor who sets exceedingly harsh standards and metes out equally severe penalties if these standards are not met. You have acquired a Self 2 Judge.

The development of such a critical Self 2 is not a mysterious process. Psychological studies demonstrate that we all begin to talk to ourselves at an early age and that this self-talk is based on what we have learned from interacting with the significant adults in our environment. An adult's communication with you as a child is a prototype for your later communication with yourself. If the influential people in your early life were harsh, critical, or judgmental, then your own Self 2 tends to incorporate these same characteristics. If your early mentors had realistic requirements and were genuinely instructive in their comments, you learn to set the same type of standards for yourself.

Based on the messages received from other people (parents, brothers and sisters, teachers, friends), you also form a self-definition, a set of controlling boundaries that can determine, in large measure, your life course. You learn to see yourself as athletic or clumsy, intelligent or stupid, lovable or unloved, okay or not okay.

When the principal figures in your early life have perfectionistic, judgmental standards, you are extremely vulnerable to the development of a negative self-image. Even if you are doing average or better than average work, for example, you may incorporate the self-definition "stupid" if you do not live up to the performance of a brother or sister or to the unrealistic expectations of a parent. Even if you are exhibiting normal energy and exuberance, you may accept your parent's critical view — "bad child."

Moreover, you will begin behaving in a way that "proves" that your self-definition is true. For example, if you view yourself as a lousy athlete, you will shy away from any activity that hints of athletic ability. The opportunity to develop physical skills is lost, as is the chance to discover your latent talents. Along similar lines, if you have the self-definition "I'm stupid," you will not assert yourself during intellectual discussions. Neither will you have the opportunity to test this definition's validity.

Through your interactions with your early world, you may also learn that your okayness is conditional, that you are noticed, loved, and accepted only under certain conditions, that is, when achieving, looking pretty, or being obedient. If you were criticized or scolded when you allowed yourself to relax or play, you may decide, "I'm okay only when I'm accomplishing something." Furthermore, this decision can persist to the point that as an adult you critically judge yourself in the same way whenever you have the opportunity to relax or have fun. This judgment, of course, will manifest itself in your moment-to-moment self-talk: "Why are you just sitting around? You've got a million things to do today. If nothing else, you could clear out that drawer. Don't be so lazy." The parental message accepted years ago continues to generate negative self-talk.

As you can see, the framework that you learned as a child for evaluating yourself and your experiences has a tremendous influence on how you now direct your life. Unfortunately, this framework does not always allow room for your emotions and needs. Important mentors can expose you to a way of talking to yourself that ultimately leads to frustration and failure. You can be taught to operate within the judgmental structure.

The Judgmental Structure

The judgmental structure is essentially a view of the world where perfection is the dominant expectation. There is always a very clear "right" way of doing things that makes any other choice "wrong." This framework leads to the constant preoccupation with what is lacking, as opposed to what is present. It leads invariably to faultfinding and blaming, with the corresponding emotional reactions of disappointment and anger.

Let's examine the effects of this toxic structure on Connie Evans. Connie is just beginning to organize her own business, an advertising service for small community organizations. The decision to work for herself has put Connie into a turmoil. Although she spent eight years in an advertising agency before her marriage and has the necessary background and experience, she finds herself full of self-doubt. Getting her project off the ground has been very difficult, as any move toward working for herself causes anxiety.

If we look to Connie's inner speech, the source of her difficulties becomes apparent. Connie is operating under the constant scrutiny of her Self 2 Judge. She is trapped within the shoulds and should nots of the judgmental web. Any move to extricate herself is met with self-punishment. If she is not immediately available when sons Shawn and Seth come home, for example, Connie must fight off her fear that she is being a neglectful mother. If dinner is not on the table at the usual time, she feels guilty. When friends interrupt her work with calls during the day, she is torn as to what to do. Should she ask them to call her back that night, or should she just talk now and not have to worry about hurting their feelings?

The dialogue with which Connie begins her work day further explains her turmoil. "Why am I doing this?" she asks herself. "Who is going to hire me? I haven't been in the work force for over ten years. There are younger women out there. I'm just wasting my time." While she gets a handle on these thoughts with the reply "Well, you can at least do a brochure for yourself. That's your business, isn't it? And get in a full day today, not just two or three hours," still, the small injection of hopelessness has an impact. At the end of the day, Connie feels depressed. Further, since she has usually managed to work at a high level for only a few hours, she observes, "You didn't do it again," and scolds herself, saying, "What's it going to take for you to do a full day's work? If you don't shape up, you're not ever going to land an account."

By examining Connie's inner dialogue, we see three Self 2 buttresses that support the judgmental structure. Each buttress, and the self-talk derived from it, interferes with Connie's work-related goals. Let's briefly examine each, the Self 2 commands (Drivers), prohibitions (Stoppers), and faulty thinking (Confusers).

Drivers

As the word indicates, a Driver is an internal push—"Get busy! Do it right! Take it like a man! Do something!" The something that we are commanded to do, depending on which Driver is in operation, is based upon our Self 2 notions of what we should do. We are instructed to "Be Perfect, Hurry Up, Please Others, Try Hard, or Be Strong"—Driver mechanisms first formulated by Taibi Kahler. Drivers generate tension. They put us into high gear. To the Self 2 Judge, a natural pace is not sufficient. We must be better, faster, stronger, and if this is not achieved, we consider ourselves inadequate.

As we speak of Drivers, it is important to realize that this term does not refer to the psychological concept of drive or motivation. Motivation or drive, like energy or enthusiasm, flows naturally from the Intrinsic Self. A Driver is buoyed up by a kind of forced motivation, a pressure from the Imposed Self that may have no connection at all to a person's inner well of aliveness and energy. A motivated writer may work on a manuscript for eight hours at a stretch, fully enjoying this creative pursuit, wishing to do nothing else. This is far different from the writer whose Judge says, "You should write. You must do it perfectly. Try hard to finish it."

Connie Evans is driven by what analyst Karen Horney once termed the "tyranny of the should." Her Imposed Self tells her, "A good mother *should* have dinner ready at six o'clock. A good neighbor *ought* to be able to chat on the phone or entertain a drop-in guest. A professional woman *must* put in an eight-hour day."

Connie has yet to learn that Drivers demand the impossible. Her day does not have unlimited hours; her energy level is not boundless; her patience is not inexhaustible. Yet her Self

2 Judge believes that all of these things *should* be. Connie's Drivers, her Self 2 "you should" commands, invariably lead her to fail.

Stoppers

Connie's Imposed Self not only pushes her to act against her feelings and needs, it also blocks her natural expression. Self 2 inhibitors are called Stoppers. Stoppers prevent us from doing what our feelings suggest. They discourage our natural spontaneity with harsh judgments, threats, and rigid requirements. Certainly, stopping ourselves from acting is sometimes in our own best interests. We learn to stop at a traffic light before crossing the street. We censor thoughts and actions that would be harmful if expressed. However, on many occasions, the actions that are inhibited and the feelings that are squelched are very important ones, crucial to our well-being. Stoppers commonly prevent us from asserting ourselves.

Connie's Self 2 Stoppers are seriously interfering with her ability to move forward with her professional goals. For example, Connie has difficulty asking friends not to call during her work hours. She would like to do so, but she stops herself with the thought "I would hurt their feelings." Connie inhibits herself in other ways as well. Her need to tell Shawn and Seth that she can no longer be available to them in the afternoon is not expressed because she equates setting limits with being neglectful. She fears that pushing dinner back an hour or so will cause her to lose her "wonderful wife" status. Moreover, because these beliefs are totally accepted, swallowed whole, we might say, Connie has no basis for testing them out.

Connie is trapped by her own Stoppers just as surely as if she were confined by another person. By conforming to these Stoppers, Connie pays a high price.

Confusers

At the end of the day, after working productively for several hours, after preparing dinner and visiting with a neighbor, Connie punishes herself with the thought "You won't ever get a client." She is unknowingly seeing herself and her accomplishments through a filter of irrational and confusing ideas.

Confusers are ways of perceiving and thinking that prevent us from clearly experiencing the world. Connie's evaluation "I didn't do it again" is one such Confuser. Viewing herself from an all-or-nothing framework, Connie believes that she must accomplish one hundred percent of a task or it doesn't count. Under this Confuser, she gets no credit for what she has done, be it two hours or five hours of work. Further, this Confuser sets Connie up for self-punishment, which leads to negative feelings. The net result is that it becomes even more difficult for her to meet her goal tomorrow.

Connie's prediction "You won't ever get a client" is a second Confuser. If Connie mistakes this negative assumption for a fact, she will reject her project without giving it or herself a chance. She will join the ranks of those who feel hopeless about the future and about their own abilities to have an impact on it.

From Judge to Guide

Although Connie automatically deals with herself in a critical, judgmental way, she would not consider relating to another person with such harshness. The discrepancy between how Connie (at least outwardly) deals with other people and how she confronts herself is commonplace. In my experience, many people are passive in their relationships with others. Yet these same people are frequently aggressive with themselves. Most people, for example, would be extremely reluctant to say to someone else, "That's stupid," no matter what the error. Yet without thought, they are quick to label their own mistakes as "stupid." Some go further and call themselves "stupid" for making errors.

Were we not operating from a judgmental Self 2 position, our relationships with ourselves would be vastly different. Instead of driving or stopping or confusing us, Self 2 would function as a guide, someone who cares for us and is concerned with our well-being. This guide would serve as a good parent or a supportive friend.

The way in which we respond to stressful situations depends very much on whether Self 2 is functioning as a Judge or a Guide. Depending on this Self 2 orientation, what one person experiences as a minor annoyance may seem like a catastrophe to another. For Bill, not getting an *A* on a graduate school term paper causes profound feelings of worthlessness. For Jeff, a rejection notice on a grant proposal, a one-year project, has little or no adverse effect.

The difference between these two reactions is due to each individual's self-talk. Bill has a very critical Self 2. He judges anything less than *A* (even a *B*) as a failure. Receiving a *B* grade on a paper easily precipitates in Bill the Self 2 critique "You failed. It wasn't a good paper. I guess you just don't have it in you. You may not be graduate material. You're not going to be successful. You're a loser."

With all his self-concern, however, Bill does not mention any specific negative consequences that will result from his *B* grade. His entire focus is on the self-evaluative notion of success and failure.

Conversely, when Jeff does not receive the government grant he has been waiting for, he has the following dialogue with himself: "Looks like you didn't get the grant. That's too bad. It means you'll have to start writing another proposal before long. If you had made it this time, it would have saved some work, and that equipment would have come in handy. But that's okay. You can make do. It's no catastrophe."

Jeff stays totally away from self-evaluative judgmental statements. The approval of his grant is not tied to his self-worth. Instead, the day-to-day consequences of his rejection notice are reviewed and the impact evaluated. While there are some negative aspects of the rejection, there are no corresponding feelings of worthlessness. Again we see that the overall level of stress experienced is very much a function of how people talk to themselves. The external event, in and of itself, is not usually the determining factor.

So What Does This Mean to Me?

I hope that this brief look at the power of what you tell yourself has begun to answer that question. To repeat an earlier assertion, depending on whether your Self 2 functions as a Judge or a Guide, your own self-talk can make the difference between a happy and an unhappy life, between fulfilling your own potential or losing sight of your own real self. Your internal dialogue may determine whether you surmount the obstacles you face or succumb to them.

Many of us "lead lives of quiet desperation" just because we have learned to judge ourselves, to punish ourselves, to suppress our natural assertiveness, and to set our goals at an arbitrarily high level. In the chapters that follow, we will see how Self 2 Drivers, Stoppers, and Confusers interfere with our growth. And we will see how to change them — to turn a critical, toxic, internal environment into one oriented toward self-support.

3
∎∎∎∎∎∎∎
Drivers

IN Nathaniel Hawthorne's short story "The Birthmark," Aylmer, an eminent man of science, marries Georgiana, a beautiful woman, flawless in all respects except one. On her lovely face lies a small but clearly perceptible red mark. Aylmer is shocked by "this slightest possible imperfection." As he focuses more and more on the birthmark, it becomes unbearable to him, "causing him more trouble and horror than ever Georgiana's beauty . . . had given him delight." Finally, he finds an elixir to remove the flaw. He is ecstatic. For a few minutes he beholds perfection, until as fate would have it, his wife dies from the aftereffects of the magic potion.

Long before psychologists began looking at the detrimental effects of rigid, judgmental standards, writers like Hawthorne described how ultimate tragedy is born from unrealistic demands and expectations. The description of one man's demand for perfection and its cost speaks vividly of the Drivers* that push many of us to act in ways that are ulti-

---

*The term Driver was, to my best knowledge, first used by Taibi Kahler. The material about Drivers in *Talking to Yourself*, however, is my own and the definitions and examples of Driver behaviors are different in some respects from Kahler's.

mately harmful. The most pernicious Driver of all, interestingly enough, is the one of which Hawthorne wrote — the Driver Be Perfect.

Be Perfect

The notion that we and other people ought to Be Perfect is strangely pervasive in our society. We forget an appointment and all hell breaks loose inside. "That shouldn't have happened," we say to ourselves. "How can you be so stupid?" Self 2 castigates Self 1.

Caught in the grip of Be Perfect, we constantly grade ourselves. It is a bizarre Pass/Fail system. One hundred percent perfect and we pass. Anything less and we fail. No matter what the task, Be Perfect is present. If we can't do something right, we don't do anything at all.

Being Perfect frequently encompasses other Drivers as well. Based on our own unique learning histories, we may see perfection in terms of accomplishment (the Drivers Hurry Up and Try Hard). We may see it in becoming a veritable Superman or Superwoman (the Driver Be Strong). Or again, Perfection may require self-sacrifice (the Driver Please Others). For some of us, all Drivers are operative. As one group member said, "I'm a dentist. I Try Hard to Please Others so that I can Be Perfect."

Regardless of the specific focus, the person conforming to the Be Perfect structure is constantly pushed to perform at very high levels. To be less than perfect is to risk severe self-punishment. This can be clearly seen in a simple example — the typical plan to diet. Most of us diet at some time in our lives. For some of us, this poses no particular problem. Desserts are curtailed, a few pounds are lost, and the diet is discontinued. For others, however, deciding when to eat or not to eat becomes a never-ending conflict surrounded by anxiety, depression, hopelessness, and self-punishment.

Jill, five feet three inches, 135 pounds, is caught in such a conflict. For the past ten years, she has seesawed between 125 and 155 pounds. Parties are a misery for her. Not only does she dislike the way she looks, but parties have food, and the temptation to eat is overwhelming. If she eats, she is likely to eat too much; if she doesn't eat, she feels deprived and will make up for her deprivation after the party when she is home alone.

Jill is hungry most of the time. Most days are 900-calorie days. She doesn't allow herself pizza or pasta or sweets. She barely eats breakfast or lunch. Yet in spite of her tight rein, Jill views herself as someone who is lacking in willpower. Along with her nearly constant deprivation, she faces a steady stream of self-deprecation as well.

If Jill is so conscientious about her 900-calorie diet, then why doesn't she lose weight? The answer is simple. Jill periodically binges. She comes home and eats anything and everything she can find: a half-gallon of ice cream, a box of cookies, a loaf of bread. She eats them quickly, without any real enjoyment, and her mounting disgust with herself simply makes her want to eat more. Jill's binges may continue for several hours or several days, during which time she regains all the weight that she has lost by her careful regimen.

Jill is caught in a diet/binge pattern, a peculiar cause-effect combination of interest to us because the Driver Be Perfect is almost always present. The decision to diet, for Jill as well as for many dieters, is a kind of New Year's resolution. It is predicated on perfection. "Until I reach 115 pounds, under no circumstances will I ever eat more than 1,000 calories a day, or have starchy, sweet, or otherwise unhealthy food," goes the contract. It takes only a casual scrutiny of this resolution to reveal its Be Perfect premise. Another clause, "If I do not keep this agreement with myself, then I am a failure and a contemptible person," makes it absolute.

Once the resolution is made, a dieter may indeed Be Perfect, as far as the diet is concerned, for one day or one week or even for a month. But there will come a day when the dieter is tired or upset or lonely or just plain too hungry to resist a certain food, and then the Be Perfect spell will be broken.

This happens with Jill every so often. At a low moment, she eats a couple of potato chips (or a cookie or a dish of ice cream). For a nondieter, or someone who isn't controlled by the Be Perfect standard, this momentary slip would not be experienced as a problem. The very idea that it would be may sound ludicrous. After all, a few potato chips have at most 50 calories. But to Jill, the weight of the potato chips—no matter how small—is enough to crack the Be Perfect structure that she has promised to follow.

With her slip, Jill begins an immediate Self 2 reproach: "Why did you do that! You're hopeless. You've been doing so well. Why did you have to blow it? You have no self-control." Jill's Self 2 criticism begins to generate negative feelings—anxiety and depression. She has dealt with such feelings in the past by eating, so now she takes a handful of potato chips.

Jill's anxiety is momentarily quelled by eating more, but it soon resounds with greater intensity, and she finds herself caught in the vicious cycle of binge eating. Each new mistake leads to more anxiety and self-punishment, which leads to further eating. The destructive consequences of Jill's Self 2 criticisms are clear. A handful of potato chips, which in terms of weight gain means nothing, has provoked a tirade against the self that has profound negative repercussions, one of which is, in Jill's case, binge eating. This *does* lead to weight gain. That a small deviation from a prescribed plan can have such a major destructive effect demonstrates the power of the Be Perfect Driver.

After a number of weeks of therapy, Jill defined her dilemma like this: "Keeping to my diet is like walking a tightrope. One false move, and I've had it. I can't walk a tightrope forever. I have to free up a little—let myself walk on a sidewalk, even make a mistake occasionally."

Sounds reasonable. We might wonder why Jill had such a struggle recognizing that her Driver was hindering rather than helping her lose weight. Yet in almost every training group that I conduct, I find that people have a hard time letting go of their familiar internal commands. Whether the Driver is Be Perfect, Hurry Up, Be Strong, Please Others, or Try Hard, it is difficult to repudiate. "Aren't Drivers good sometimes?" group members ask. "What would I do if I didn't push myself? What kind of person would I be?"

Many people fear that without Drivers they would end up lying lazily in the sunshine all day. Worse yet, they would tell everyone off, become self-centered or vulnerable. They fear that life would pass them by. In actuality, without our internal commands we generally accomplish more. We become easier to live with. Our self-respect increases.

Many people believe that their Drivers alone are holding them together. This is simply not so. Drivers push us and prod us and direct us away from our natural pace. They set us on an unrealistic course, and because of their unremitting demands and their blindness to reality, in the long run they are detrimental to the very tasks they are supposed to support. If you doubt this, listen to the following descriptions of Driver effects by various group members:

"I'm a first child. My father taught me all of the Drivers, particularly Be Strong. I push myself to the point that I get sick."

"I ended up with severe depression. I was so busy pleasing other people that I forgot to take care of me."

"I make lists and Try Hard to complete them. A little voice says to me, 'Other people would have done this. Why haven't you gotten it done?' Then I get defiant and don't do anything."

"I had to do an oral report in class, and I couldn't eat or sleep in thinking about it. My Be Perfect got the best of me. I ended up not being physically able to do it."

Notice that the end result of obeying one's Drivers is frequently failure. Invariably, we rebel or collapse in the face of such relentless pressure. We go on what I call a "Sit-Down Strike." This Sit-Down Strike occurs when we fall off the tightrope. Because we can't do something perfectly, we end up avoiding it completely. We turn off, burn out, rebel, or get depressed.

Alcohol or drugs frequently aid in this Sit-Down Strike. Thus Linda comes home from work each night, pours herself a couple of martinis, and collapses on the sofa. She sees no other choice. Without the help of alcohol, she would continue to worry about today's mistakes and plan for tomorrow's crises all evening. By the end of an already stressful day, she is all too happy to have this martini-induced option of rest and relaxation, which she does not give herself. The only problem is that to rest and relax she must knock herself out. She has learned no other means of turning off her Be Perfect, Hurry Up, and Try Hard demands.

Linda lacks an alternative to both the Driver and the Sit-Down Strike. This is the Permitter, the inner affirmation of one's Intrinsic Self. In contrast to Drivers, Permitters allow room for flexibility. They loosen the grip of our internal commands and allow us to ease off the tightrope onto a sidewalk. Permitters allow us to say, "It's okay" to ourselves — "it's okay to relax; it's okay to take my time; it's okay not to finish it all tonight." Moreover, unlike the rebellious, defiant, or exhausted reaction of the Sit-Down Strike, Permitters give us a direction that allows us to proceed forward with our goals and plans. Instead of demanding perfection, for example, a Permitter says, "It's okay to be human" and "It's okay to make mistakes." Such permission leads to feelings and behaviors far different from the "I'll do nothing" decision of the Sit-Down Strike.

Hurry Up

The second Driver, Hurry Up, pushes us to do things quickly. It commands that we do more and more in less and less time.

Those of us trapped in the Hurry Up vise are impatient with ourselves and others. We are ever aware of the clock and of how much has been accomplished within a certain time frame. One woman caught in Hurry Up described the experience like this: "My watch is constantly burning a hole in my wrist. There's never time to do what I want. I scold myself constantly: 'You're taking forever to do that. Stop dragging.' I push the kids the same way: 'Hurry up and make your beds. Hurry up and eat your cereal.' I don't allow them or me to take our time."

Hurry Up is one of the easiest Drivers to identify, and, interestingly enough, a prime place to spot this Driver is while driving. If you want to see if you are affected by Hurry Up in this area, ask yourself the following questions: Do you find yourself annoyed when a car in front of you pauses for two or three extra seconds when the light turns green? Do you weave in and out of traffic to get someplace five minutes sooner? Are you quick to use your horn? If your answer is yes to any of these questions, it's likely that you have a Hurry Up Driver, at least in this one area.

Of course, Hurry Up appears in many other places as well. And paradoxically, as with all Drivers, it ultimately interferes with the real purpose of our actions. I am recalling a visit to the Louvre that my husband and I made during the first year of our marriage. With only two hours to see this grand museum, we rushed around trying to find the familiar masterpieces and had little time to enjoy or savor what we were seeing.

As we recognize Hurry Up in ourselves, we begin to see it pushing around other people as well. I once told a class that I would give them five minutes to write what they would say to themselves if they arrived late for a meeting. This exercise can tease out the negative self-talk that occurs when a Driver such as Hurry Up or Be Perfect is not obeyed. In giving the class only five minutes to do a fairly complex exercise, it's likely that my own Hurry Up Driver was in force. But there was also a Hurry Up in at least one class member. With seeming annoyance, one participant asserted, "We don't need that long!"

Those of you who are familiar with the book *Type A Behavior and Your Heart* have perhaps realized that the Hurry Up Driver is a major component of Type A Behavior. Reflecting a constant sense of time urgency, impatience, and an excessive competitive drive, Type A Behavior has been associated with coronary heart disease and heart attacks. Authors Friedman and Rosenman state, "Overwhelmingly, the most significant trait of the Type A (person) is his habitual sense of time urgency or 'hurry sickness.'" The pressure created by the constant struggle over day-to-day tasks to be accomplished and moment-to-moment obstacles and interruptions to be overcome can cause a person whose internal command is "Full steam ahead" to react with anger and irritation. According to Friedman and Rosenman, this behavioral characteristic predisposes people to the increased risk of heart attacks.

As it does with all Drivers, society frequently reinforces those who Hurry Up. Setting short deadlines and meeting them is rewarded with promotions and acclaim. The cost of the overwork is frequently not experienced until later, when friends, family, and important parts of one's self have been discarded and left far behind. Too late, one discovers that the quality of one's life has suffered.

The great environmentalist John Muir is said to have "viewed with sadness" the distinguished visitors who came to Yosemite, calling them "time poor." According to his biographer, Edwin Way Teale, Muir "chose to be time rich first of all." He once wrote his sister, "I have not yet in all my wanderings found a single person so free as myself. When in the woods, I sit at times for hours watching birds or squirrels or looking down into the faces of flowers without suffering any feelings of haste." How many of us caught in our Hurry Up routines could say the same? For that matter, how many of us allow ourselves even thirty minutes each day to contemplate the beauty of nature, or to allow our thoughts to drift? Perhaps many of you do so more than I. My Hurry Up Driver is one that I continually have to combat.

Unfortunately, as with other Drivers, simply deciding to take some time off or to relax each day has little effect unless what we say to ourselves during the time off or the relaxation changes. I can recall once going through a relaxation exercise all the while thinking of what I had to hurry up and do when I finished. "Why is this tape taking so long?" my train of thought went. As you might guess, I was worse off physiologically after my "relaxation" than I was before I started.

The Permitter opposing Hurry Up states, "It's okay to relax and take my time. Everything does not have to be accomplished today or even tomorrow." For those of you thinking that you could not possibly give yourself this permission, you may wish to consider Friedman and Rosenman's warning: "You are only finished when you are dead." Changing from Hurry Up to a genuine belief in the okayness of taking one's time does not occur without thought or without practice. Yet through a reorientation of one's Self 2 Judge, such a shift can be made.

Perhaps here is a good place to counter an objection that some of you may raise: "But I can't take my time. I work in a crucial position. I have to hurry." Other Permitters draw forth similar objections, most of which rest upon a misunderstanding of what Permission actually involves. Perhaps an illustration will clarify this issue further.

I was recently working with a nurse to lower the anxiety she was experiencing when she worked in the operating room. I think you will agree, that here, of all places, speed is of the essence. After all, another person's life is often at stake. Within this stressful occupation, however, hounding oneself to Hurry Up does not help. In fact, here as everywhere else, pushing past one's capacity means making errors.

The Permission "It's okay to take the time I need to respond accurately" was very effective in lowering my client's anxiety during a difficult operation. Far from hindering her effectiveness in the operating room, this Permitter greatly enhanced it. Of course, people who work under such high-pressured conditions must be especially cautious about generalizing a crucial need for alertness and speed in one area to other situations where a broader degree of Permission is possible.

Be Strong

The Be Strong Driver tells us that certain needs and feelings are unacceptable, even despicable, for ourselves and for others. An individual with a Be Strong Driver regards any need as a weakness to be overcome. Feelings of sadness, hurt, or loneliness are intolerable. According to the Be Strong command, people should be able to handle *on their own* all problems that come their way.

Because the Be Strong Driver says, "You must do it all yourself," many people who need help are unable to ask for it. Be Strong individuals may never enroll in a self-awareness class or even read a book like this, because help of any sort precipitates a drop in self-esteem. Even when such persons override the Be Strong Driver enough to come into therapy, they may despise themselves for having needs or feelings. Not infrequently, someone in my office will start crying (a totally human response) and then immediately begin a tirade against himself or herself, "I don't know why I'm doing this. This is so stupid. I'm acting like a baby." Some people go even further to stop their "weak" reactions. They clench their fists or bite their lips, anything to distract themselves, because the expression of sadness is experienced as a humiliation.

As with all Drivers, the Be Strong command represents an accepted, even admired, way of behaving in our society. This is particularly true for men. The strong, silent movie hero exemplifies society's ideal of the self-reliant individual who knows how "to take things like a man," that is, without visible emotion or feeling. Even the experience of pain is supposed to be borne as stoically as possible. Of course, the Be Strong socialization process can shape the behavior of women as well. One of my female clients, for example, was so affected by the Be Strong Driver that she did not allow herself to ask for a local anesthetic during a painful operation in which she had a mole removed. She wanted to, but she would have faced severe self-reproach if she had expressed this need to her doctor.

The Be Strong Driver is developed under circumstances where important others are severely critical of softness or vulnerability. Having had the experience of being ridiculed or punished when sadness or sensitive feelings emerged, children begin to treat themselves in the same manner.

The blunting of one child's sensitivity and compassion toward wild animals can be understood if we examine an experience recalled by Lyndon Johnson in Doris Kearns's book *Lyndon Johnson and the American Dream:*

> In the fall and the spring, I spent every moment when I wasn't in school out in the open. With other boys, I went hunting squirrels and rabbits. I carried a gun and every now and then I pointed it at the animals, but I never wanted to kill any of them. I wanted only to know that I could kill if I had to. Then one day my daddy asked me how did it happen that I was the only boy in the neighborhood who had never shot an animal. Was I a coward? The next day I went back into the hills and killed a rabbit. It jumped out at me from behind a bush, and I shot it between the eyes. Then I went into the bathroom and threw up.

Years later, Johnson gave male visitors to the LBJ Ranch rifles and cajoled them to shoot a deer or an antelope in his presence. According to Kearns, Johnson was putting his visitors' manhood to the test, as his father had once challenged his own. In our terminology, Johnson's Self 2 had incorporated his father's definition of masculinity and strength, overriding his own intrinsically negative response to the killing of an innocent animal.

The Permitter "It's okay to have feelings and to express them" opposes the Be Strong Driver. Hurt feelings, sad feelings, tender feelings, vulnerable feelings, and needy feelings are all acceptable. Permission to express these feelings with others is equally important. Allowing oneself to cry alone is not the same as expressing sadness to another person.

Please Others

The Driver Please Others says that we are okay only when other people like and approve of us. For a person controlled by the Please Others Driver, losing this approval even for a moment can lead to high levels of anxiety and depression. Even when the disapproving person is unimportant, there remains an intense fear of rejection.

Those of us with a Please Others Driver often have a difficult time asserting our own needs and feelings. We find it difficult to say no to requests and demands from others. If we are not careful, we find ourselves in the position of one man who described himself as "spending my entire life doing what other people have wanted me to do."

In talking of the Please Others Driver, I am not referring to the give-and-take inherent in any good relationship. Pleasing another person can be enjoyable and rewarding. However, many people please others at their own expense. They develop an exquisite sensitivity to the nuances of another person's emotional state while remaining oblivious to their own. For example, it is not uncommon for persons caught in the Please Others Driver to fail to recognize their own feelings of anger or resentment until long after a provocative incident has occurred. The ability to distract oneself so effectively derives from the preoccupation with another person and the closing off of one's own Intrinsic Self.

The Please Others Driver has affected women in particular. According to sociologist Suzanne Keller, a basic tenet of the traditional feminine role is the command that "women should live through and for others." This is, of course, a direct injunction to Please Others.

In effect, many a woman has yoked her life to that of her husband or her children. She has transplanted her center or mechanism of control into someone else. This other person's feelings, not her own, become her signal for reacting. "When George was home," Norma states, "I was always on the lookout for anything that might trigger his anger. I went around paving the way for him — making sure the kids weren't too noisy, stepping in to locate something he couldn't find, doing anything to keep him calm. I was his valet in almost every sense of that word. Even when I was visiting someone, I would base my departure on the mood I determined he would be in when I got home. I never considered my own feelings at all. I spent nine years of marriage monitoring his."

"It's okay to please myself" is the Permitter that Norma lacked. Pleasing yourself means considering your own feelings and needs. It means allowing yourself to pursue your own unique agenda. It does not mean that you will not also choose to please others. But pleasing another person will be a choice, one that takes your own feelings as well as the feelings of the other person into consideration. The Please Others Driver gives you no choice. One step off the tightrope demand of constant approval from others means a disastrous fall in your own self-worth.

Before leaving the Please Others Driver, there is one additional characteristic that bears mentioning. Individuals operating with Please Others generally take on the Drivers of the persons with whom they are relating. Thus a woman may find herself hurrying at five o'clock to clear the room for her husband's arrival. If it were not for her need to please, she would not alter her own behavior in that fashion. She would not periodically get caught in the Be Perfect and Hurry Up demands of her spouse. It is just this incorporation of the standards of others that leads Please Others people even further away from their own feelings.

Try Hard

The fifth Driver, Try Hard, was initially the most difficult for me to understand. I have told groups that perhaps this difficulty rested on the fact that I frequently get caught in the Try Hard myself. Try Hard involves the push to take on more and more — more and more projects, more and more invitations, more and more responsibilities. Try Hard is impervious to the setting of appropriate limits.

I recently had a chance to change a negative situation involving my own Try Hard Driver. After several months of buying a local newspaper, I realized that I was pushing myself to read it each day and to tear out certain articles, the idea being that I should keep up with local issues. If I was tired after coming home from work, I stacked the paper in the corner, with the resolution that I would Try Hard to look it over the next day. What usually happened was that I faced the weekend with a stack of newspapers that I nagged myself to read, while my house grew increasingly cluttered with clippings.

I finally decided to give myself permission to let go. I stopped buying the newspaper, to the great benefit of both my house and my sanity. The honest truth of the matter was that I didn't really want to read the paper. I only felt that I should. This is the crux of the Driver Try Hard. It pushes us to accept a burden without concern for our emotional and physical limits.

In perhaps no area is there more chance of the Try Hard Driver pushing us past these limits than when we are caught in a rescue operation. The concept of the rescue operation was first introduced to me by family therapist and author Shirley Luthman. It is an important concept crucial to our well-being, for when we rescue someone, we take responsibility for that person and for his or her problems. In attempting to help this person, we often get pulled in past our own limits. Setting limits, even very appropriate ones, about how much help can be given, at what time of night one does not want to be called, how long a conversation can last, or how much financial assistance can be supplied, goes against the dictate Try Hard.

Helping professionals (psychologists, physicians, nurses, police officers, and others) are particularly vulnerable to the

Try Hard Driver. Placed in professional situations where their jobs involve helping people in need, they often ignore their own personal limits and take on the problems of their clients as if these problems were their own. The ultimate consequence is what Dr. Christina Maslach, in an article in *Human Behavior,* has called "Burn Out." Maslach states, "After hours, days, and months of listening to other people's problems, something inside of you can go dead, and you don't give a damn anymore."

Jenny found herself in this position of unexplained alienation from her friend Martha, whom she had gone out of her way to help on a number of occasions. She had loaned Martha money and had put her own academic performance in some jeopardy to help Martha complete a report. Having gone to such trouble for her, Jenny could not understand why Martha seldom called or wanted to get together.

In trying to help Martha solve her problems, Jenny had forgotten to consider her own limits. Now Jenny feels resentful and taken advantage of, and Martha feels guilty. Jenny and Martha would have fared better if Jenny had chosen a position that included the support of another person *and* a sensitivity to her own limits. This balance can be achieved only by steering clear of Drivers like Try Hard, which leave no room for one's own feelings and needs.

Opposing Try Hard are the Permitters "It's okay to say no" and "It's okay to let go." In other words, we can choose *not* to try hard. We can decide not to participate on five committees, or even on one committee, if we do not want to participate. We can decide not to Try Hard to spend time with a new acquaintance and not to take on another project, no matter how worthy. In short, we can recognize our own limits — in work, in friendship, and in intimate relationships.

Finally, we can give ourselves permission to succeed. "It's okay to give my diet, my book, my job search enough time, backing, and energy to succeed." Working in conjunction with other Permitters like "It's okay to ask for the support I need in meeting my goal; It's okay to acknowledge the real difficulties inherent in my project; and It's okay to set limits in other areas," we no longer need to try hard. We can simply meet our commitments to ourselves.

Driver-Related Costs

As we have previously mentioned, the end result of obeying our Drivers is paradoxically just the lack of accomplishment, the vulnerability, and the interpersonal difficulties that we feared would occur if we did not honor their relentless commands. Drivers take us along a pernicious and far-ranging course, whose costs are reflected in our behaviors, our feelings, our levels of stress, our interpersonal relationships, and our self-esteem. Thus Aileen, whose Hurry Up Driver blares all day at work, comes home at 5:30 and sleeps until the next morning. Because she ignores her internal signals of fatigue and tension at work, by the end of her shift she is wiped out.

Aileen's exhaustion has certain consequences, one of which is the curtailment of social activities, a vital ingredient of her well-being. What Aileen does to replace this lack will depend upon her own learning history. She may drink more than usual, or she may find herself stopping to load up on fast, fattening foods on her way home from work, knowing that she will be too tired to cook. Either alternative adds weight, and as she finds that her clothes no longer fit, her self-esteem begins to drop. She has less energy and enthusiasm for her job.

We could, if we desired, develop this downward spiral even further. Let's assume, however, that at this point Aileen consults a therapist. To the therapist she may say, "I have a weight problem" or "I don't feel very good about myself." It is unlikely that she would say, "I drive myself too hard at work." Yet that is her problem. Her other difficulties are simply consequences of the Driver Hurry Up.

If Aileen were to examine her behavior closely, she would probably discover that there are relatively few times during her day when she actually has to rush. Her usual Hurry Up behavior (reading while she eats lunch, walking rapidly from one place to another, skipping breaks, growing impatient with conversation, returning messages at once) rests upon her internal push. If she knew the costs of the Driver, she would perhaps consider turning it off.

So it is with other Drivers. Their promised glory fails to materialize. The Be Perfect writer whose critic sits frowning over his or her shoulder suffers writer's block — accomplishing little or nothing. The Please Others husband or wife becomes a resentful martyr. The Be Strong loner commits suicide. The Try Harder volunteer burns out.

The picture that I am painting is, of course, extreme. For most people, Drivers only hinder creativity, they simply generate bad feelings, they merely interfere with interpersonal relationships. With most of us, Drivers do not destroy completely our push toward growth. Yet the demands of the tightrope are severe. Any fall can lead to a sense of failure, to depression, and to a loss of self-esteem. The glittering coin whose face offers us the chance to grasp our image of perfection hides on its underside despair and self-hate. Pick up the coin, and you hold both possibilities.

Your Driver Profile

To better understand how you have learned to drive yourself, you may wish to do the following exercise. Draw a circle in the center of a piece of paper. This circle represents you. Around this center circle, draw five other circles as well, each representing an important person in your life. The people chosen may be living or dead. You may not even know some of them on a person-to-person level. The circles may stand for a group of people or the church. If book characters or public figures have had an important influence in your life, these can also be acknowledged. When each circle is drawn and labeled, list specifically any Drivers (Be Perfect, Hurry Up, Try Hard, Please Others, or Be Strong) that you learned from this significant person in your past. When this is complete for each person, go back and note also the Permitters that you acquired from those past mentors.

As you begin to recognize the origins of your own Drivers, you gain further distance from them. This toxic process, through which the judgmental position is upheld, becomes less integrally a part of you. Now you have the choice of continuing to talk to yourself in such a way that your Drivers are obeyed or developing new Permitters on which to base your self-talk.

4

· · · · · · ·

Stoppers

"**I**F I have an idea," Sheila began, "I first say to myself, 'What I'm thinking is probably not that important or someone else would have already said it.' Then if someone does express my idea, I tell myself, 'You were an idiot not to have spoken up!' I really can't win with myself. Even describing this right now makes me think, 'How silly!'"

Many of us, like Sheila, interfere with our own spontaneous self-expression and thus confine ourselves to limited areas because of our own self-talk. Do you ever find yourself in this position of inhibiting the natural unfolding of your actions and feelings? If so, you are most probably familiar with Stoppers — those internal self-messages that say *no, don't*, and *only if.*

Stoppers were the first form of self-talk that caught my attention. I began noticing Stopper effects when I asked people in assertiveness workshops why they were unable to express their feelings or act in accordance with their desires. I found that all too frequently an internal signal — a negative judgment, a confining rule, or an anxious concern — had stopped them. Thus a man does not approach a woman (or vice versa) for fear of seeming "on the make." An argument is avoided because a person concludes "I should be above this." The term Stopper was originally applied by psychiatrist Eric Berne to negative messages like "Don't be," "Don't grow up," or "Don't be normal." These injunctions are also called Witch Messages. I have expanded the Stopper concept to include Catastrophizing, Negative Self-Labeling, and Setting Rigid Requirements.

Before describing each Stopper process, let's examine one situation in which all of them tend to occur. Imagine yourself here — at a social gathering where you don't know anyone. Maybe it's the social hour after a professional conference. Perhaps it's a "Drop by, we're having some friends over" invitation from a casual acquaintance. No matter. Both situations are basically the same — you and a group of strangers and a feeling of "What do I do now?"

After allowing yourself time to get your bearings and help yourself to a drink, you look around and spot someone across the room you think you might like to meet. Maybe the person you see looks particularly interesting or attractive. Or perhaps you notice the individual who offered some controversial comments at your conference workshop. Whatever the source of your interest, if you are *not* talking to yourself in a negative manner, or put another way, if your Self 2 is functioning as a Guide rather than as a Judge, chances are that you will walk up to the person, introduce yourself, and make an opening comment. Even if you have some initial reluctance to do this, your action will be supported with statements to yourself like "Hey, what can you lose? This is a social gathering. You're here to talk. I bet the man over there would enjoy meeting you. Go ahead," or "That's the woman who made those interesting observations. She would probably like to know how someone reacted to her comments. If not, that's okay too, but give it a try."

On the other hand, if you are listening to your judgmental Self 2, you will probably not act. Your original impulse to extend yourself will be dampened by your inner dialogue. "Ah," you begin, "there's the woman I've been wanting to meet. I think I'll go over and introduce myself." Fine so far. Only notice now how Self 2 Stoppers begin to surface. "Wait a minute," your Judge commences. "Just because you want to meet her doesn't mean that she wants to meet you. What if you walk over, and she sees you coming and turns away. That would be awful. And even if she's interested in meeting you, how can you be sure that you won't be boring. What have you got to say that's all that important? I know! If she looks in your direction and smiles, then walk over. See? She's just smiled. Wait a minute. How do you know she was smiling at you? If she smiles again, go . . ."

In relating this Stopper dialogue to groups, I usually ex- aggerate toward the end to help people see the "no risk" wall that they are carefully constructing around themselves. Of course, a person carrying on this kind of self-dialogue will rarely make it across a room (or even make it two or three feet for that matter) to converse with another person. A self- dialogue like the one above results in self-rejection. Can you determine the number of Stoppers in this brief self-dialogue? There are six — two examples of Catastrophizing, two Nega- tive Self-Labeling, and two Rigid Requirements. Let's exam- ine in detail each of these Stopper processes.

Catastrophizing

The first two Stoppers in the above dialogue are examples of Catastrophizing, a term first coined by psychologist Albert Ellis. Catastrophizing is the internal rehearsal of all the hor- rible, catastrophic events that might possibly occur if you were to engage in a particular behavior.

Catastrophizing interferes with the realistic solution to the equation "Action equals Benefit-to-be-Obtained over Risk-to- be-Taken." When you Catastrophize, you exaggerate the risk factor so much that you decide to do nothing. In the imagined party scene, the Self 2 Judge Catastrophized that the woman across the room would not want to become acquainted ("Just because you want to meet her doesn't mean she wants to meet you") and that she might even turn away. Because this improbable scenario was considered "awful" in its eventuality, the opportunity to act upon the desires of the Intrinsic Self was rejected.

The key phrases in Catastrophizing are "What if" and "That would be awful." The phrase "So what if" is one neutralizer. As you become more growth-oriented, you will find that most "That would be awful" self-talk does not focus on the realistic consequences of an action but on the self-evaluative ones. In other words, most times you would suffer little external harm but a great deal of self-imposed suffering if your Catastrophes actually occurred. Thus, when someone Catastrophizes "It would be awful if I asked for a raise and didn't get it," the "awful" relates to feelings of embarrassment or injured pride at being turned down. The realistic consequence of not getting the raise is often, paradoxically, an increased chance of getting one the next time.

If you find yourself blocked by fears and Catastrophes, try writing down each one as a "What if" statement. Some examples are: "What if Geoff doesn't ask me out again?" "What if my presentation isn't well received?" or "What if I try out for a part in the play and don't get it?" Next, determine if your "What if" fear involves a realistic consequence or a self-evaluative one. In other words, does not getting the part in a play lead more to a genuine loss or to bad feelings about yourself? Self-evaluative consequences, as you will see later, can be drastically reduced as you alter your own self-talk. Examine the catastrophes listed below. Do any of these "What if" fears inhibit you?

It would be awful
if every person in the world didn't like and approve of me
if I ever made a mistake
if I couldn't find a perfect solution
if someone didn't want to see me again
if I were wrong

if my opinion were challenged
if someone got angry at me
if I were disapproved of
if I got angry
if I got emotional
if I lost my job
if my relationship didn't work out
if I were criticized
if I couldn't think of anything to say
if I were rejected
if I blushed or if my voice were shaky
if everyone didn't consider me to be a nice person
if someone didn't listen to me
if someone knew more than I did

Negative Self-Labeling

The second Stopper process found in the beginning example is what I call Negative Self-Labeling. Negative labels are arbitrary judgments attached to natural and healthy Self 1 impulses. Labels like "boring" and "not that important" can make it very difficult to act on signals from the Intrinsic Self. These labels come from a Self 2 Judge whose critical eye is ever ready to punish and ridicule a push toward growth.

The impulse to be assertive is very vulnerable to the effect of Negative Self-Labeling. Each of the four areas of assertive expression, in fact, is associated with a plethora of such labels. If you want to express positive feelings toward someone, you may be concerned about sounding "insincere" or "gushy" or being a "kiss-ass." If you have an impulse to say something positive about yourself, labels like "conceited" and "bragging" may frighten you into silence. Your assertion of negative feelings may be squashed by concerns about "nagging" or being "mean." You may not set limits or say no, because you label yourself as "selfish" or "unfeeling." Self-initiation is stopped if you tell yourself that what you want to say or do is "unimportant" or "dumb."

In addition to blocking self-assertion, Negative Self-Labels can limit your creativity as well. "I spent three hours writing three sentences," Millie told one class. "Every word I wrote, I labeled: 'That sounds funny.' 'That doesn't make the point.' 'That word is outdated.' 'Don't sound so cute.' As you might guess, I was soon so disgusted with myself and my paper that I didn't want to spend one more second on it." I hear examples like Millie's over and over. The Self 2 Judge punishes with negative labels to the point that a person's creativity is squelched, or at the very least, the fun is taken out of it.

Contrast Millie's description for a moment with that of author Llewelyn Powys, who describes in *The Creative Process* how he ignores any negative labels. Powys writes, "My own method is to give no thought whatever to the form of what I am writing. I put down my ideas as they present themselves pell-mell in my mind, fanciful, sentimental, bawdy, irreverent, irrelevant, they are all equally welcome. In going over my work, however, I am prepared to spend a great deal of care in endeavoring to find the just word or an adequate balance for any particular paragraph."

Powys's "critic," as he explains, comes to the fore only after his material has had unhindered access to his paper. No Stoppers interfere with his flow of words or thoughts. Powys goes on to state, "I consider the greatest difficulty to be overcome by immature, untrained writers is lack of confidence. They are all too self-conscious. When once the pen is in the hand, it is important to forget about the opinions of others and to write away after your own fashion with careless, proud indifference."

Stopper-produced inhibition, through the mechanism of Negative Self-Labeling, can occur with sports and leisure activities as well as with creative pursuits. For example, many people refuse to take up tennis or bridge or skiing because they cannot tolerate the self-punishment evoked by being a beginner. They fear that their efforts will be seen as inept or stupid. Here again comes self-rejection. Having such a critical view, they find it is safer to confine themselves to those few activities that have already been mastered.

Even when Stoppers do not completely prevent a person from tackling new activities, they can interfere with learning and drastically reduce enjoyment. Timothy Gallwey's *The Inner Game of Tennis* describes the usual ways in which people talk to themselves when learning this familiar game. Criticizing and judging past behavior is a common occurrence, as the following example from the *Inner Game* demonstrates: "I'm hitting my forehand rotten again today. . . . Dammit, why do I keep missing those easy setups. . . . I'm not doing anything the coach told me to do in my last lesson. You were great rallying, now you're playing worse than your grandmother. #!*$@&%!"

Negative Self-Labels ("rotten," "worse than your grandmother") employed in this manner frequently interfere with an action by generating tension. Moreover, these unpleasant feelings all too often cause a person to avoid the activity in the future.

Negative labels are invariably harsh self-judgments on behaviors that can be interpreted in a different manner. The labels "stupid," "a klutz," "inept" can be replaced by the label "beginner," one that is much less negative and actually more accurate.

The labels we choose derive, in part, from how the significant others in our pasts saw us. If our mentors had strong standards of perfection, perhaps our beginning athletic attempts were called "clumsy" instead of appraised as a "good start." After all, it's easy to see imperfection and much more difficult to reinforce growth. Many of us need to reevaluate our labels so as to limit their destructive effects. We need to realize that most negative labels are not based on truth or honesty or a willingness to see reality but on a harsh, critical stance that we have learned to apply to ourselves and to others.

In evaluating your negative labels, it is also important to consider the motives behind any action. For example, your motive in voicing negative feelings may not be to nag or to be mean but simply to clear the air and to avoid the buildup of resentment. Certainly, care must be taken as to *how* you voice these feelings, but your need to express them is human and natural, two positive labels. Similarly, your motive behind playing tennis may not be to rival Steffi Graf, but to get some exercise. Beginners probably get more of that anyway, so what does it matter that your game has some distance to go?

A final consideration regarding Negative Self-Labels comes from listening to your Intrinsic Self. If you do, you will often get a very different perspective from that offered by your Imposed Self. Your Self 2 Judge, for example, may consider an issue "too petty" to bring up, but you may find yourself tossing and turning all night thinking about it. If this is the case, it is important to remind yourself that the issue may seem petty to someone else, but your feelings are signaling that it is important to you. Perhaps once you bring it up, you will receive new information that will make the issue inconsequential. Until then, however, you must push aside your Negative Self-Labels with a recognition and acceptance of your genuine feelings.

Listed below are some commonly used Negative Self-Labels, some of which may be familiar in your self-talk repertoire. You may notice that the last six labels in the list do not seem to fit. At first glance these labels (nice guy, superman, superwoman, good parent, gracious host/hostess, good person) seem positive, not negative. And so they often are. Yet such labels can also be used by the Self 2 Judge in a negative, destructive way. Thus many a "nice guy" allows himself to be taken advantage of rather than risk losing his positive image.

Many a superwoman fails to take time for self-nurturing. Be careful of positive labels. They can also limit your potential for growth.

1. Nagging
2. Cold
3. Compulsive
4. Dull
5. Uninteresting
6. Aggressive
7. Castrating
8. Immature
9. Egotistical
10. Ungrateful
11. Irresponsible
12. Unfeminine
13. Harsh
14. Bossy
15. Parental
16. Domineering
17. Selfish
18. Wrong
19. Demanding
20. Illogical
21. Irrational
22. Thoughtless
23. Hysterical
24. Crazy
25. Insensitive
26. Pushy
27. Impolite
28. Bitchy
29. Stupid
30. Dumb
31. Shrill
32. Sissy
33. Weak
34. Ugly
35. Nosy
36. Incapable
37. Competitive
38. Unmasculine
39. Adamant
40. Unladylike
41. Too much
42. Soft
43. Overactive
44. Troublemaker
45. Childish
46. Willful
47. Self-pitying
48. Silly
49. Stuck up
50. Unimportant
51. Too idealistic
52. Petty
53. Frigid
54. Nitpicking
55. Self-centered
56. Overly emotional
57. Nice guy
58. Superman
59. Superwoman
60. Good parent
61. Gracious host/hostess
62. Good person

Setting Rigid Requirements

Setting Rigid Requirements is the third Stopper process that occurred in the situation at the beginning of the chapter. The statement "I'll walk across the room and approach the woman

I would like to meet if she looks in my direction and smiles" is a Rigid Requirement. So is the "If she smiles again" addition. Notice the small word *if*. With this one word, a set of conditions is prescribed that must be met before an action can take place. All too often, these conditions narrow choices and block feelings and actions. The old adage "*If* you can't say something nice, don't say anything at all" is a common rigid requirement — one that shuts off totally the expression of negative emotions. Below, a number of Rigid Requirements are listed. Are any of these in your Stopper repertoire?

I'll follow my feelings
if it is vital
if someone is not in a bad mood
if I cannot live with the situation as it stands
if no one else is around to see me
if I can't get my spouse to do it
if the other person will be assertive back
if I have all the facts or information
if I have done everything else perfectly
if the other person can take it
if I am feeling good about myself
if it's what I should feel
if I am sure about what I feel
if I am justified
if I am dealing with a peer
if I won't hurt anyone's feelings
if I will still be liked
if no one will be angry with me
if my assertion is without flaw
if I can be unobtrusive
if I'm perfect
if it's part of my job
if it's a matter of principle
if I know the outcome
if the time is right
if I don't antagonize

if it's really going to bug me
if I can be witty, eloquent, and brilliant

Rigid Requirements frequently stop behaviors that do not fit the Self 2 Judge's ideas of what should be. Thus a person who has learned to follow the Driver Be Strong will often have the corresponding requirement "I'll express myself *if* I can do so without being emotional." When followed, this requirement can limit the expression of anything of real importance, hence emotion. Along these same lines, a person whose Judge says Please Others tends to have the Rigid Requirement "I'll speak up *if* I'm sure that I won't hurt anyone's feelings." Since not hurting someone else's feelings is only partly within our control, this requirement can block the assertion of all limits and negative feelings. A final example of a Rigid Requirement controlling Self 1 expression will be familiar to those with the Drivers Hurry Up and Try Hard. It goes something like this: "Okay, *if* you finish cleaning the house and sort out your income tax receipts, *then* you can relax." Self 1 signals are not accepted and acted upon until certain requirements are met, even when internal signals of fatigue or tension are strong.

The antidote to the Rigid Requirement *if* is the Permitter *even if.* Thus, rather than say to myself, "I'll ask a question *if* it's really important," I can say to myself, "I'll ask my question *even if* it is *not* important." To the requirement "I'll speak up *if* I'm sure I won't hurt anyone's feelings," I can state, "I'll speak up *even if* I hurt someone's feelings." If my intent is positive, speaking up is the best course, even if I risk hurting someone. If I don't express myself now, my feelings will generally come out later in a destructive way. Many friendships and marriages have been destroyed because resentment was allowed to accumulate behind the requirement of not hurting feelings. Only when the resentment grew big enough was this requirement pushed aside. Then it was often too late to work out problems that could have been dealt with early on.

Witch Messages

A final form of Stopper, what Eric Berne called the "Witch Message," is a negative injunction that says, "Don't: Don't grow up; don't change; don't be yourself; don't be sexual; don't be different." Some of us even accept the injunction "Don't be." It is easy to see that these messages oppose the growth and development of the Intrinsic Self. Witch Messages are all the more pernicious in their effects because they are learned at an early age when our survival often hinges on their acceptance.

"Don't be different" is a common Witch Message transferred from parent to child. To win approval children must conform to their parents' ideal of what a child should be. This makes it very difficult for them to acknowledge and accept their own growth pulse. Thus their direction may not be the unique combination of abilities and interests of their Intrinsic Selves, but a preordained path set prior to birth by their parents. The ideas "My son should be an engineer like his father" or "My daughter doesn't need to be concerned about her college major because she'll just get married" are different forms of the Witch Message "Don't Be Yourself."

The assertion of your right to listen to and honor all parts of yourself is the best antidote to a Witch Message. It is sometimes useful to assert this right in your own mind to the person from whom you learned your negative injunction. Within a therapy context, I sometimes ask my clients to affirm to someone in their past this resolve to honor the Intrinsic Self. Thus a young person may assert to a parent, "I can't live my life the way you want me to. I *won't* live my life the way you want me to. I'm a different person from you. I want you to accept me for who I am." This confrontation with an absent parent in an empty chair can have great emotional impact. Whether or not the same confrontation is ever made in "real life," this assertion will often release a person to follow his or her own direction.

Stopper-Related Costs

Even as you identify examples of Catastrophizing, Negative Self-Labeling, Setting Rigid Requirements, and Witch Messages, you may not see any real reason to alter this way of talking to yourself. In other words, you may not be aware of the costs of these inhibitory processes. Basically, Stopper-related costs, like the Driver-related costs discussed in chapter 3, will be reflected in five areas: in your feelings, your behavior, your interpersonal relationships, your sense of self-esteem, and your level of stress.

To put these costs into perspective, let's examine several areas where Stoppers dominate. One common focus is on time spent on nonwork pursuits. Labels like "lazy" or "nonproductive" frequently cut off many Self 1 interests and activities and confine a person to a very narrow path. Only when this path is followed does a person escape the nagging labels of the Self 2 Judge. Thus, over time, life can become a routine of get up, go to work, come home, have a drink, watch television, and go to bed. Weekends are for recuperation from the past week and preparation for the next. Along these same lines, the Stopper No Time can presage the gradual elimination of enjoyable hobbies and activities. Yet along with a temporary relief from self-punishment, a high cost is paid for this kind of self-deprivation.

In all likelihood, an individual's feelings will signal the first indication of this price. These feelings may hide in words like "Life is not as exciting as it once was" or "My marriage has lost its romance" or "I've burnt out with my job," but whatever the descriptive phrases, there is a stagnation of the Intrinsic Self produced by the tight Stopper rein. Over time, these feelings of boredom and ennui may deepen into depression. As vital ingredients of emotional nourishment are discarded, a person's world shrinks into a narrow, unrewarding place. Depression is the Self 1 signal that too much has been eliminated.

A second example of Stopper-related costs can be seen in the interpersonal consequences that result when self-assertion is blocked. The failure to assert negative feelings, for example, leads to "gunnysacking" the buildup of resentment toward other people. Gunnysacking produces periodic explosions or the more subtle, but equally harmful, process of withdrawal. Both of these reactions lead to strained interpersonal relationships. Moreover, with a gunnysack weighting us down, we are less free to deal with each situation in a clear, uncontaminated fashion.

Shyness provides a final example of Stopper-related costs. The shy individual is blocked, quite often by anxiety-producing self-talk, in reaching out to other people. Having once been considered shy myself, I know that shyness doesn't necessarily result from an absence of thoughts but from an absence of thoughts considered acceptable to express.

The self-imposed inhibition that is shyness leads to isolation from others and feeds a person's low self-esteem. Jan, for example, has great difficulty engaging in small talk. She labels her ideas as "commonplace," "already known," and "uninteresting," thus stopping herself from sharing just the kind of information that makes up beginning conversations. Her Rigid Requirement "I'll speak up *if* I can think of something new to say" results in all too many missed opportunities. Her Catastrophe "It would be awful if I said something awkward or out of line" makes spontaneous interaction impossible. Because these Stoppers so effectively stifle Jan's communication, she appears to be uninterested in other people. Some people even see her as aloof. What Jan fears most usually happens. She is ignored and left out by others. The tragedy is that this rejection occurs only because Jan has already rejected herself.

In the chapters that follow, we will examine how to remove from our paths the Self 2 Stoppers that interfere with our growth. Before we do, however, there is one further form of negative self-talk at the disposal of the Self 2 Judge. The next chapter will introduce us to Confusers.

Your Stopper Profile

To clarify how you have learned to stop yourself, you may wish to determine your Stopper history. To do so, repeat the exercise that you completed earlier in regard to Drivers. Again draw a circle in the center of a piece of paper. This circle represents you. Around this center circle, draw five other circles as well. Each of these circles represents an important person in your life. The people represented may be living or dead. You may not even know some of them personally. The circles may stand for a group of people or the church. If book characters or public figures have had an important influence on your life, these can also be acknowledged. When each circle is drawn and labeled, write inside it any Catastrophes ("What will the neighbors think"), Negative Labels ("You're selfish"), Rigid Requirements ("Ladies don't get angry"), or Witch Messages ("Children should be seen and not heard") that you learned from your interactions with these significant others. Also write any permissive messages (messages that oppose these Stoppers) that the important people in your life offered you, messages like "Be yourself" or "Children should be seen and heard" or "To your own self be true." Knowing where your negative messages come from can give you an increased ability to deal with them later.

5
·······
Confusers

To make sense of the constant barrage of information with which we are confronted each day, we all arrive at a system for evaluating our experiences. We develop a kind of short-hand, a way of simplifying what we perceive. We sort events and people into categories — right or wrong, good or bad. We draw conclusions and operate on the basis of certain assumptions. We magnify some experiences and ignore others. The benefit of this shorthand is that we simplify our environments. The risk is that this distillation takes us away from reality. In our simplification, we ignore important factors and misperceive others. Robert Pirsig, author of *Zen and the Art of Motorcycle Maintenance*, puts it more eloquently: "We take a handful of sand from the endless landscape of awareness around us and call that handful of sand the world."

Aaron Beck, a well-known psychiatrist who has done pioneering research relative to the causes and treatments of depression, has described five ways of thinking that distort everyday experience and thus predispose an individual to psychological distress. These five processes are not new. They have been described by general semanticists in years past. Yet even for those of us who will never suffer from severe depression, these processes are very important for they are

Confusers, and as such, they selectively alter our day-to-day experiences. With two added to Beck's list, the Confusers are as follows:

1. Arbitrary Inferences
2. Misattribution
3. Cognitive Deficiency
4. Overgeneralization
5. Either/Or Thinking
6. Vague Language
7. Magnification

Arbitrary Inferences

An Arbitrary Inference is a conclusion that has been drawn without careful consideration of the facts involved. It is a very common Confuser, partly because our language lends itself to the mistaken view that inferences are facts. Thus if Jim makes the statement "Mark doesn't like me," Jim assumes that he is stating a fact. Yet this information may not have come from Mark's saying to Jim in a serious manner, "I don't like you." Instead, Jim may have come to the conclusion on his own, after putting together the evidence "Mark hasn't called lately; Mark didn't want to play golf the last time I asked." Thus the statement "Mark doesn't like me" is not really a fact. It is an inference. It is a conclusion drawn on the basis of other events, such as Mark's lack of recent contact. In actuality, Mark's feelings toward Jim may not have altered at all. Mark may have good reason for his unavailability.

According to general semanticist Harry Weinberg, author of *Levels of Knowing and Existence,* a factual statement is "one which is made only after observation and which is verifiable by accepted standards." On the other hand, an inferential statement is one that goes beyond observation to draw a conclusion. As you can see, not only is Jim's view that Mark doesn't like him based on an inference, but even his evidence for this conclusion has not been distilled to the factual level. The statements "Mark hasn't called lately" and "Mark didn't want to play golf the last time I asked" are also inferences. Jim can consider his first statement to be a fact only if he has an answering service that always works or if he has been at home every moment, his line has never been busy, and there have been no problems along the phone cable. If he is not certain of these factors, his factual statement must be "I have not connected with Mark although he may have tried to call." The same careful scrutiny must occur with his second statement if Jim wishes to assume that it indeed has a factual base.

Like Jim, many people ignore this very important distinction between facts and inferences. Yet when we are dealing with inferences, there is always the chance that what we are stating or believing is not true. We cannot count on inferences in the same way that we can rely on facts. Weinberg gives a dramatic example of this discrepancy when he notes how many presumably "unloaded" guns kill people every year. The inference is that the guns are unloaded. The fact is that they are not.

Making inferences in and of itself is not a negative process. The problem is that we draw conclusions in an arbitrary fashion, that is, with very little supportive evidence. Moreover, we fail to recognize that our conclusions may be incorrect. In important areas, this can lead to desperate consequences. When our inferences relate to our basic opinions about ourselves and others, we also are playing with a loaded gun. Here too our inferences have the capacity to do great harm. To provide just one example, in his research on depression, Beck found that an important characteristic of depressed individuals was their tendency to make Arbitrary Inferences about themselves and about their futures that were overwhelmingly negative.

In my own experience as a therapist, I see that a tremendous amount of psychological pain is based on the habit of making Arbitrary Inferences. Inferences like "I'll never establish another relationship" or "I won't be able to support myself alone" or "I'll never be happy again" are blatantly false. I see them proved untrue time and time again as I work with someone in therapy. Yet they are accepted as true and often acted on to produce destructive consequences.

Because inferences typically have more to do with a person's basic belief system than with the actual facts involved in a particular situation, the same circumstance can lead to a variety of inferences. The critical factor is the basic belief of the person drawing the conclusion.

To illustrate this process in a vivid way, I asked one class to respond to the following situation: "Mary sees her friend Paul on the street. She waves, but Paul appears to ignore her. Mary responds. What is her response?" The class gave a variety of answers. Each response related to the inference that the class member had Mary make about Paul.

"If Mary said to herself, 'Oh, no. Paul must not like me anymore. He's ignoring me on purpose,' she'd be depressed," one member began.

Another quickly proposed, "On the other hand, she might think to herself, 'Wow, Paul doesn't recognize me. My new haircut must make me look great.' Then she might feel excited."

A third member offered, "What about her thinking, 'I can't wait to tell Paul that he walked right past me without speaking. I can tease him about that for the next three weeks.'"

A fourth alternative: "She could generate anger if she thought, 'How dare Paul not speak to me! He's a conceited boor. Who does he think he is!'"

Perhaps the best response of all came with the last suggestion: "If Mary says to herself, 'I wonder why Paul didn't wave. When I see him again, I'll ask him,' she won't have any strong reaction. She may be curious, but that's about all."

Notice how many different responses were evoked from one situation — reactions ranging in degree from mild curiosity to moderate distress — all based on the particular inference that Mary made.

The inference that Mary chooses, of course, does not occur simply by chance. It is ultimately connected to her basic beliefs and attitudes. Because of this predetermining set and the inferences that come from it, Mary will probably exhibit the same emotion in many diverse situations. Eric Berne calls such characteristic emotional reactions "rackets." Further, once Mary has made an inference, she has started a process that can become a self-fulfilling prophecy. In other words, what Mary predicts may actually happen. This is true because inferences have great power to affect a person's feelings and future behavior.

If Mary makes a negative inference, for example, she is likely to feel depressed or angry. She will then tend to behave in a hostile or withdrawn manner in any future interaction with Paul. By behaving in such a manner, Mary will generate a counter response from Paul that is also likely to be negative. Thus Mary's inference "Paul doesn't like me" may ultimately prove true.

The negative inference "It's hopeless" provides another powerful example of a potential self-fulfilling prophecy. This is a particularly harmful belief whatever it is applied to, be it the possibility of learning something new, the idea of developing a relationship, the prospect of finding a better job, or any other self-initiated behavior.

On the feeling level, this inference produces depression. Behaviorally, a Sit-Down Strike occurs. Without the belief that our efforts will ultimately lead to a meaningful outcome, we lose the motivation to make those efforts. The person with the inference "I'll never lose weight," for example, will be too depressed to take the necessary steps to reduce food intake and increase calorie expenditures. In like manner, the thought "It won't make any difference" will inhibit any efforts to alter a toxic situation, one which may not change on its own accord.

In working with people in therapy, I find that the inference "It's hopeless" is *the* major roadblock to change. Until this particular message stops blaring away, a person will not take hold of the opportunities that are there and will continue to squash the budding impulses of the Intrinsic Self. The inference "It's hopeless" puts one into the position of victim. Essentially, this inference turns off the internal motor. No wonder the car refuses to run.

Positive Inferences

Arbitrary positive inferences are generally not as problematic as negative ones. Positive inferences, in fact, often lead a person to behave in a manner more conducive to happy consequences. Faith and trust, attitudes generated by positive inferences, help to buffer people against the negative events in their lives. Evidence suggests that these protective inferences are very beneficial to a person's physical and emotional well-being.

When are positive inferences destructive? Like their negative counterparts, positive assumptions cause difficulty when they lead to the distortion of reality and when they prevent us from taking all available facts into consideration. It is unlikely, for example, that people thinking about robbing a bank spend much time contemplating the time they are going to spend in prison. More likely, the inference made is a positive one, that there will be money to solve problems and buy happiness. A similar positive inference, disguised as a belief in fate or luck, spurs the compulsive gambler on. "I'll recover my losses in this next play. Then I'll stop," the gambler asserts, a positive inference usually not confirmed in reality.

We need only look back briefly in history to see the dreadful effects of one man's arbitrary positive inference. In his book *Inside the Third Reich*, Albert Speer, Hitler's armaments minister, described how, nearing the war's end, in the face of repeated defeats, Hitler continued to believe in victory: "I can only explain Hitler's rigid attitude on the grounds that he made himself believe in his ultimate victory. His religion was based on the 'lucky break' which must necessarily come his way. . . . The more events drove him into a corner, the more obstinately he opposed to them his certainty about the intentions of Fate."

Dr. Harvey Powelson, former director of the psychiatric clinic at the Berkeley Student Health Service, introduced to me a concept that he called "inverse paranoia." In the framework that I am presenting, this term describes another form of arbitrary, positive inference that ultimately proves harmful.

Typically, this inference is made in a love relationship, where one partner behaves in a manner that says "I want out" or "I don't care for you." Yet, at the same time, he or she verbally conveys the message, "I love you." "Inverse paranoia" involves a crucial lack of suspiciousness that keeps one hanging on even in the face of very negative behavior. Here, the positive inference "He really loves me" or "She will change" prevents the injured party from letting go. This inference is based on the overweighting of what the partner says and the underweighting of what the partner actually does. Again, reality is distorted.

While we all make inferences and will no doubt continue to do so, there are several ways to prevent these inferences from becoming Confusers. The first step is to make the crucial distinction "Am I stating a fact or making an inference?" Compare the facts and inferences that follow:

Inference	Fact
I don't have any friends.	No one called me today while I was home.
You're angry with me.	I perceive that you are frowning.
I'm not a good speaker.	Someone left the room in the middle of my speech.

Inference	Fact
I'm not graduate material.	I made a *C* on my first graduate exam.
I'm not attractive to women.	The woman I just looked at did not return my smile.
I'll never get over my depression.	I've been in therapy for four sessions, and I'm still depressed.
I can't count on this therapy to cure me.	I've been in therapy for eight months, and I'm feeling worse.
I'm going crazy.	I feel anxious frequently, and I don't understand why.
I can't write.	What I have just written doesn't sound good to me.
I'm a failure as a teacher.	Half of my class failed their midterm exam.
She's going to come back to me.	She sent me a birthday card.
I'll only have one drink.	I'll forget to count.

Are you clear about the difference? If you discover that what you are telling yourself *is* based on an inference, your second step is to ask yourself "What are the facts supporting this inference?" Unless these facts are overwhelming, it would be extremely wise to take the third step of checking out your conclusions. This is an important step to follow if you are to prevent your beliefs from moving farther and farther from reality.

This was the step taken by Susan, a member of one of my first "Talking to Yourself" workshops. An incident occurred during the period when Susan was attending the workshop, where she had the opportunity to check out an Arbitrary Inference. The incident occurred in her choral group, an important pastime for her. Susan explained: "While at choral rehearsal, I noticed that the woman directly in front of me had moved during the break to another place. I felt my stomach turn, as I thought to myself, 'Oh, no. I must be singing off-key.' Then I remembered what we had discussed, and I decided to check out my inference at the next break. I asked the woman why she had moved. Her reply surprised me. She explained that the man sitting next to her was singing so loudly that she couldn't tell if *she* was singing off-key. If I hadn't asked, I would have concluded that I was at fault, and I would have felt bad. Who knows? I might even have stopped attending the chorus."

"What if people are dishonest when you try to check something out?" someone asked. Well, this is sometimes the case. However, the information to be gained from feedback is so important that it is worth the risk. One value of talking with a therapist or working within a group is that in such a situation there is an increased opportunity for honest feedback.

Misattribution

A second common and destructive Confuser is Misattribution, the direction of blame or responsibility away from the real causative agent onto something or someone else. Misattribution is particularly toxic when applied to feelings. Many of us genuinely believe the myth that other people cause (have control of) our feelings; for example, "You made me angry" or "Talking to my friend depressed me." The idea that someone else *made* you feel anything is almost always a misattribution. Your reaction to any situation depends to a far greater extent on your own value judgments and your own self-talk. In other words, you can choose to be angry at your friend for breaking a date at the last minute, or you can tell your friend that you don't like this behavior without feeling very upset one way or another. Depending upon the direction of your attributions, you can feel angry, depressed, relieved, or neutral in exactly the same situation. And, of course, your behavior will tend to fit the feelings that you have generated. In the situation just described, one person would spend the evening nursing a depression, whereas another would take the free time to do something enjoyable.

The importance of a correct attribution (that you make yourself angry or depressed or happy by what you choose to think, perceive, and do) is that you take back your power to control your own life. You also assume the responsibility to take care of yourself. As redecision therapists Bob and Mary Goulding note, "Most of the difficulty people have is not staying in the here-and-now, by anticipating the future or rehashing the past. There is usually no way of feeling bad if I stay in the present, in this place, unless this is a bad place, and then I will get the hell out of it." The responsibility for your own happiness, in other words, is completely your own.

Misattribution also frequently occurs in regard to behavior. Abusive behavior (child abuse, spouse abuse, and self-abuse), for example, is often blamed on something external to ourselves like "I was drinking" or "I was upset by the noise" or "I couldn't take *it* anymore." In external abuse, the injured party may even be blamed for the assault! "You made me hit you. I didn't want to do it." Thus abusers can persuade themselves that they had no other choice.

Just as the structure of our language promotes the development of other Confusers, our language directs us toward Misattribution. The small word "it," for example, as in the statement "I couldn't take *it* anymore," aids in the misdirection of responsibility. Through the use of this common and seemingly harmless pronoun, we throw our own power and control out of the window. To illustrate: Nancy is considering the prospect of completing her Master's degree. "*It* just seems too hard," she tells me. "How do you make it too hard?" I ask her. The difficulty is rarely in the task itself, but in our driven, punishing response to the task. Another example: Jennifer tells me about a curious feeling of panic. "*It* came over me as I was driving here today." She describes this panic right after telling me that she is considering taking on a new position of increased responsibility.

I comment: "You describe your panic as if it simply flew in the window and lit on your head. Might not you be telling yourself something with your panic?" As Jennifer takes responsibility for her own feelings, she is able to decide that she is telling herself not to take on another burden — the new position. She recognizes that her panic is her Intrinsic Self warning "No! Too much!" *It* did not occur randomly.

In *Anatomy of an Illness*, Norman Cousins notes "that 90 percent of pain is self-limiting, that it is not always an indication of poor health, and that, most frequently, it is the result of tension, stress, worry, idleness, boredom, frustration, suppressed rage, insufficient sleep, overeating, poorly balanced diet, smoking, excessive drinking, inadequate exercise, stale air, or any of the other abuses encountered by the human body in modern society." Most people do not recognize this basic statistic and instead misattribute their pain to something else. Thus instead of seeing your stomach cramps as a result of the pressure and subsequent tension that you produce in your constant self-demand to succeed, you may take the shortsighted view, "It's my ulcer acting up again." Then treating the ulcer as some entity apart from yourself, you give "it" a dose of medicine and consider the problem solved. Or you may convince yourself that your stomach pain is most certainly due to cancer, totally ignoring the fact that you are tolerating a number of situations that are in conflict with your real feelings and needs. The list of possible Misattributions is endless. And their cost is very high.

Cognitive Deficiency

A third Confuser is Cognitive Deficiency, the failure to be aware of the full picture. Cognitive Deficiency is not the same as intellectual impairment. Many very intelligent people get caught in this Confuser, because they do not take all factors into consideration when drawing conclusions about themselves or other people. Cognitive Deficiency is a kind of tunnel vision. Depending upon whether you tend to externalize (direct blame outward) or internalize (direct it inward), this tunnel focus can lead you to overrate the importance of either the external factors or the internal factors operating within a situation. This can cause you to blame either yourself or other people unjustly.

Take Harry, for example. Harry's application for the university of his choice was turned down, leaving him ashamed and confused. Harry interprets his rejection as a notification from authority that he is not okay, that he is not competent or up to the university's standards. He makes this interpretation in spite of the fact that he has always been successful in his studies and has a top standing in his high school class.

In his thoughts, Harry focuses all of the blame for his not getting accepted on himself and his own ability. No consideration is given to the large number of students applying for the few available spaces at this prestigious university or to the fact that most of the students are, like Harry, honor students at the top of their classes. He neglects to consider as well the personal and political bias that can influence any selection process. He has one factor in his equation. Acceptance equals a competent student. Rejection equals incompetence.

Were Harry to take the full picture into consideration, his equation would include all of the information listed above, and more. Acceptance would perhaps be viewed as a sum total of student competence + staff bias + number of students applying/number of spaces available + geographical location + minority status. This equation would give a more realistic picture. It would also serve as a buffer against Harry's self-punishment, allowing him to make further efforts.

If Harry tended to externalize instead of internalize, he would probably not put himself (his grades, test scores, essays, extracurricular activities) in the picture at all. He would instead focus on the flaws of someone else. "It's all Dr. Henderson's fault. He didn't take the time to write me a good letter of recommendation. That's why I didn't get in" or "That university only admits rich kids." Here the equation is also inaccurate, generating unnecessary anger that could also undermine subsequent action.

Denial

Denial is a form of Cognitive Deficiency. With Denial, there is not only a failure to note relevant information, but also the desire *not* to see. Openness to the full picture would lead to pain or to an undesired change in behavior. Many people deny problems in relationships, for example, because to face them would be very painful and would necessitate some action. Women who wear fur coats usually do not allow themselves to think about the animals who were cruelly trapped to obtain the fur.

The antidote to Cognitive Deficiency is what semanticist Alfred Korzybski called the "etcetera." The "etcetera" reminds us to account for as much relevant information as possible before we make a judgment. The attitude of "what more" opens our narrowed focus so that we see beyond our own belief systems. I often reinforce the notion of the "etcetera" by having someone list all the possible reasons for a particular result. "Put as much information as possible into your equation," I instruct. If someone's tunnel focus is generating self-blame, I ask for possible factors operating within another person or within the situation. If someone is directing all attention to another person, I ask the individual to consider the effects of his or her own behavior. The full picture usually decreases anger and self-punishment.

Overgeneralization

A fourth Confuser is the tendency to Overgeneralize, to recognize only the similarities between people or between events and to ignore the differences. Statements like "All men or women are alike" or "I can't do anything right" are Overgeneralizations. We have taken one or two experiences, usually negative ones, and from them have drawn conclusions about the entire world. Racial, cultural, and sexual prejudice is based on this Confuser.

Overgeneralization reduces one's flexibility, one's ability to see differences, and again, one's capacity to respond to the reality of a situation. Many anger-generating messages come from the tendency to Overgeneralize about another person. Statements like "He *never* thinks about me" or "She *always* complains about *everything* I do" generate feelings of anger and hopelessness. Notice the push toward Overgeneralization in words like *always, never, everything,* and *every time.* These words promote the distortion of reality. When such words are focused on the negative behavior of another person, they produce anger. When they relate to our own actions, they generate depression. How could a person not react to self-messages like "*Everything* I do is wrong" or "I'll *never* find anyone to love" or "I'll *always* be neurotic."

Korzybski used the methods of "dating" and "indexing" a situation as a means of interfering with the tendency to Overgeneralize. Dating — attaching a time (day, hour, year) to a situation — helps us to recognize that what we feel, think, and believe at one time differs from what we experience at another. The dating statement "Right now, I feel very angry with you" contrasts with the general statement "I hate you." The dated self-judgment "I wasn't a good mother to my child that month in 1954 when I was so depressed" contrasts with "I wasn't a good mother." Of course, the above statement could be altered still further, as we will see when we talk about another Confuser, Vague Language.

"Indexing" means acknowledging the uniqueness of each person and each event. In other words, rather than the notion "Men are more qualified than women for upper management," a statement becomes "Man 1 (Tom) is more qualified than Woman 1 (Theresa) for Position 1 (marketing manager). Man 1 (Tom) is less qualified than Woman 2 (Denise) for Position 1 (marketing manager)." By recognizing the differences between people and between situations, indexing allows for a more accurate assessment of reality and thus puts us in a better position to deal with our world.

Vague Language and Either/Or Thinking

In his book *People in Quandaries,* Wendell Johnson describes how the two Confusers, Vague Language and Either/Or Thinking, often lead to great unhappiness. He notes how frequently the "good things of life" are described in vague words like *success, happiness, wealth,* and *accomplishment.* Of course, these terms encompass many specific events that differ for different people. Success to one person may mean making over $40,000 a year. For another, success may mean becoming a millionaire before the age of thirty. Of course, the first person is likely to attain the good feelings that come from a self-acknowledged success, more than the second, whose criterion is so much higher.

Because it is such a vague concept, many people do not have a clear-cut definition of success. Success is an elusive, never-to-be-captured experience. Although many people have actually attained the trappings of success (money, property, advanced degrees, friends, recognition), they do not consider themselves successful. Because success is so ill defined, nothing ever gets counted ("Oh, so this is how it feels").

If a second Confuser, Either/Or Thinking, intervenes, the thought chain expands from "I'm not a success" to "Then I must be a failure." The final result is a great deal of self-evaluative pain.

When a marriage ends, there is a strong tendency to engage in Either/Or Thinking, adding self-generated distress to what is already a painful situation. The partners in a divorce frequently consider that they are failures, "One-(or more) time losers." Yet often both partners have experienced significant growth during the marriage. Author and therapist Shirley Luthman once said that people frequently use a marriage to grow up. When this growing up process is completed, there may be a need for the partners to go their separate ways. Certainly such a marriage was not a "failure" in the total sense in which that word is so frequently used.

Actually, there is a great amount of territory between success and failure. This territory needs to be taken into account if a person is to avoid the kind of excessive negativity that Either/Or Thinking and Vague Language can cause. Put another way, a person needs to learn to be specific and to think in percentages. Thus if you make the statement "I haven't accomplished anything this year," you probably mean, "I haven't accomplished 100 percent of what I think I should have accomplished." If "what I should have accomplished" is defined clearly and if you are encouraged to break out of the Either/Or structure, then you can probably report "No, I can't really say I've accomplished zero percent. It's more like 50 percent or 60 percent." This new perspective attacks the view "It's either 100 percent or nothing," where everything from 1 to 99 percent doesn't count.

A subcategory of Vague Language is the Unanswerable Question. In *People in Quandaries*, Johnson describes how people frequently ask themselves questions that simply cannot be answered, questions like "Why was I born?" "What would have happened if I had reacted differently?" "Should I have married?" or "Was my decision the right one?"

Sometimes people have thoughts or feelings they consider out of the ordinary. These thoughts, whether sexually or aggressively tinged, are quite disturbing. Under these circumstances, the question "What does this mean?" motivated by the concern "Am I crazy?" is frequently asked. Although fantasies can give us clues about what is bothering us, there is no way of knowing precisely what a thought or a fantasy means. Violent thoughts ("What if I stabbed my spouse with a knife?"), for example, sometimes arise when we have not allowed ourselves to assert negative feelings to a spouse. Sexual fantasies, when we look beyond their exaggerated format, often signal us to be more aware of needs that are not being met in our sexual relationships.

Many of us, however, don't view our thoughts or fantasies as a kind of projective test that creates an opportunity for self-discovery. Instead, we recoil from them even as we push ourselves to get to the bottom of the matter. Unfortunately, coming from a critical, judgmental position, our interpretations of these unanswerable questions are invariably negative. We decide that we are abnormal, perverted, out of control, or crazy. We would eliminate many problems for ourselves if we just labeled the question "What does this mean?" as unanswerable.

Magnification

The seventh and final Confuser is Magnification, the process by which we overestimate the importance of an event or a situation. Magnification again allows us to reaffirm our basic beliefs at the expense of reality. Thus people who have a negative self-view will often survey their every move with what appears to be a magnifying glass. A woman who has learned to see her self-worth in terms of physical beauty will give far too much emphasis to the negative effect of a blemish or an extra pound. A man who is basically unsure of himself will magnify the importance of a sexual encounter in which he is unable to perform.

The behavior of other people can also be subjected to this kind of scrutiny. A person with low self-esteem often gives great significance to any slight or perceived slight. By magnifying negative qualities and events, the "rightness" of the original belief in one's own worthlessness is confirmed. Of course, positive events are magnified as well, but not necessarily because of a basically positive self-view. The rejected lover who finds deep meaning in a Christmas card sent by a former sweetheart is magnifying the importance of a positive event to avoid accepting the reality of the loss. Such Magnification and subsequent distortion of reality rest on the belief that the lover is nothing without the loved one.

As you may have already ascertained, Magnification can lead to tremendous problems. When a life-or-death importance is placed upon a decision (whether to take one job over another, whether to live alone or with a roommate, whether taking a leave of absence is the "right" thing to do), so much anxiety is generated that action of any kind is blocked. A misunderstanding or a disagreement with one's mate can be magnified into the end of the relationship. The person who operates by Magnification lives on a stormy sea, struggling to overcome each approaching wave. This is a life lived in turmoil.

The antidote to Magnification is the active process of "bringing it down to size." "It" here refers to the situation, the importance of a decision, the catastrophic consequence of an action, the difficulty of a project, and so on. Bringing it down to size may involve discussing a particular problem with someone who is not involved. It may mean waiting until the next day to take action. It frequently involves breaking a huge project that rests ominously on the horizon into small, workable steps.

All too often a decision to be made or an action to be performed is considered too difficult or too dangerous just because it has not been broken down into its component parts. Doreen, for example, was very upset because she couldn't decide whether to stay in her apartment alone (which was enjoyable, but expensive) or try to find a roommate (cheap, but often personally difficult). She went back and forth on her decision, magnifying its importance by her view that any choice would be irreversible. She had forgotten to break her decision down into the several smaller decisions that in reality would make her larger one for her.

Once she did this, her problem became "Do I like anyone who has contacted me about being my roommate?" This was a much simpler question to answer, based as it was on concrete information and upon her feelings. Once she found someone whom she did like, the decision to share her apartment was not nearly so difficult to make.

I—You Messages

Over and above the specific antidotes mentioned throughout this chapter, there is one additional approach to combatting Self 2 Confusers. This approach involves the use of "I" messages, a technique first emphasized by Dr. Thomas Gordon in his book *Parent Effectiveness Training.* "I" messages, which state feelings and opinions, differ from "You" messages, which attack with negative labels the integrity of another person.

In communicating assertively with other people, "I" messages are much more likely to be well received than "You" messages. If you question this, think of how your reaction to another person would differ depending upon whether a "You" message (You're wrong) or an "I" message (I disagree) was directed toward you. If you respond like most of the people to whom I've asked this question, you would prefer hearing "I disagree," a statement that is clear, honest, and direct but that avoids the assaulting negative label *wrong.* This same principle applies to the communication of negative feelings in general. Rather than the "You" message "You're insensitive," the "I" message "I feel bothered when you're late for our tennis date" is both more precise and more effective.

It occurred to me, after I had taught this assertive technique for several years, that the shift from "You" message to "I" message is more than a practical communication tool to be used when interacting with other people. It is a vital focus for a new form of communication with ourselves. If incorporated at a deep level, "I" messages provide both a vehicle for and an affirmation of a profound alteration in our views of ourselves and of other people. They are really the key to the internal change that we have been talking about all along, a turning away from the vague yet rigid judgmental position toward an outlook oriented around growth and feeling.

Let me give a specific example. When, because she is lonely and bored, Betty goes out with a guy she really doesn't like and returns from her date even lonelier than before and angry with herself to boot, it is important that she forego her usual "You" messages to herself. These messages ("You are so stupid; You just can't learn; You were an idiot to go out with him") need to be replaced with "I" messages like "I don't want to go out again with someone I don't like just because I'm lonely and bored. I need to make my life more interesting so that I'm less vulnerable to acting against my real wishes." Notice that "I" messages do not get Betty off the hook with herself or paint a rosy picture. They simply stay with the facts and with Betty's feelings, as close to the behavioral level as possible. Negative judgments are avoided. Why? Because they do not help, and, as we know, they actually make most situations worse.

The negative judgments embodied in "You" messages are at the root of many Confusers. In Betty's "You" messages "You are so stupid," "You just can't learn," and "You were an idiot to go out with him" we see, in fact, traces of five Confusers.

What better example of an Arbitrary Inference can be found than Betty's statement to herself "You just can't learn"? How many times has Betty been out with this guy anyway? Two or three times? Does this really constitute "not learning"? we might challenge.

What does Betty mean by stupid anyway? Her Vague Language is a rather severe self-punishment for the specific crime of going out on a date and failing to have fun.

Do you see Betty's Either/Or Thinking? She is telling herself that either everything works for her, or she's stupid. There is also Magnification. Betty's one date, which lasted all of five hours, is construed as so important that it constitutes the universe's final opinion of her intelligence and character. Finally, we see Cognitive Deficiency. Betty's tunnel vision is causing her to overemphasize the negative. What about all the decisions she has made that were positive? Don't they belong in the picture as well?

Most of us, like Betty, live in that neighborhood somewhere down the hill from perfection. Some of us are pleased when we progress forward. On the other hand, many of us are angry because we are not already on top. We see any progress as a reminder of our own deficiencies rather than as signals of our growth. The old adage of the glass of water sitting on the table applies here. The optimist describes the glass of water as half full; the pessimist sees it as half empty.

By now, you have no doubt seen just how closely related Drivers, Stoppers, and Confusers are in their negative effects upon the Intrinsic Self. I separated them initially to give you a clearer understanding of each Self 2 process. However, in reality, the self-dialogue combines bits and pieces of each to build a strong case against simply being ourselves. Also, as we have already seen, based on the particular set of shoulds and should-nots that form our basic beliefs, the Drivers, Stoppers, and Confusers of each person's Self 2 band together to reinforce a particular theme. This theme excludes parts of the Intrinsic Self that are considered "not okay" while carefully preserving a person's ideal image.

When someone has grown up believing that other people's opinions are very important, that not making waves is preferable to standing up for one's own self, and that self-worth comes from other people's approval, that person generally will be propelled by the Driver Please Others. Any tough parts of Self 1 such as anger, independent strivings, or intellectual rigor will be stopped with Negative Labels like "impolite, pushy, or rude" or Catastrophes about rejection and disapproval. Confusers will also be present. One woman caught in the Please Others constellation, for example, was limited in expressing her anger by Either/Or Thinking and Vague Language. Having grown up with vague, fairy-tale notions from books and movies of what it meant to be a "lady," she felt that any forceful expression would destroy this cherished self-image.

Along these same lines, a person with a Be Strong Driver tends to experience self-hate and humiliation if any soft feelings are exposed. Softness is labeled as "weakness"; sadness and sympathy directed toward oneself are considered to be "self-pity." Confusers are also present. A person caught in the Be Strong constellation will often magnify the amount of time spent in sharing sad or sensitive feelings. To illustrate, one man who had shed all of five or six tears during one therapy hour concluded that he had better pull himself together before he completely collapsed.

By now, I have probably given you sufficient information to recognize Self 2 Drivers, Stoppers, and Confusers in yourself and in others. Chapter 6 begins the second portion of this book by outlining a step-by-step procedure for changing your internal dialogue from one that is repressive and dictatorial to one that allows for self-nourishment and personal growth.

6
■ ■ ■ ■ ■ ■ ■
Changing Your Tapes

IF you have discovered, through our discussion thus far, that Drivers, Stoppers, and Confusers are influencing (if not actually running) your life, you may be wondering what to do about it. Perhaps you are aware of your negative self-talk and the tension that it generates, but find that you can turn it off only by exhaustion (running marathons, working long hours), by distraction (the use of alcohol or drugs), by intense involvement with something else (food, love affairs, too numerous projects and demands), or by avoiding many people and activities and confining yourself to a limited and limiting arena.

There is, fortunately, another way, a method that allows you to follow your internal signals and turn off the blaring messages imposed by your prior learning. This method involves five basic steps:

1. Be Aware: Listen to your own self-talk.
2. Evaluate: Decide if your inner dialogue is supportive or destructive.
3. Identify: Determine what Driver, Stopper, or Confuser is maintaining your inner speech.
4. Support Yourself: Replace your negative self-talk with Permission and Self-Affirmation.
5. Develop a Guide: Decide what action to take consonant with your new supportive position.

The following questions will allow you to put this method into practice:

1. What am I telling myself?
2. Is my self-talk helping?
3. What Driver, Stopper, or Confuser is maintaining my inner speech?
4. What Permission and Self-Affirmation will I give myself?
5. What action will I take based on my new supportive position?

Going through the five-step method by answering these questions may seem difficult at first. As is often the case when learning a new skill, your initial attempts to alter what you tell yourself may feel awkward or mechanical. Don't let that discourage you. With practice, the entire process becomes automatic. It is indeed possible to contradict your negative self-talk and replace it with self-support.

Gaining Distance

Separate yourself from your critical Self 2 messages. The judgments of your Imposed Self must no longer be automatically accepted. You must examine and discard them, if necessary. The first three steps, with the questions "What am I telling myself?" "Is my self-talk helping?" and "What Driver, Stopper, or Confuser is maintaining my inner speech?" will allow you to gain distance from your own self-talk. What you say to yourself will become a behavior to be examined, and, if so desired, to be changed. Once you have established some distance from what you have learned in the past and have evaluated your heretofore unchallenged beliefs and self-messages to see if they are helping or hindering your development, you will have cleared the way for the final stage — the development of self-support. Let's examine the first three steps now in detail.

Step 1: Be Aware (What Am I Telling Myself?)

Listening carefully to your own self-talk is the first step toward changing it. Until you know what you are telling yourself and see how your internal messages affect you, there is no possibility or incentive for altering your inner speech. Some people, as we have already mentioned, are not aware of the automatic tapes that influence their lives so much. Like the self-instructions that gradually fade into the background with complex skills such as driving a car or operating a new piece of equipment, a person's self-talk may go underground, leaving unexplained feelings but no awareness of the internal messages causing them.

If this is the case with you, it is important that you begin to examine the areas where your self-talk is most likely to be accessible. As you begin to ask yourself the crucial question "What am I telling myself?" you may find it useful to write down your reply. What you discover may surprise you. At the very least, you will begin to view your self-talk from a different perspective.

Be aware of external triggers

External events are frequent triggers of negative self-talk. Foremost among these external triggers are compliments, criticism, new projects or activities, and periods of intimate sharing. You can utilize these events to discover something about your own inner speech.

Compliments

Negative self-talk is frequently observed in a person's response to compliments. What seems on the surface to be a positive stroke from another person may, in fact, serve as a cue for severe self-reproach. For example, when someone tells you, "You look nice today," do you respond, "Thank you. I feel good today," or do you describe everything about yourself that doesn't look nice — "Oh, my hair is getting too long. I've got to get it cut" or "Don't you think I'm getting too fat?" Along these same lines, if your work is praised, does it provoke the apology "If I had more time, I would have polished it a bit more," or the agreement "I'm really glad you like what I did. I've been feeling good about this project myself." The way you respond to compliments can give you a beginning awareness of your inner speech.

Criticism

Another trigger of negative self-talk is external criticism. For many of us, the pain of criticism comes not so much from the attack by another person but from our own internal response to the attack. For example, if a family member were to ask, "Do you think the house is clean enough to have people over after the meeting tonight?" would you respond, "I know this house isn't clean. I'm just not a good housekeeper. I'm messy. Okay, I know I'm messy. There's nothing I can do about it"? In other words, would you magnify tenfold any critical message directed toward you? With my clients, I have frequently used the illustration "Someone throws a stick at you, and you pick it up and beat yourself with it." Examine how you pick up the stick, and you will become better acquainted with your own critical Self 2 messages.

New projects and activities

Being faced with a new project or activity is another trigger for negative self-talk. Self 2 Drivers, Stoppers, and Confusers are summoned by new projects with ferocious intensity. In almost every class I teach, the beginning of a new exercise provokes someone's negative self-talk. For example, when I ask all the class members to write down situations where their self-talk is negative, someone usually confesses, "I know of a situation where I treat myself badly, but I notice that I'm punishing myself even as I'm writing it down. I'm thinking, 'Will this be boring to the class? Is my situation too personal? Is this what you want?' I feel surrounded! My critical Self 2 is lurking everywhere!" If you begin looking at your internal response to new situations, you too may find your negative self-talk more pervasive than you ever imagined.

Intimate sharing

Talking about your intimate feelings with another person is a fourth way to discover negative self-messages. I sometimes find, for example, that a client is initially unaware of any thoughts that might be contributing to an upset. Yet when I ask "What did you say to yourself when such and such happened?" I will often hear something like "I told myself that I was a coward" or "I decided that I acted really stupid" or "I'm afraid that I babbled like an idiot when I talked to my date" or "I found out that I'm inept at playing handball." There is no way that these self-deprecating comments would not have caused bad feelings. Yet until these thoughts are brought out through conversation with another person, they go unrecognized. This is, by the way, one positive role that a therapist can play. By simply identifying negative self-messages as they pour forth, therapists can help their clients "see" what they are telling themselves.

Be aware of internal triggers

As important as external events are, the best way to get in touch with your own inner dialogue is to monitor your internal signals. These include feelings, physical symptoms, avoidance thoughts, and avoidance behaviors.

Feelings

Your feelings provide the best single path to your inner speech. By feelings, I am referring to bodily sensations of anger, joy, sadness, remorse, excitement, or lethargy — not to disguised self-judgments like "I feel that I am stupid" or "I feel that I can't do anything right." These latter statements are examples of negative self-talk parading as feelings. While these statements will indeed produce feelings (depression and anxiety, for example), they are self-judgments. This distinction is an important one because a judgment can be changed. This change, in turn, will produce an alteration in feelings. When you can recognize "I'm not feeling stupid, I'm feeling depressed. I'm telling myself that I'm stupid" or "I'm feeling anxious because I'm concluding that I can't do anything right," then you have taken the first step toward gaining control of your own self-talk and ultimately the feelings that accompany it.

Negative feelings are frequently signals of negative self-talk. A sudden shift in emotion, particularly one that seems to occur out of the blue, is a high probability signal that you have just said something to yourself.

This happened to Cheryl one evening when she returned home from a conference where she had been one of the featured speakers. Just as she was about to put her key in the door, she felt what had been a sense of elation suddenly disappear. "It was almost like a trap door opened, and I fell from my pleased, positive mood to feeling really down," Cheryl related. "This happened all in what seemed to have been a two-second period. I wasn't dreading going home, as far as I knew, so I asked myself, 'What's going on here? What am I saying to myself?' The answer was right there, once I asked the question. I had been feeling good about my speech, thinking to myself, 'That was the best speech I've ever made. Everyone seemed to like it.' That was followed immediately by the question 'Will I be able to keep this up?' That was where my depression began."

Such unexplained feelings of anxiety, lethargy, or hostility, as well as sudden bursts of energy and enthusiasm, often rest on an internal statement of which we are initially unaware. By asking yourself the crucial question "What am I telling myself?" or more specifically, "How am I scaring myself?" or "How am I depressing myself?" often enough, over a long enough period of time, and by listening, really listening to your reply, you will let your Self 2 messages begin to surface. Once they do, write them down. By keeping a record of your own self-talk, you will have examples to work with as you begin to make the shift to self-support.

Physical symptoms

Tension-produced symptoms such as a stomachache, difficulty in breathing, rapid heartbeat, and others often indicate that negative self-talk is taking place. Over the years, our language has noted this correlation between mind and body in phrases like "You're a pain in the neck" or "This job is a real headache." Many people, in fact, experience their reaction to negative events as a physical symptom. "I never feel angry; I just get a headache," Robert tells one class. For Robert, feelings of anger are bypassed and translated directly into physical pain. Thus a headache is Robert's signal to ask himself the question "What am I telling myself?" In answering his question, Robert may find that he is tolerating a situation that is toxic to him. By blocking his own anger, he has had no action signal to motivate his assertive response.

Muscular tension is another signal that negative self-talk is on the scene. Such tension, as we have just seen, is often the manifestation of a conflict between a feeling and the negative self-talk that is preventing that feeling from emerging. In his book *The Disowned Self*, Nathaniel Branden says, "A child discovers very early, often wordlessly and subconsciously, that he can deflect his awareness away from the undesired feelings, and further, that by tensing his body and constricting his breathing, he can partially numb himself to his own state."

Thus many people smile as they describe painful or humiliating experiences from their pasts. The smile serves the delusion that it is really not so bad, even as it prevents the full awareness of pain. As people become conscious of this process and the accompanying self-talk that upholds it ("You're not so bad off; other people have worse experiences; don't be a big baby," and such), they are often able to let go and fully experience for the first time feelings of rage and sadness that have been blocked. These feelings, along with the childhood messages in which they are wrapped, then become available for examination.

A firsthand account of this kind of experience was described by Ira Kamin in his article "Dropping the Smile for Awhile":

> When I first started going to therapy I was in such pain I was numb. I told my therapist horror stories. I told him I felt like someone was twisting my arm behind my back. I told him I was getting pinched twenty-four hours a day. I told him I couldn't stand the pain, even though I couldn't feel it anymore.
>
> He said, "Do you realize you've told me all this with a big smile on your face?"
>
> "No," I said. . . .
>
> It took me less than a summer to cry with my therapist.

Permission to drop the smile and to experience one's own feelings is unfortunately not always available outside of therapy. At the first sign of distress, many people respond with the pseudosupportive statement "Don't cry" or "Don't feel bad" or the punishing prohibition "Stop wallowing in self-pity." If we do not contradict these messages, we squelch our feelings, locking them inside the tension of a smile.

Before leaving the notion that physical symptoms are sometimes signals for negative self-talk, I would like to share a personal experience with you. One day, as I was feeding my cat and the raccoons who visit each night, I noticed myself having difficulty breathing. I immediately asked myself the question "What are you telling yourself?" and quickly realized that I was pushing myself to hurry up and get everyone taken care of. I was walking rapidly and rushing up and down the stairs with a tense preoccupation with getting everything done. Naturally, my breathing reflected the fact that my Drivers were going full blast. When I gave myself permission to take *my* time, my breathing returned to normal. The point I would like to make, however, is that I realized that I was pushing myself only when I considered my physical symptom to be a possible signal for negative self-talk.

Many people do not permit this possibility and instead attribute their physical reactions to something entirely different. An anxiety-based stomachache may be interpreted as cancer, generating still more tension. Psychogenic chest pain may be considered the beginnings of a heart attack. Even when medical tests show that no physical problem is present, a person may not realize that negative emotions can provoke physical pain. When the stress-related symptoms actually lead to physical damage, a psychosomatic condition such as an ulcer results. The underlying, unrecognized factor is all too often negative self-talk.

Avoidance thoughts

A third internal signal that negative self-talk is lurking underground is the avoidance thought or fantasy. When you find yourself thinking "I have to get out of here," "I want to go back to bed," or "I need a drink," there is a strong chance that you are escaping from internal pressure. Thus Sally found herself fantasizing about going away to a desert island. "Maybe then," she told herself, "I could get some letters written and some books read." As Sally and I examined her everyday situation, it became clear that she was trying so hard to please others that she had no time for herself. She suddenly realized why her Self 1 (her Intrinsic Self) wanted to transfer to a desert island. Of course, even there she would not escape from her real problem—her internal Please Others and Try Hard commands.

The same dynamic was behind Jim's "I wish I were dead" rumination. "I really am not suicidal," Jim explained to one group. "I just keep having the thought 'I wish I were dead.'" As Jim became aware of his underlying messages "You've got to succeed; you've got to make it this year," and the way he was pressuring himself, the grip of this frightening thought loosened. "You know," Jim told the group the next day, "I had that thought again last night, and I was able to laugh it off. I haven't stopped pressuring myself yet, but I sure have a signal now that tells me 'too much.'"

Avoidance behaviors

Akin to avoidance thoughts are avoidance behaviors, what some of us call "procrastination." Some people find themselves eating, drinking, having a cigarette, watching something they don't particularly want to see on television, or curiously eager to clean the house rather than confront what they have actually chosen to do. Glenda described this kind of behavior around her decision to apply for a job. "I feel locked in, stuck, immobile," Glenda said. "I spend hours cleaning out a drawer or straightening up my desk. It seems I'll do anything to distract myself from what I really want and need to do—call about a job." Glenda's delaying behaviors are a clear signal to her that she has not confronted her underlying negative self-talk. Messages like "They won't be interested; I'm not sufficiently prepared; I may sound incompetent" are generating the anxiety that leads to her avoidance.

The following exercise will help you to discover your negative self-talk. It will also disclose your best signals for uncovering your inner speech.

1. Think of a recent compliment. What was your verbal response to it?

2. What criticism have you faced? What was your internal and external reply?

3. List a project or activity that you have begun or considered beginning. What did you tell yourself as you started or failed to start it?

4. What beliefs about yourself have you shared in intimate conversation with another? Were these beliefs negative or positive?

5. Think of a situation (time, place, surroundings) where you tend to feel negative about yourself. What do you typically say to yourself while in this situation?

6. Consider a time when you generally feel positive about yourself. What are you telling yourself in this circumstance?

7. Do you have any common physical symptom? What is your symptom telling you?

8. Do you find yourself engaging in "wistful thinking"? Do you often procrastinate? If so, from what negative self-talk are you escaping?

This exercise is not an easy one. Each question takes significant time and thought. If you draw a blank in responding, you may wish to follow the suggestion I gave to Debbie when she found herself unable to make sense of her behavior.

After losing six pounds, Debbie began breaking her diet plan and eating more than usual. She felt terrible about herself, but had no idea why she had gone off her diet. The only conclusion she had drawn was that she was masochistic and really didn't want to lose weight.

After assuring myself that Debbie's increased consumption wasn't based on a reaction to a starvation regime (a common occurrence with many dieters that plunges them into a diet-binge pattern), I asked her to shut her eyes and replay the day she had begun eating more than she had planned.

"I was feeling really well," Debbie began. "I had lost six pounds that week and had bought a new dress that I actually looked good in. I was excited and wanted to see exactly how much weight I had lost that day. When I got on the scale, I saw a two-pound *gain*! At that point, I told myself that I was just fooling myself, that I was never going to lose weight, and that it was unfair for me to have been so good only to gain two pounds. I was furious. I felt like throwing the scale across the room. Instead I started eating."

By replaying the events of her day, Debbie discovered what she had been totally unaware of — her negative self-talk. This discovery allowed her to understand other occasions when she had reversed her weight loss after reading her scale. Had Debbie not gone through this replay procedure, she would still be punishing herself. Now she has something specific to tackle as part of her weight loss plan.

Stepping Back

As you become acquainted with *your* negative self-talk, you will have completed Step 1 of the five-step program. Yet even now you may find yourself unable to gain distance from your habitual self-punishment. Many people are, in fact, exquisitely aware of their self-messages, experiencing them as waves of self-contempt or as periodic doses of toxicity. Yet these messages continue unabated.

Why do we have such difficulty gaining distance from our own inner speech? One answer is that we have frequently swallowed whole the negative messages from our pasts without questioning their validity. Eva demonstrated this to one class when she began to reverse her negative statement "I really acted dumb." With the encouragement of the class, she was able to substitute a less punishing evaluation of herself. The moment she did so, however, she quickly retreated "Wait a minute," she exclaimed. "I shouldn't be saying 'I'm not dumb.' I *am* dumb!"

Our unquestioning acceptance of negative judgments also results from the fact that significant others in our pasts have frequently failed to oppose our negative self-talk. During childhood, negative messages were perhaps reinforced by many people and many experiences. As we grew up, we continued to surround ourselves with individuals who were not supportive, or we did not put our negative beliefs to a test. By not revealing them to anyone, we had little chance of correcting our harsh self-judgments, even if the current environment was itself very positive. Now, I hope, you will choose to begin a careful evaluation of your inner speech.

Step 2: Evaluate (Is It Helping?)

Only when you expose just how destructive your negative dialogue is do you begin to gain distance from your own Self 2 messages. This is accomplished by examining the impact of your negative dialogue in five important areas — your feelings, your level of stress, your self-esteem, your behavior, and your interpersonal relationships.

As you answer for yourself the question "Is my self-talk helping?" with the realization "No. What I'm telling myself isn't helping at all!" you begin to disengage from it. The recognition that your negative self-talk is generating feelings of anger, depression, and anxiety, as well as undermining your problem-solving ability, helps you to challenge a heretofore accepted way of talking to yourself.

Do not ask yourself, "Is my self-talk true?" or even "Is my self-talk realistic?" Most people believe the pronouncements of the Self 2 Judge and so remain stuck in the judgmental framework when such questions are asked and answered. You can break this perpetuating negative cycle only by shifting to the growth-oriented evaluation "Is my self-talk helping?" Thus Carla's Judge warned her that she hadn't accomplished anything for the past ten years, so why did she expect herself to change now. "That's true," Carla exclaimed and settled even more firmly into depression. "Maybe so," I replied, "and if you keep listening to your Judge, ten years from now you can tell yourself the same thing. Your Judge has prevented you from using your talents and abilities by just this kind of self-talk. The question is not 'Is it true?' but 'Is it helping?'"

As *you* begin to realize that your own self-talk is leading to negative consequences, you may find it useful to specify exactly what these consequences are. In this regard, try the following exercise. From your previous list of self-messages, choose several typical examples. Then ask yourself, "Is what I am telling myself helping?" If your answer is no, see if you can determine what the negative costs are in each of the five basic areas: feelings, behavior, self-esteem, interpersonal relationships, and level of stress. If you like, compare your responses to those in the two situations that follow.

Situation 1: Squelching yourself

Charles has been invited to a friend's party and, although he hasn't any other plans, he is hesitant about going. He has an all-too-familiar litany of excuses. He decides to consider their effects.

"What am I telling myself?"

"I'm telling myself that there's no reason for me to go to Jan's party. I won't meet anyone there, and I'm just no good at small talk. I'll be boring, and it will be boring."

"Is this self-talk helpful?"

"No!"

"How is it affecting my feelings?"

"That's clear. I'm getting really depressed. I feel lousy."

"What is the effect on my behavior?"

"I won't go to the party, so I'll just sit here alone all night."

"How does my self-talk relate to my opinion of myself?"

"I'm putting myself down with what I say."

"How is my self-talk affecting my relationships with other people?"

"To be sure, it's not helping me meet anyone new. My friends are going to get tired of my never showing up at their parties."

"What about my level of stress?"

"I feel conflict when I'm so pessimistic, because I would like to go to the party and have a good time. I guess I'm making my stress level go up."

At this point, Charles can evaluate the various costs of his negative self-talk in very clear terms. Understanding these costs will help tilt his decision in the direction of his own growth.

Situation 2: Pressuring yourself

Penny's best friend Sharon has gone through a severe depression. In order to help her through this period, Penny invited Sharon to spend several months with her. Penny, however, finds that she herself is quite distressed. She examines her self-talk.

"What am I telling myself?"

"I am asking myself, 'Should I have taken this on?' I'm not always able to talk with Sharon. What if I make things worse? I should do more for her. I don't have enough time. How can I tell the difference between helping and interfering?"

"Is this self-talk helping?"

"No."

"What is the feeling cost?"

"I'm feeling confused and afraid. I'm going to get depressed myself if I don't stop beating myself up about this."

"What effects does my self-talk have on my behavior?"

"I overextend myself and later resent it. I don't set limits. Then I withdraw."

"How does it affect my self-esteem?"

"Instead of feeling positive about helping Sharon, I feel bad about myself. I can never do enough."

"What about my relationships with others?"

"Being oversolicitous and then withdrawing is confusing to Sharon. I'm not helping her by feeling so guilty."

"What is my stress cost?"

"It's really high. Again, I can see that I'm going to be depressed myself if I don't let up."

Of course, *your* self-talk may affect you in only one or two of these five areas. However, the clearer you are about any negative consequences, the more objective you will become. At the end of this chapter there are three additional examples that illustrate the complete answering of the question "Is my self-talk helping?"

Step 3: Identify the Driver, Stopper, or Confuser

Pointing out the Driver, Stopper, or Confuser on which your self-talk is based has two important consequences. First, by recognizing the beliefs that underlie your negative inner speech, you obtain a better understanding of the source of your self-punishment. This in turn leads to increased objectivity and the chance to lessen the impact of your old tapes.

When a woman says to herself, "There I go again, trying to be the Bionic Woman," she establishes some degree of distance from her Be Strong Driver. When a man decides, "I'm overreacting when I predict that this performance evaluation will ruin my chance of a promotion. After all, this is just one person's opinion. There will be three others," the strength of his negative inference is reduced. When someone comes to the realization "I rarely assert myself when I feel angry, because I tell myself that I'm being picky. That's a negative label. I don't have to let it control me anymore," a large part of that person's assertive problem has been eliminated.

As a member of one group wrote, "I find it useful to type out my negative self-talk in specific areas. When I put it in writing, it is much easier to see the harmful operating agents at work. And as I type each step and as I read them later, I recognize the beliefs that support the statements and that have been operating premises for years. The cycle of positive growth begins to snowball just as powerfully as any negative cycle ever could!"

The second important consequence of identifying your Drivers, Stoppers, and Confusers is that by pinpointing the source of difficulty, you also direct yourself toward a positive alternative. A springboard of sorts is set up for changing your destructive internal message into one of self-support. Thus one person decides, "Here I am telling myself that I have to Try Hard to send everyone I know a Christmas card. I don't have to do that. It's okay for me to let go of that demand this year. It simply doesn't fit with the fact that I'm now working." Another realizes, "I've been calling myself lazy all day. I have the right to do nothing sometimes. This is my day off. I'm not going to spend it Hurrying Up."

A shift in your self-talk will inevitably affect what you do, what you feel, and what you believe. When you move from negative to supportive self-talk, your feelings will lighten; you will become more assertive, less driven. Further, in the very process of changing your self-talk, you will challenge your basic beliefs, the source of both your self-talk and your behavior.

"Why not just change my basic beliefs and be done with it?" you might ask. The answer to this question lies in the understanding that these beliefs form your core experience about yourself and your world. They are not easily challenged. Further, these beliefs lead you to behave in ways that invariably prove them true. They become self-fulfilling prophecies.

Only when you try out new behaviors do you begin to challenge your basic beliefs. Thus if you have the conviction "No one likes me. I'm not likable" and you decide to question this assumption and join in group conversation, you are likely to find that other people are friendly and responsive. The belief then undergoes some alteration like "Maybe some people like me." If you choose to wait until the belief itself changes before behaving in a friendly way toward others, there will be no source of modification.

Of course, in order to join a group and behave in a manner conducive to other people's positive response, your self-talk must also change. You must push past, at least momentarily, the constant self-preoccupation and self-deprecation that inhibit a natural conversation flow. Only then will your behavior change in a way that truly allows for the correction of basic beliefs.

As you alter your self-talk, you will set up a corrective mechanism for challenging the entire structure by which you live your life. As changes in self-talk lead to changes in behavior, the external environment will usually respond to support your growth. This can be seen in three specific situations, one involving a Driver, one a Stopper, and one a Confuser.

Situation 1: Diffusing a Driver

Gayle has been on a diet for several months. Although she has lost quite a bit of weight, she hasn't yet met her goal of 135 pounds. Lately her diet hasn't gone very well. She has, in fact, exceeded her calorie limit on a couple of occasions. Gayle suspects that the culprit is her fear that she will not meet her weight loss goal by the time she and her husband take the Hawaiian vacation they have planned. Gayle wants to turn off this mounting pressure.

Question	Reply
What am I telling myself?	I'm saying, "If you don't start losing weight faster, you won't be thin enough for your trip to Hawaii. You promised yourself that you would look good."

Question	Reply
Is my self-talk helping?	No. This pressure is making me feel anxious, which means I eat more. I'm seeing myself as a failure. I'm getting irritable with the kids. Pressuring myself is making me gain weight, not lose it.
What Driver, Stopper, or Confuser is operating?	It's a clear Hurry Up. There's also some Be Perfect in there. I can't go to Hawaii unless I look perfect.
What Permission and Self-Affirmation will I give myself?	I will allow myself to take my time. Even if I go to Hawaii at this weight, I'm fine. After all, I've lost enough already so that I look okay in shorts. If I get off my back, I'll start losing weight again anyway.
What concrete action do I want to take today to lose weight?	I'll take a walk tonight. Also, I'll make sure that I buy the proper foods at the market so I'm not tempted to blow my diet. And I will do something nice for myself. This self-punishment has been depressing.

Situation 2: Squelching a Stopper

Jeannie is beginning to feel that her life is passing her by. Except for work, she rarely goes out. Although she has ideas of what she might like to do, somehow she never manages to carry them out. One idea is to join the Peace Corps. Jeannie has not acted on this impulse, however. She decides to find out why by exploring her own self-talk.

Question	Reply
What am I telling myself?	I'm saying to myself, "I'd like to join the Peace Corps." Then I think "Oh, come on, Jeannie, you're doing it again. Another pipe dream. You're being silly. The Peace Corps looks good from a distance, but once you find out about it, you'll be wrong again. Everyone's going to think, 'There she goes again, living in a fantasy world.'"
Is my self-talk helping?	No. It's keeping me isolated and depressed. It's stopping me from trying things out.
What Driver, Stopper, or Confuser is operating?	I'm stopping myself by calling my idea a *pipe dream*, by labeling myself as *silly*, and by saying that if it doesn't work out I'll be *wrong*. I'm also catastrophizing that other people will disapprove of my pursuing my idea and that they won't like me.
What Permission and Self-Affirmation will I give myself?	I will tell myself that it's okay to have fantasies and dreams. I will also say that if I find out that the Peace Corps is not what I want, I'm not wrong. I've simply learned something new on which to base my actions. I'm a levelheaded person as well as someone who likes to dream. It's okay to let my friends know the dreamer part of me.
What specific action will I take to help me resolve my problem?	I'm going to make an appointment to talk with the Peace Corps representative. Then I'll decide my next step.

Situation 3: Confronting a Confuser

Craig has decided to change jobs after being dead-ended by a major reorganization in his company. He learned this week that his application for a particularly desirable position in another firm has been turned down. Craig responds with anxiety and depression. He finds himself procrastinating about applying for other jobs. He begins to explore his own self-talk.

Question	Reply
What am I telling myself?	I'm saying that I will never find another job in my field.
Is my self-talk helping?	No. I'm getting so fearful of rejection that I don't even feel like looking for another job. All I'm doing in my spare time is sitting around feeling bad.
Is there a Driver, Stopper, or Confuser in operation?	I'm drawing a negative conclusion about what's going to happen. Telling myself "I'll never find another job" is a Confuser. I've made a negative inference. The fact is that I didn't get the job I wanted. That doesn't mean that I won't find another.
What Permission and Self-Affirmation will I give myself?	I'm a qualified person. I do a good job. I have special skills that a lot of companies can use. It's okay for me to assume that I will get a job, at least until I have given it a better try.
What action do I want to take to help me achieve my goal?	I've got a stack of resumes sitting on my desk ready to be sent. If I stop assuming it's hopeless, I'll feel more like mailing them.

7

. . . .

The Language
of Self-Support

LEARNING to talk to yourself in a positive way is something like learning a new language. Fluency takes time, practice, and dedication. In helping people alter their self-talk, it has been interesting to me that the final two steps, those involving self-support, are the most difficult. Here people get stuck. Here they can't think of what to say. Why should this be surprising? Steps 4 and 5 require something new — new attitudes and new beliefs. It would not even be farfetched to suggest that these steps demand a new relationship with one's self, one that may contradict years of programming. Let us look now at this new language and see just what it involves, and how it can be developed. Let us clarify Step 4 — supporting yourself through Permission and Self-Affirmation.

Supporting Yourself

The best way to become acquainted with self-support is to try it out, preferably in a group, in individual therapy, or with a wise and nurturing friend. If you are very careful, this friend can even be yourself. Before beginning, however, join me and one class in listening to Elizabeth's struggle to replace her judgmental self-talk with a new language, one oriented toward growth.

ELIZABETH: I recently ran for city council and lost by some three thousand votes. I keep torturing myself with the idea that maybe I could have won, if I had received the endorsement of a particular community organization. At least I should have tried to get it.

PAM: Elizabeth, would you describe out loud to the group what you usually tell yourself about losing the election. Only this time, also go through the five steps involved in changing your tape, the ones I've just described.

ELIZABETH: My negative talk usually starts out, "Elizabeth, you should have asked for the support of the Commission. If you had made any effort, the other candidate wouldn't have received their approval. You were really dumb not to go after it. The Commission only endorsed so-and-so because he asked, and you didn't."

PAM: That's enough of the negative. It's clear that you're aware of punishing yourself. Move on to Step 2.

ELIZABETH: Let's see. I'm to say to myself, "Let's step back a moment. Is what you're saying to yourself helpful?" No. I am depressing myself by dwelling on something that's over. I can't do anything about it now. As to Step 3, I suppose I'm trying to Be Perfect again. (*Here Elizabeth's tone and pace suddenly changed. She rapidly continued.*) Anyway, there's a real question as to whether or not I did do the right thing. Actually, the Commission should have invited me to speak to them, so that they could hear both candidates' views. They shouldn't have been so biased. He probably promised them something for their endorsement.

GROUP: (*Laughter.*)

ELIZABETH: Besides, I did give three speeches each week, and I knocked on three thousand doors.

PAM: Would anyone like to give Elizabeth feedback? Was what you heard self-support?

The class consensus was that while Elizabeth had effectively gone through the first three change steps (being aware, determining the destructiveness of her inner speech, and recognizing the Driver in operation), she had not developed and expressed any genuine support for herself. Instead, Elizabeth was *blaming* and *justifying* — blaming the Commission for not inviting her to speak and justifying herself for not really having had the time to appeal to them anyway because her hands were full.

By what she said, Elizabeth demonstrated that she had not, in fact, escaped from her judgmental Self 2 position. In shifting blame from herself ("You should have asked for their support") to the community organization ("They should have invited me to speak"), Elizabeth remained in the right/wrong framework. The only difference now was that the organization, not she, was at fault. Of course, Elizabeth's emotional response also changed with the shift in the focus of her blame. She no longer felt depressed; she felt angry. The group's laughter occurred exactly at this point of emotional transition. Unfortunately, while anger may feel better than depression, shifting blame will not allow Elizabeth to let go of this old situation or of her negative feelings. Yet this shifting of blame is as far as many people ever get. It is a poor substitute for self-support.

Elizabeth's comment "Besides, I did give three speeches each week, and I knocked on three thousand doors" is an example of justification, a second way the judgmental position masquerades as self-support. Distinguishing justification from self-support is often difficult. There is, however, a difference, a very important one. Justification explains away negative self-talk while at the same time upholding the judgmental belief upon which it is based. Self-support, on the other hand, demolishes both the self-talk and the underlying belief.

When Elizabeth made the comment "Besides, I did give three speeches each week," her voice signaled that she was not supporting herself. Even the introductory word "besides" indicated that an excuse was in the offering. Elizabeth clarified her message when she observed, "When I made that statement, I was still trying to convince myself that I *was* perfect by justifying what I had done. I just don't want to give that up, do I?"

Based on the feedback she had received and her own increased awareness, Elizabeth began again. This time, in a firm solid voice, she stated, "I deserve credit for running in the election, whether or not I did everything perfectly. I got nine thousand votes; I established an effective election committee; and I pushed back prejudice against women by running. It's okay for me to be proud of myself."

Elizabeth's last statement *was* an example of self-support. By stepping outside Self 2's standard of perfection, she was able to affirm herself and acknowledge her own growth. This time, the examples of her accomplishments were apart from an arbitrary win/lose criterion. Her self-support included both Permission and Self-Affirmation.

Permission

Webster's dictionary defines Permission as "giving an opportunity." Giving yourself Permission provides you with the freedom to make mistakes, to have feelings, and to experience yourself as human, all without self-punishment. Paradoxically, by giving yourself this flexibility, you insure that you will function at your highest level of effectiveness.

Subjectively, Permission is experienced as a relief, as the lightening of a burden. This relief can be very important for someone struggling under the depressing weight of negative self-talk. Richard, for example, was having difficulty writing. He had, in fact, not worked on his novel for over three months. The thought of sitting down at his desk was enough to knot his stomach and convince him that he needed a drink.

After taking him through a standard relaxation procedure, I asked Richard to imagine himself beginning to write, making sure to remind himself that he was just jotting down ideas and that he need not try to make his writing sound perfect. Moreover, I suggested that he was in no hurry at all. He would have plenty of time to rewrite and revise later. All he wanted to do was to put his ideas down on paper. After he had written for ten minutes or so, he was to allow himself to do something pleasant like relax in a hot tub, have some juice to drink, or read a magazine.

Richard was able to visualize this scene with no increase in tension. Afterwards he offered, "In the way you described it, beginning to write was like entering a soft space. I could go on like that forever." The soft space of which Richard spoke was created by replacing his Drivers with Permitters. "It's okay to take your time" and "It's okay to make mistakes" substituted for Hurry Up and Be Perfect.

I've often thought of self-support in terms similar to Richard's soft space. To me, it brings to mind the idea of a pillow cushioning a fall, or a protective buffer that absorbs and dilutes any external assault. A similar analogy appeared in an article about addiction written by psychologist Nicholas Cummings. Cummings likened the person addicted to drugs or alcohol to "an unfinished house that has only an attic and a basement." When such persons experience a negative emotion, they fall "from the attic straight to the basement." When this fall begins, an addict will run "quickly to the bottle, the pill, the needle. So, indeed, the first thing we have to teach them is how to build a floor in the house, because you cannot live just in elation or depression." In our terminology, this floor is built with self-support—Permission and Self-Affirmation.

Let's review for a moment the basic Permissions that oppose the Drivers, Stoppers, and Confusers of the judgmental position. Briefly, these Permitters are:

1. It's okay to be human; it's okay to make mistakes.
2. It's okay to follow my own pace, to take *my* time.
3. It's okay to listen to, honor, and act upon my own feelings.
4. It's okay to please myself.
5. It's okay to support myself and allow myself to succeed.
6. It's okay to say no to activities that do not reflect my intrinsic feelings at the moment.

At the core of all Permission is a decision to honor and trust one's own Intrinsic Self. Such trust goes against everything some of us have been taught, bringing up fears of being "selfish" or not a "good person." Moreover, it goes against the common notion that other people's feelings are more important than our own.

When I made a similar statement about trusting and honoring one's own feelings to Sharon, one of my clients, she responded strongly, "But I can't follow my feelings. They have always gotten me into trouble."

"Are you sure about that?" I asked. "Aren't most of the decisions you regret based on going against your feelings?"

After some thought, Sharon agreed. "Yes," she said, "I married a man I didn't want to marry and stayed in that marriage for five years because I was afraid of my feelings. I knew all that time that I wanted out, but I didn't trust what I was telling myself."

Trusting in your feelings is far from easy. Even when you begin to operate from this new position, one foot may remain behind, stuck in the old judgmental mold. Such was the case with Mitch, during a class exercise, when he began to make the leap toward self-support.

"I want to take up scuba diving," Mitch began. "I've wanted to do it for a long time, but I tell myself that I shouldn't. It costs too much; it's dangerous; it's not productive. I don't know anyone else who's into diving, so I would be doing it just for me. I'm too old to start something new like that. Everyone would think I was crazy."

As Mitch's assignment was to counter his negative self-message and to substitute a positive, supportive one, he continued, "To change this, I guess I could say to myself, 'Taking up scuba diving may not seem productive, but actually a lot of ideas can come to a person when he's away from his desk and just relaxing. Even though it would be just for me, I might not be so depressed all the time, so I would be better company for my family. Maybe I'm not too old. It might be good for me to get the exercise.'"

During the group feedback, several class members praised Mitch. "You were able to turn around the objections you listed and see a positive side to each of them," one person said. "That sounded better." But even as Mitch was being given positive feedback, one student seemed disturbed. "It sounded to me like your scuba diving has got to be productive in order to be okay," she offered. "In other words, unless scuba diving is going to let you solve some work problem or improve some relationship within your family, you can't justify doing it. Sounds to me like you're still into Please Others and Be Perfect. What about scuba diving just for fun?"

In one sense, Mitch had fallen into the same trap with his scuba diving that Elizabeth had been caught in earlier with regard to her political defeat. He was trying to appease his Imposed Self with the assurance that his diving would not be contrary to its internal commands. Mitch had not really asserted the Permitter "It's okay to please myself."

Had his self-talk been truly based on such a Permitter, Mitch could have stated, "It's important for me to listen to my insides and to nurture myself. I have the idea that I would enjoy scuba diving, and that's reason enough for me to act. It's okay to do it for the sheer pleasure that it could bring. Whether I become more productive or a better husband and father isn't relevant. It's okay to do it for myself."

There are four additional Permissions that deserve special consideration because of the difficulty in getting past society's prohibitions against them. These are (1) the Permission to Need, (2) the Permission to Have, (3) the Permission to Accept Limitations, and (4) the Permission to Feel Good.

Permission to Need

There is a strong taboo against having or admitting to having needs. The very idea provokes intense reactions: "Can't you use another term? Neediness sounds so desperate."

The "Do your own thing" experiments of the seventies and eighties produced a general assumption that if you needed another person, you simply did not have your act together. Although the aspects of this movement that spoke against desperation or addictive relationships were clearly positive, the movement itself seems to have gone too far — so far, in fact, that many of my clients castigate themselves unmercifully for having needs or being needy. In so doing they forfeit their chances for positive, intimate relationships.

There is no life without need. The way we tell an inanimate object from an animate one is need. Plants need sunshine. People need other people. When I need desperately, it is probably because I am not allowing myself to act in ways that meet my needs. I am usually stopping myself with my own self-talk, with some rule or label, and making myself into a victim.

In one group I asked, "Where did you learn that it's negative or shameful to have needs?" Jane replied with strong emphasis, "The starving Armenians. As a child, anytime I felt sorry for myself or needed anything, I was reminded of how ungrateful I was being and that at least I had food on the table, had two legs, and two eyes. Ungrateful. That is the main block that I have to being needy." "Guilt," I wrote on the chalkboard.

Stan, one of the men in the group, added, "I simply learned not to ask. I kept my needs to myself. My attention was

always on making my mother happy. I grew up with a dominant mother, and then I married a dominant wife. I have no
concept of needing anything, except perhaps relief."

Elisa added, "If I want and get something, other people
will be jealous. They won't like me. In my family there was
never enough to go around. There was not enough affection
or attention or love."

So how does one resolve the Either/Or dichotomy between
waiting like Sleeping Beauty for Prince Charming and in the
process being a first-class Victim or the equally out-of-balance
decision that one can and should be totally self-sufficient? As
I shared with Jill, one of my clients, a stunning redhead who
had never been married, "The self-victimizing that occurs
with neediness comes from the idea that you yourself are not
capable of meeting your own needs, not in a vacuum, but by
interacting with another person, or as many other people as
are required. If you were hungry, you would not punish yourself for being hungry, you would go out to a restaurant. If
you are lonely, you need to do the same thing — establish a
connection."

The very idea that neediness is shameful prevents any
positive move toward its resolution, such as answering a personal ad or joining a support group. Thus, there is no action,
and the sense of desperation, hopelessness, and also neediness is increased.

I am reminded of Paula, another client, crying desperately
at the thought of her current relationship not working out.
Her sadness in large part resulted from her own internal persecutor who had decreed that she could not have sex with
anyone else without viewing herself as a bad person. Another
person might be convinced of his persecutor's pronouncement that he is a "failure" if he does not make a particular
relationship work.

Again, we cannot overemphasize how such judgmental
accusations have the power to damage our own self-esteem
and our self-control, and to prevent us from acting. The term

Stopper is just that, an inner barricade by which the Real Self is stymied.

Once, when I was in the process of fighting my own needs by attempting somehow to be a female Mahatma Gandhi, a very dear friend told me the story of the red hat. I have repeated the story many times, tailoring it in detail to the situation of the client with whom I was working. It always seems to get the message across. It goes as follows:

Once upon a time a woman decided that she wanted a red hat. So she went to a store and asked the salesperson to show her a red hat. The salesperson replied, "I'm sorry, but we don't sell red hats at this store." Now, instead of immediately leaving the store and going to another one, the woman began a rather common internal dialogue. "I bet if I just wait awhile, they'll get in some red hats." So she waited and waited until the store was about to close. She even decided to come back the next day, and the next. Over time, as she thought further, she figured that maybe she was not quite attractive enough for the salesperson to sell her a red hat, so she began a self-improvement course, lost some weight, cut her hair, and so forth. Still, no one in the store produced a red hat. She became very sad at this point and began to cry, looking desperate and secretly thinking that somehow if she's sad enough, someone just might round up a red hat. She saw other people go past the store wearing red hats, but this just convinced her that she must try all the harder to make herself "good enough" to deserve one. Somehow, she never thought to believe the information given her the first time she asked — "We don't sell red hats!"

This story had a profound effect on me at the time because I was dating a man who had said to me, even before we got involved, that whenever a woman fell in love with him, he always fell out of love with her. In other words, he was not available in a love relationship. He didn't sell red hats.

I have told the story with several variations. One is that the woman doesn't even tell the store clerk what she's looking for. So she never gets information as to whether the store does or doesn't sell red hats.

So many of my clients are stuck in relationships with men or women who say up front, "I don't ever want to be married," or "I don't love you." The illusory self-talk that keeps them there in a depriving situation is "If I am good enough, you'll change." The inner child from the past is hoping to win the unavailable parent's love by trying hard, so very hard, one more time. It is a setup for a relationship *not* to work.

Permission to Have

A similar inner barrier is the refusal to allow yourself to have something in your life. For some people, the inner Judge has set up clear rules against hoping or believing or trusting. It is as if the pain of believing or trusting an unreliable or even sadistic parent became too great, and the child decided never to love or trust again.

In other cases, the child decided to protect his parents by not having or acknowledging that he has more than they do. This is particularly true when either parent is caught in a Victim position, and the child feels that he must save that parent before he is entitled to or deserving of a life of his own.

With Claire, a client, who had faced severe deprivations and disappointments from an extremely self-centered mother, the protective aspects of the Judge were highlighted. Claire was afraid to let herself want anything, hope for anything, or experience having the love and affection that she actually had. Like the bars in a cage she had created especially for herself, Claire was unable to move past these inner prohibitions: "Don't want; Don't ask; Don't believe; Don't have."

As I asked her to alter her self-talk and to repeat after me, "I can get married. I can have a nice place to live," Claire explained, "I'm disconnecting from what I'm telling you. A part of me keeps thinking that a monster is out there." I asked Claire if she could tell the scared, distrustful part of herself that a "monster" (her critical mother who ridiculed and denigrated her simple requests as a child) used to be there. In truth, her cage had served to protect her somewhat from this monster, but now, the cage was just a cage, preventing her from moving on with her life. With sadness and grief, Claire began the process of dissolving the bars of her self-constructed prison. The very next week, she called to let me know that she had taken a new job.

Permission to Have Limitations

One of the hardest permissions to give myself has been the permission to have and to acknowledge my limitations. This has been particularly true in my work with clients. Here, I have had to confront over and over, often painfully, that I am not God, that I cannot prevent someone from harming herself, nor can I make someone change. The shame I used to feel because of these limitations was experienced, in particular, when I needed to hospitalize someone. I erroneously assumed that I had failed as a therapist. Actually, nothing is farther from the truth. An individual's need for hospitalization has nothing to do with my worth as a therapist. But it does point out that I cannot work magic.

As John Bradshaw writes in *Healing the Shame that Binds You*, "What our healthy feeling of shame does is let us know that we are limited. It tells us that to be human is to be limited. Actually we humans are essentially limited. . . . Healthy shame is the basic metaphysical boundary for human beings. It is the emotional energy which signals us that we are not God — that we need help. *Healthy shame gives us Permission to be human.*" (Italics mine)

When our Judge will not give us this Permission, tragic results follow. Without humility, battles are fought that cannot possibly be won. Impossible demands are made upon ourselves and our children.

It is interesting that one major aspect of physical illness is its automatic "time out" from the demands of the Judge. Illness offers a series of permissions, unavailable to many of us in normal times. In their study of cancer, the Simonton group, authors of *Getting Well Again*, asked their patients to list the positive aspects of having cancer. The patients freely acknowledged five such benefits: (1) Having permission to get out of dealing with troublesome situations or problems; (2) receiving attention, care, and nurturing from others; (3) having the opportunity to regroup psychologically to deal with a problem or find a new perspective; (4) finding incentives for personal growth or for modifying undesirable habits; (5) not having to meet the high expectations of themselves or others.

Notice that four of these five benefits have to do with Permissions to have needs and limitations. Many of them harken back to a childhood experience of sickness, bringing out the best in a parent. I know several people whose best memory of childhood involved being sick. Only then did their parents touch or hold them, or offer a respite from demands and pressures. This rarely experienced nurturing overrides any memory of the physical pain or distress of the illness. How tragic that one's own Judge replicates the same harshness and lack of nurturing except when illness intervenes. How relevant are such factors in causing illness? We do not as yet know. However, this notion certainly bears introspection and consideration.

The frank assertion of boundaries is an antidote to this state of affairs. This assertion can come only from the inner permission, "It is okay to say no." James gave himself this inner permission and confronted his boss, telling him that he could not deal with the mixed messages and contradictory demands from his two supervisors. The boss listened and made the necessary changes. For James, this was a new experience. His past method of dealing with such a conflict would have been to blame himself, work superhard to adjust to the problem, and finally burn out and quit, feeling ashamed and like a failure. His newfound permission to have limitations led to a different and better outcome. Had his boss not seen his point, James was prepared to resign without going through the cycle of shaming and depleting himself first.

Permission to Feel Good

In writing my first book, *Self-Assertion for Women*, I remember working on a particularly witty section and experiencing a growing sense of elation and excitement, upon which I immediately got up and went downstairs to make myself a cup of tea. It was almost as if I could not allow myself to feel that good.

Some years later, I was attending an outdoor rodeo with my mother. Something occurred that caused me to laugh aloud. My mother, at that point, hushed me. Where her discomfort came from, I don't know, but the experience provided for me an awareness of the process by which I learned to hush myself rather than face an outside censor. I wonder how many children are yelled at or hushed when they experience joyful or elated emotions and express the noise and physical exuberance that goes with such feelings. Unfortunately, I think the answer is a lot. For certain, many of my clients present a phobic-like response to feeling good.

Why do so many of us lack this important and basic permission to feel good? Why is there the cultural superstitions of the "Evil Eye" from which one must shield any signs of happiness or well-being? Why do we avoid sharing our successes with our friends? Why do some of us refuse to enjoy what we have? Do we believe that it will instantly vanish?

We fear, quite simply, the experience of loss. If we never allow ourselves to have anything, so the thinking goes, we will spare ourselves the pain of loss. Unfortunately, this thinking is a lie. We will still have to face all of the grief. We will simply have forfeited the joy.

I see people over and over taking self-talk loops away from the happiness of the now — fear loops, depression loops, regret loops. "I treated my daughter so badly when she was little" begins the regret loop. Three hours later, one can still be running around in that loop, generating anxiety and depression, and helping no one because we cannot change the past. In contrast, by staying in the now, I can ask myself,

"How can I amend my behavior toward my daughter now? What apologies and explanations need to be offered? Who am I treating badly now by living in the past?" Similarly, consider the scare loop, "I won't be able to support myself in the future. It's hopeless." Why not ask instead, "Is there something that I can do now to create a skill or job for myself? If not, then let it go."

Many great philosophers have centered their energy on staying in the now, seeing this as the key to happiness. I believe this true for myself as I recall one of my happiest times. I was on my horse, who was eating grass, while I lay my head across his neck and looked at the tiny wildflowers around his nose. The sun was shining and my Judge was asleep, and I was free to simply be.

Self-Affirmation

Self-Affirmation is a positive declaration about your own self. At its core is appreciation and respect for the Intrinsic Self. Its focus is on personal growth. Because Self-Affirmation is tied to the Intrinsic Self, it makes little difference whether or not you meet the external demands of society or the requirements of your Self 2 Judge. For that reason, Self-Affirmation may make little sense when viewed in terms of other people's values. Thus a woman with the Drivers Hurry Up and Try Hard — Type A Drivers — might, to the amazement of her friends, affirm herself for choosing to take more time off, rather than for accepting a prestigious or financially rewarding assignment. A man with a Be Strong Driver might regard his newfound ability to cry as a major growth step, one opposing the stifling message of his past, "Take it like a man."

Resting as it does upon the acceptance of your own growth as the basic criterion for reinforcement, Self-Affirmation requires you to look within to your own center to decide when you have made progress. The old saying "It's not where you are on the track that counts. It's where you started and how far you've come" is relevant here. If more people were able to operate from the growth perspective inherent in this maxim, self-support would not be so difficult. Yet people frequently ignore or discount positive changes in themselves, because these changes do not meet their external standards of what should be.

Jamie, for example, related to me two instances in which she had attempted to support herself. In the first situation, she had experienced her negative feelings evaporating as she had completed the final steps of the tape change method. With her second attempt, she did not fare so well. She was unable to neutralize the depression she felt about her inability to assert herself with two people at work. In fact, as she found the method not working, Jamie felt even more depressed.

Because she had written down her answers to each question in the five-step program (What am I telling myself? Is my self-talk helping? What is it costing? and so forth) I was able to examine her responses very carefully. Nothing caught my attention until I came to Step 4. Here, Jamie gave herself Permission to take the long time it seemed that she needed to become more assertive. She told herself that is was okay to be slow about it, and she affirmed that she would try to give herself credit for even tiny assertive steps.

Do you recognize Jamie's problem? Do you see the judgmental perspective inherent in terms like *long time, slow,* and *tiny*? As we talked, Jamie was able to say, "I'm patronizing myself, patting myself on the head. I'm saying, 'It's okay for you to be backward.' I guess I'm so used to judging myself that it creeps in even when I'm trying to be supportive."

Jamie *was* still judging herself. She had a preconceived notion of how much time she should take to master the task of being able to assert herself in all problem situations. Jamie only focused on how she was lacking when she compared herself to this ever-present "should." As with most judgmental standards, Jamie's was not all that realistic. Moreover, it kept her from recognizing how far she had come. She was not appreciating the fact that by asserting herself she had already solved a number of problems in her love relationship. Note Jamie's basic judgmental framework and the no-win consequences of it in the diagram on the opposite page. Contrast this framework with the Growth Model.

As Jamie came to realize, it would have been surprising if she had found herself feeling better after completing the five-step process. Her Permission and Self-Affirmation were tainted with subtle judgments. As such, they could not neutralize the effects of her original negative statements. She had been caught in the no-win perspective of the judgmental position.

While it is important that we affirm ourselves for "doing," as in Jamie's attempt to give herself credit for her newfound assertiveness, it is imperative that we learn also to acknowledge our okayness in "being." What psychologists have termed "unconditional positive regard" relates to this basic affirmation of the Intrinsic Self. Simply stated, unconditional positive regard means that whatever we choose to do for others or not do for them, whatever perfection or lack of it we manifest in our work, whoever loves us or doesn't love us, we are worthwhile. Our self-worth is not based on externals, but on the unique individual each of us is, an individual who may not have been nurtured or appreciated in the past, but who was and remains okay.

By talking directly to that little child who is still within, we permit the emergence of feelings of love and compassion and the decision to support and protect that precious part of ourselves. When Amy spoke to the little five-year-old girl inside, her whole manner changed: "You're a beautiful, lovable child whether or not you please your mother. You don't need to keep trying so hard to get people to like you. I'm not going to allow you to tolerate a bad environment, you're too special." Amy's expression to herself here is true Self-Affirmation.

As you now begin to support yourself through a new and possibly foreign language, the following guidelines may prove useful:

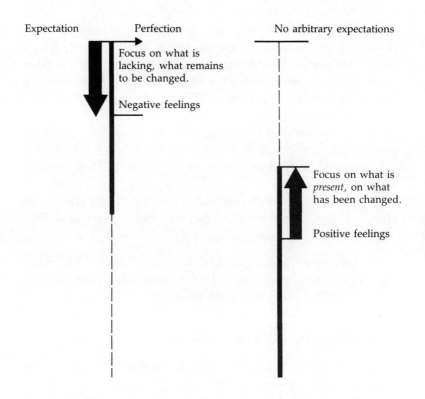

The Judgmental Position

The Growth Model

Expectation   Perfection

No arbitrary expectations

Focus on what is
lacking, what remains
to be changed.

Negative feelings

Focus on what is
present, on what
has been changed.

Positive feelings

1. *Forget what should be.* Give yourself credit for the steps you have taken, without judging their size or weight. Don't require a major breakthrough for self-acknowledgment. Writing one page of a report counts, for example, not necessarily finishing the entire report.

2. *Be specific.* When you spend two hours on a project, give yourself credit for two hours. Don't say, "I spent some time on . . ."

3. *Focus on something besides accomplishment.* Stated more positively, praise yourself for effort, for improvement, for allowing yourself to express or to experience your feelings. Give yourself credit for being aware of a negative process, even if you have not yet changed it. Notice any assertion of your Intrinsic Self.

4. *Learn to think in percentages.* For example, if you reduce your negative self-talk by 10 percent, then you have made a step forward, even if you are still overly critical 90 percent of the time.

5. *Encourage yourself.* Remind yourself that you are a valuable and lovable person right now, whether or not you accomplish, improve, or change anything.

In the comparisons that follow, notice how Self-Affirmation is possible within a growth framework, whereas it finds no place within the judgmental position.

Situation 1: Dealing with conflict

Susan and her husband, Jim, have spent the last week fighting about Susan's desire to accept a promotion in her firm. The new position will require Susan to travel several days a month, and Jim doesn't want her to be away from home that often. Describing her week, Susan says:

JUDGMENTAL EVALUATION: Jim and I aren't compatible. None of my friends has a husband as rigid and traditional as Jim. But I guess my friends aren't as cowardly and wishy-washy as I am either. We just don't have a good marriage.

GROWTH EVALUATION: It's been a difficult week, but I think that Jim and I have become clearer about each other's feelings. Not long ago, I would have given in at the slightest indication that Jim didn't like something. This time I've stuck to my position, in addition to hearing his.

Situation 2: Taking new risks

Joe has taken on a project that requires knowledge of several new accounts. In order to complete this assignment, he finds that he must ask other people in the office for specific information. This is new for Joe, who has always prided himself on his independence. Describing his problem, Joe says:

JUDGMENTAL EVALUATION: You're in over your head here. You should have mastered this by now. I bet the guy before you wasn't such a dunce. Those people probably think you're a poor manager.

GROWTH EVALUATION: It's hard for me to ask questions, but I think it's positive that I'm doing so, anyway. I don't think I could have asked for help a few years ago. I would have made mistakes and suffered through a lot of unnecessary trial and error. I'm finally turning off that Be Strong Driver.

Situation 3: Being a beginner

Eleanor is taking a class in public speaking to help her master her fear of giving oral reports at work. Having just completed her first speech, she says:

JUDGMENTAL EVALUATION: That was bad. You stumbled three times; you dropped your notes; you didn't gesture once. Everyone else gave a much better speech. Your topic was too technical. They didn't understand half of it.

GROWTH EVALUATION: Hey! One down, ten to go. You did it, kid. That was hard for you, but you did it. The important thing was not how it sounded (you can improve on that later). The important thing was that you got up there and made a speech.

Notice that each judgmental evaluation began with the premise of perfection and then demonstrated what was wrong with each person's effort. There is little chance for good feelings to derive from this stance. Like the little girl one teacher told me about, who was upset about her test score of 98, we wail about the two points missed rather than acknowledge the 98 points received. The growth model, on the other hand, is capable of generating tremendous positive feelings. Since there is no arbitrary expectation, any progress, any step forward, is acknowledged and appreciated.

For many of us, the judgmental position is the only one we have known. Our self-talk quite naturally flows from it. For that very reason, we have to be quite assertive in combatting these Self 2 messages. In Barbara Gordon's book *I'm Dancing As Fast As I Can,* there is an example that gives some sense of the magnitude of this struggle. After spending her birthday away from the hospital where she was working to overcome her psychological and Valium-induced problems, Gordon returns, "filled with a heady sense of accomplishment." She elaborates: "That night before I fell asleep, I said to myself, 'You did it, Barbara.' But my exhilaration was interrupted by a crack from my smart-ass self, that mocking, negative part of me that wouldn't let me alone. 'Terrific,' she said. 'Next week you can go to sleep-away camp.' I tried to silence her and remember the day. The struggle between the two of me must stop or I won't be able to live."

This struggle between Self 1 and Self 2, between the judgmental and growth positions, will invariably begin when you make the transition from your old language to the new. What was once underground may surface with a frightening intensity. As Gordon describes it, "I was forty-one, engaged in a battle with myself tougher than any fight I had ever had. Melodramatic or not . . . , I would have to fight as hard for me, and against me, as I did against the bad guys. If only I knew how to do it."

Pick a situation and try out for yourself both the judgmental and the growth evaluations. Determine which feels better, which motivates you for the future. Also decide which evaluation you now use most frequently.

For those of you having difficulty with the growth evaluation, you might try talking to yourself as you would talk to another person. Dr. Geraldine Alpert, a good friend of mine and fellow clinical psychologist, shared with me the question she asks her clients who are not supporting themselves. She asks, "What would you say to a child whom you loved if he or she were to have made the kind of mistake you just made?" For many people, an entirely new set of responses is called into play when a problem is broached from the perspective of talking to a loved one. Dr. Alpert then goes on to ask a second question, "How about being as good a parent to yourself as you are to your child?"

Creating a Buffer

One of the major benefits of self-support is that it allows you to create a protective barrier or buffer against the toxic situations in which you may find yourself. Nowhere does Epictetus's maxim "Man is troubled not by things but by the view he takes of them" apply more than here — in situations where you confront negative input from the outer environment. Only through an internal mechanism of self-support can you achieve a state of calmness under fire and security under stress.

By definition, a buffer is a shock absorber, a protection against outside influences. The buffer provided by your own self-support will stabilize you and keep you centered in the face of disappointment, criticism, rejection, or disapproval. Equally important, a buffer of self-support can protect you from the critical Judge of someone else.

Most people have received destructive feedback from another person at some time in their lives. There are, in fact, tragic examples of how negative judgments have influenced individuals without a protective buffer to turn away from their own Intrinsic Selves. When the individual giving the feedback happens to have society's seal of approval (parent, teacher, physician, therapist, or others), there is even more chance that the critical message will be swallowed whole because it carries the weight of authority.

Self-support provides the cushion that can keep you from going under in the face of negative feedback. Author Ayn Rand received a large number of rejection notices before *The Fountainhead* was accepted for publication and subsequently sold millions of copies. Would you have persevered under similar circumstances? Without a buffer of self-support, it is extremely difficult to deal with rejection. Like criticism, rejection never feels good. If you have a buffer or cushion, it simply doesn't have to feel so bad.

I have, on some happy occasions, helped a client create a buffer against a specific external event. Within one therapy session, this cushion of self-support can make the difference between despondence and self-acceptance. Over time, people develop the skill to construct these buffers for themselves. As one of my clients puts it, "It's like I have this beautiful multi-colored shield between myself and the person giving me negative feedback. With its protection, I can be there, and at the same time feel okay about myself. It's amazing how it softens any blow."

The first time I was aware of creating an internal buffer for myself, I was teaching a class on child development, an area where I have little practical expertise. I presented to the class a fairly technical lecture on learning theory and its application to behavioral problems in children. At the break, several students approached me and criticized my topic as being "too technical" for them. I was able to listen to their criticisms and even make some changes in my lectures, which made the class more rewarding for them and easier for me. What pleased me most, however, was that my own self-talk cushioned me from any destructive internalization of their criticism. For a Be Perfect, Please Others individual like myself, this was no small feat.

The buffer I used was the internal reminder "I'm okay even if I'm not liked and approved of every minute. I don't have to be a perfect teacher." I repeated this Permission to myself even as these students were sharing their concerns. I won't go so far as to say that I enjoyed the criticism. I can say that I didn't get particularly depressed or upset about it.

It is important here to emphasize that a buffer does not block incoming information. (I heard the students' criticisms and made some of the changes they requested.) Neither does it direct criticism back through means of a counterattack. (I did not turn their objections around and accuse them of being lazy or unwilling to work.) A buffer simply neutralizes the judgmental component inherent in most criticism. It allows the information to be received and dealt with while minimizing any self-evaluative pain. Instead of picking up the stick that someone has thrown and beating ourselves with it, we learn to pick it up, examine it, use it constructively, and then throw it away.

To summarize, a buffer protects us from the judgmental component of another person's criticism and from any judgmental additions of our own. It works by introducing Permission and Self-Affirmation against the Be Perfect, Hurry Up, Be Strong, Try Hard, or Please Others claims of another person. A buffer detoxifies criticism.

When therapy is successful, a person often comes to a point that might seem incomprehensible if viewed solely from an outside perspective. The environmental stress that originally brought the person into therapy may have remained unchanged. The process of altering the stressful situation may even have stirred up more immediate difficulty (a quietly toxic marriage may be moving through a turbulent divorce). Yet the inner environment is vastly altered. When in the face of equal or additional stress, you feel congruent, alive, and calm within yourself, you will know that a genuine turnabout has occurred. A cushion has been created, a buffer constructed, and self-support has become a basic internal ingredient.

8

∎ ∎ ∎ ∎ ∎ ∎ ∎

Developing Your Guide

WHEN you have made the transition from a critical, punishing orientation to a supportive one, the question arises, "What now?" If you are a Be Perfect dieter who affirms "It's no tragedy when I don't stick to my diet one hundred percent. It's okay for me to be human. I've already lost five pounds, and I'm doing well," you are at a critical point. If you are not careful, the judgmental position will again dominate, saying "Well, don't do it again. One mistake is all you get!" Reverting to the old standard is a dangerous possibility.

On the other hand, it is not in a dieter's best self-interest to eat another handful of potato chips or move on to a bowl of ice cream. A direction is necessary, a plan for action, if you will. You have seen the negative consequences of the Be Perfect tightrope. What is needed is a sidewalk, a flexible plan that allows for mistakes yet moves in the desired direction. What is needed is a Guide.

In contrast to a Judge, a Guide sets forth an action plan that allows you to be human, to experience and accept your feelings, and to operate in cooperation with your Intrinsic Self. By avoiding the destructive pitfalls of Drivers, Stoppers, and Confusers, a Guide helps you to formulate an action plan that is both realistic and useful. The development of such a Guide is the fifth and final step involved in changing your tapes. This Guide will differ greatly from the Judge who has heretofore sat heavily upon your shoulders. Let's examine the basic features of both Judge and Guide in the comparisons that follow:

The Self 2 Judge	The Self 2 Guide
1. A Judge ignores your Intrinsic Self. It operates totally on preconceived notions of what should be.	1. A Guide takes into account your Intrinsic Self: your feelings, your day-to-day fluctuations in mood, your changing priorities and desires.
2. A Judge is inflexible. No change is allowed because of altering circumstances or feelings.	2. A Guide is flexible. It allows your action plan to vary with changing circumstances.
3. A Judge does not consider the environment. It operates within the rarefied atmosphere of "what should be" and ignores "what is."	3. A Guide considers the environment in which a particular behavior is to be developed. That environment is altered as part of the action plan, if necessary.
4. A Judge knows nothing of small steps. The message "Do something" is never amplified by the instruction "This is the first step."	4. A Guide is satisfied with small steps. Rather than demanding, "Accomplish such and such," a Guide asks, "What step can you take to move forward in your growth?"
5. A Judge relies on Drivers, based on the assumption that you would not move if you were not pushed. Drivers are considered necessary mechanisms of control.	5. A Guide permits no Drivers to interfere with the action plan. There is no Hurry Up, Try Hard, or Be Perfect. The Guide assumes that given the proper environment, you will grow in the manner that is best for you.
6. A Judge uses punishment, not reward. Its focus is on what is lacking, not on what is accomplished.	6. A Guide incorporates ample positive reward into each step.

Referring back to the initial example, a dieter's Guide might say, "It's likely that you ate those potato chips because you let yourself get too hungry and had nothing else on hand to eat. The next time you're going to be at school late like this, why not bring a piece of fruit with you? Then you'll have something good to tide you over, and you won't be so tempted to hit the vending machines."

Notice that when Self 2 is functioning as a Guide, a workable plan is set forth, a sidewalk approach to meeting the stated goal. The dieter's hunger is not criticized or ignored. It is taken as an important need that must be integrated into any workable plan. Notice also that special measures (bringing a piece of fruit) are considered necessary because of the special circumstances (being at school late in the evening) that the dieter faces. Working with the realities encountered rather than ignoring them is an important function of the Self 2 Guide.

There are five basic principles that enable a Guide to function in a nonpunishing yet effective capacity. These are (1) small steps, (2) sensitivity to the environment, (3) sensitivity to yourself, (4) ample reward, and (5) self-assertion. Skill in applying these principles is very important. Let's consider each principle in detail.

Small Steps

One of the simplest, most basic principles the Guide employs is the use of small steps. According to Dorothy Tennov, author of *Super Self*, a step "should be large enough to be discernible, small enough to be accomplished." If a step is too large, it will be avoided. If it is too small, it will go unnoticed.

Most of us, when we err, do so by making our steps too large. In writing a report, we decide to complete it in one six-hour block. We diet by setting a five-pound weight loss goal each week. We list twenty items to accomplish in one day. Of course, the larger the step, the less likely we are to meet it, and the more we set ourselves up for discouragement and self-punishment.

After having a very difficult time finding an exercise that she *would* do, Jane decided to apply to herself the small step principle. It originally seemed to her that she was using this principle when she told herself that it was okay to jog only once around the track. She thought she was using it when she gave herself permission to go to just one dance class each week. But these behaviors dwindled away to nothing. Jane finally recognized that as small as these steps might seem to her Judge or to another person (a quarter-mile jog is certainly a minute step to a twenty-six-mile marathoner), they were too large for her.

Therefore, Jane decided to find an exercise that was indeed a small step, one that would start her moving toward her goal of becoming more physically fit. Living in a house with three flights of stairs, she decided that running up and down two of the flights might be a good place to start. She tried this out and found that running three times in a row, up and down the stairs, felt okay. Over the course of two weeks, her batting average hovered around .500. "That's okay," she told herself, remembering that Be Perfect usually ends in Do Nothing.

The practice of making one's first step small enough seems simple. Yet it frequently goes against the Self 2 Judge's Hurry Up, Try Hard command. When anxiety is great, a first step may need to be small indeed. One of my clients, for example, set as her first step the goal of simply counting the pages of the chapter she was supposed to read. Once she looked at it, her fear lessened enough for her to move to the second step of reading the chapter headings.

Many problems that loom huge and frightening on the horizon become manageable when the steps are made small enough. If you find yourself avoiding some task that you want to tackle or ignoring a goal that you want to pursue, your problem may simply be that your first step is too large. Break it down. A basic rule of thumb is to continue your task reduction until your first step becomes one that you can make without depression or dread. Once you have finished this step, you can renegotiate with yourself about the next one. Along these lines, consider how you might apply the small step principle to housecleaning, writing a paper, beginning an exercise program, or making a career change.

In regard to cleaning the house, if your first step is something on the order of "clean the bedroom," you have probably *not* made your step small enough. Cleaning the bedroom is in itself composed of many steps — vacuuming, making the bed, picking up clothes, and dusting. If you happen not to be in an energetic mood, your "clean the bedroom" command will leave you sitting on the couch watching one more television program or engaging in some other avoidance behavior. A better step might be "Hang up five items in the bedroom."

As to writing a term paper, the Self 2 Judge would tend to demand, "Stop bellyaching, and sit down and write it." A Guide, on the other hand, might offer, "Read and underline the first article on the topic. Don't try to decide what you're going to write yet. Just read the article." If all of the material has been read, a Guide might suggest, "Jot down five questions that you want to answer in your paper," or it might ask, "What's the easiest section to write? List your ideas about that section." Notice that these steps gently lead the reluctant writer into the material. Usually, this brief exposure will prove sufficient to capture the writer's interest, and more will actually be accomplished than the small step would indicate. If this "fire" doesn't ignite, the writer will still be one step ahead. In working with people with test anxiety or with writer's block, I have found the principle of small steps to be a very effective tool for change.

Sensitivity to the Environment

When Jane chose to exercise by running up and down the stairs, she made certain that this exercise could be accomplished in her own home. Although she lived near a track, her experience had taught her that the effort involved in driving there and back was simply too great to maintain her exercising, a program still very low in habit strength. Again, she decided that it was better to do something at home than do nothing on the track. This choice involved a sensitivity to her environment.

If you are to be maximally effective, you must develop this sensitivity. When you recognize the importance of your environment, you gain a useful tool for facilitating your desired behavior. Unfortunately, if you have a strong sense of how something ought to be, you may fight your environment rather use it for your own benefit. You may expect yourself to have "self-control" under any circumstances and punish yourself if this control disappears in the face of strong environmental demands.

In working with people who want to lose weight, I often find this strong need to deny the reality of environmental control. People expect their weight to fall off with ice cream in the freezer and cookies in the cookie jar. They expect themselves to push aside the hot bread and butter sitting on the table in front of them. They want to continue cooking for the family in all the regular ways. Yet weight loss comes from controlling in advance any tempting foods, by not having them routinely available.

This same sensitivity to the environment is important with most other goals. If you want to improve your grades or become more productive in your work, for example, you must keep any nonwork distractions to a minimum. An effective Guide makes the alterations necessary to insure that your environment supports positive behavior. Again, this requires accepting what is, rather than what you think should be.

For Nola, sensitivity to the environment involved constructing for herself a work space. The hassle of getting out her sewing materials and making a space for herself on the dining room table only to have to clean up in preparation for dinner usually meant that Nola avoided an activity that she really enjoyed doing once she got down to it. A small purchase of a secondhand table and the assertion of her need for a permanent area cleared the way for her to pursue her goal. Constructing this kind of supportive environment for herself was simple, of course, after she had squelched her Judge's "you should be able to work anywhere" belief.

Sensitivity to Yourself

The third hallmark of an effective Guide is sensitivity to the feelings and needs of your Intrinsic Self. This includes two different aspects — sensitivity to your moment-to-moment feelings and sensitivity to your current capability level.

Sensitivity to your feelings

Sensitivity to your feelings involves the willingness to listen carefully to your own inner experience. Many people have learned not to trust their insides. They ask others, "What should I do? What decision should I make?" rather than listening to and honoring their own feelings and responses. Yet relieved of the muddying effects of Drivers, Stoppers, and Confusers, your feelings give you the clearest, most complete feedback possible about your own unique direction.

When I was a child, my grandmother and I used to play a game where one of us would search for an object that the other had chosen somewhere in the room. When the object was being approached, we would give the progressive feedback "You're warm, you're getting warmer, you're hot, you're hotter, you're almost on fire!" The opposite message was broadcast when the object was being evaded. The immediate feedback that was so much a part of this game is analogous to the role your feelings have in guiding your direction.

When you allow yourself to operate in conjunction with your Intrinsic Self, you will invariably experience a sense of unblocked flow. You will often feel excited, happy, energetic, or enthusiastic. You may also feel angry or sad or tired, and if you do, these feelings will be accepted and supported. You will allow yourself to experience them fully and finish them, so that you will not accumulate resentment in your gunnysack or block your expression of grief through depression and muscular rigidity. In short, you will not experience the conflict that occurs when you are fighting yourself. Neither will you deaden your own sensations with shoulds and should nots and criticisms.

Instead, when Self 1 and Self 2 operate as one, you will listen to and honor your feeling signals, whatever they may be. If you are relaxing in the sunshine, you will not need to tell yourself to get up. You will act when your feelings signal your readiness to do so. Since you are not on a Sit-Down Strike, your basic energy pulse is alive to activate you whenever a thought or an external issue captures your interest. Similarly, because your experience of grief or anger is being neither fueled nor squelched by the messages of your Imposed Self, your emotional expression becomes a healing and time-limited experience. As one person having connected to the power of her feelings for the first time exclaimed, "I just can't stop talking about all my plans and new ideas. I feel so excited. I never thought that I could be this happy."

Just as feelings of aliveness and oneness inform you that you are on the right track, anxiety, depression, and lethargy tell you that you have wandered away from your own Self 1 signals or that you are fighting against them. The now well-known experiments by Stanley Milgram on obedience to authority give us a dramatic example of this latter process. As I described them in *Self-Assertion for Women*, Milgram's studies examined the amount of electric shock a subject would willingly administer to another person when instructed to do so by someone in authority. In a result that baffled and outraged many people, Milgram found that a majority of subjects (62 percent) obeyed an authority's command, even to the point of delivering what was thought to be 300 volts of electricity to another person.

The 300-volt shock was given even though it was clearly labeled as dangerous. It was given when the victims (actually accomplices of the experimenter) cried out in pain that they did not want to continue participating in the experiment. And it was given over "powerful reactions of tension and emotional strain." As Milgram notes, "Persons were observed to sweat, tremble, stutter, bite their lips, and groan as they found themselves increasingly implicated in the experimental conflict." Very few subjects, however, listened to their own internal emotional responses when authority demanded, "You have no choice; you must go on."

Milgram also used a group of female subjects in one of his experiments. He initially thought that female subjects might give the victim less severe shock than male subjects. We know that women tend to express less aggression than men on a voluntary basis. On the other hand, a study by Sandra Bem has shown that women who conform to the traditional feminine sex role have more difficulty than men in standing up against external pressure. Milgram found this latter tendency to dominate. Women were just as obedient as men, 62 percent giving the victim maximum shock. Interestingly enough, this one group of women reported higher tension associated with their compliance than any of the twenty groups of obedient males.

Thus women refused to heed even more powerful signals than men when they were put in a position where obedience was expected, in a situation where they *should* obey.

This same unwillingness to honor one's feelings occurs in less startling examples as well. For instance, in dieting, keeping hunger at a manageable level by recognizing and accepting its validity is one of the most important factors in a successful weight loss program. Paradoxically, I often ask people on diets to eat more—more breakfast and more lunch—so that by the end of the day, their hunger will not precipitate a to-hell-with-it binge on any and everything available in the house.

Depression is another signal that frequently indicates that we have lost touch with the needs of the Intrinsic Self. The woman I mentioned before, who was experiencing a new-found excitement about her plans and activities, had been depressed for several years. Her feelings were telling her that her needs were not being met. As her Stoppers were neutralized and she began again to engage in the outdoor activities that she had once enjoyed and to reevaluate her work situation, her depression lifted. Operating in a manner similar to physical pain, her depression was the signal that told her to change directions.

Sensitivity to capability

In addition to recognizing and accepting your feelings, a sensitive reading as to your current level of functioning — your capability level — is vital information for your Guide. If you are a person who says, "Don't ask me to do anything until I've had my third cup of coffee," you are speaking of a low morning-capability level. The comment "After six o'clock, I'm too pooped to do anything except watch the tube" demonstrates a sensitivity to a reduced capability at the end of the day.

In *Super Self*, Dorothy Tennov distinguishes "Five levels of capability — from most capable (Level One) to least capable (Level Five)." Level One capability involves the capacity for peak performance. This is the level at which you can do your best work, tackle your most difficult projects, do your hardest thinking. Alternatively, Level Five is good for relaxing or for doing, at most, routine tasks. Capability levels are based on recurring physiological cycles (such as sleep, temperature) as well as transitory influences (illness, depression, fatigue, good news).

It goes without saying that the Self 2 Judge has little sensitivity to or sympathy for these differing capability levels. The

Be Strong battle cry is "full steam ahead," regardless of the internal feedback. "Hurry Up" ignores any need to pace yourself. Alternatively, rigid requirements like "Before you start your project, get your desk cleared off" can underutilize your high energy level. Folding clothes or answering routine letters while you're raring to go at Level One will set you up for failure. Similarly negative expectations ("It's probably a pipe dream") can take the fizzle out of your Level One enthusiasm. In short, both overemployment and underemployment of your current capability level can lead to negative feelings. One vital function of your Self 2 Guide is to match your internal level with the external demands that you face.

Many of the clients whom I see have set themselves up for self-punishment by a lack of sensitivity to their own current capability. They attempt to do complex, high-level tasks while at low energy levels, and failing, consider themselves incompetent, lazy, or stupid. Moreover, a lack of self-nurturing combined with an overabundance of Drivers has frequently resulted in a general reduction in overall capacity. Many people become inundated in what I call Exhaust Time. Because they push themselves too far, for too long, they become depleted, depressed, and burnt out.

Exhaust Time, the lowest level of capability, *can* be pleasurable, but only if self-demands are kept to a minimum. Exhaust Time is for sitting in the sun, reading for pleasure, taking a nap, or doing nothing. It is a time for restoration and self-nourishment. Many people don't believe in Exhaust Time. They operate as if it didn't exist. The same insensitivity to the environment that we found earlier occurs in regard to this inner state as well. Worse still, many people punish themselves for any low-level capacity. This self-punishment can dampen a naturally lowered energy cycle and push an individual into depression (see diagram).

If you expend a great deal of high-level energy on work, you may find that you are allotting only Exhaust Time for yourself or for your mate. A working couple, for example,

Energy Cycle–Capability Cycle

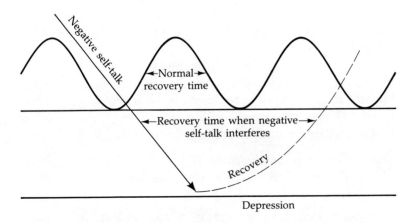

Depression

may get together only during periods of Level Five capability and yet expect their relationship to be fun and romantic and exciting. By Friday evening, when they finally are out on the town together, it is no wonder that conversation is dull, and that sex later is an unimaginative, routine affair.

In the same vein, the allocation of Exhaust Time for personal pursuits frequently leads to a mediocre result. Joe, for example, works as a tax attorney. He overworks actually — a fifty- or sixty-hour week. The time that Joe has left over after work is mainly Exhaust Time. He spends it playing racket ball, puttering around the house, and reading books about his own financial planning. Joe doesn't find much time, however, for what he says is top priority — developing a relationship. He generally doesn't feel like socializing on Friday or Saturday nights since he has worked all day. He never has time for lying on the beach, browsing around a museum, or going to a new place where he might meet someone.

Although Joe punishes himself for not getting out more ("What's wrong with you? Have you lost interest in women?"), he lacks the desire to do so. Joe's work takes all of his high-level time, leaving him exhausted and without the need for any social stimulation. The effort involved in meeting new people is simply too great to occur at Level Four or Level Five capability.

At the end of a weekend, during which he has worked nine or ten hours, Joe criticizes himself: "Another weekend blown. You're not going to meet anyone unless you get out more. Why didn't you go to the party Friday night?" As Joe looks at his internal message, he asks himself:

STEP 1: What am I telling myself?

I'm telling myself to stop making excuses and get going.

STEP 2: Is my self-talk *helping*?

It might help if I said it on Friday afternoon. On Sunday night, no, it doesn't help. It depresses me.

STEP 3: What is the Driver, Stopper, or Confuser?

Try Hard. I tell myself that I shouldn't want to lie around here all weekend. I should be out trying hard to meet someone.

STEP 4: What's my Permission and Self-Affirmation?

That it's okay to listen to my own feelings and act upon them. That means I can relax and do nothing if I want. I deserve some time for me.

STEP 5: What is my Guide, my action plan?

I'm going to stop working for a while on Saturday. I'm going to relax all day and see if I feel like going out on Saturday night. I'll let a few people know I'm interested in meeting someone and see what happens. Maybe it's time to talk to my boss about an assistant. One thing's for sure, unless I have more time to unwind and recuperate, I won't get out.

Notice that Joe's action plan is based on a sensitivity to his capability level. This sensitivity necessitates that Joe change his environment (by increasing his time at home) to give himself an opportunity to pursue his goal of forming a relationship. The same may be true for you. Whether your goal is to take time to meet someone, to write a book, or to develop a new interest, there must be enough available energy for you to move beyond your Exhaust Level.

Ample Reward

A fourth attribute of a Guide is the use of reward rather than punishment to motivate behavior. Psychologists have long demonstrated that new behaviors can be developed and that current habits can be strengthened through simple reinforcement principles. Moreover, in contrast to the numerous negative side effects that accompany punishment, reinforcement fosters positive feelings and attitudes.

You can use self-rewards to increase desired behaviors and to decrease unwanted ones — to study more, to smoke less, to develop a new skill. Rewarding yourself will produce changes that simply will not occur if you are motivating yourself with shoulds and self-punishment.

There are two aspects to rewarding yourself. First, in and of itself, positive reinforcement will help you to maintain a high level of psychological functioning. Just as you need food for physical energy, you need to nurture yourself for maximum psychological well-being. You can do this by providing a generous supply of internal and external rewards. Second, positive reinforcement allows you to reinforce yourself after the completion of each step in your action plan, insuring that your new behavior will be maintained and strengthened.

Reinforcement related to general well-being

In therapy, when I see clients who are depressed, one of the first things that I examine with them is the number of enjoyable activities in which they are currently engaged. I frequently find that there are a very small number of such pastimes. Most have been replaced by self-imposed work or family demands, so that there is virtually no time to listen to music, to read a novel, to go swimming, or to participate in other relaxing or invigorating pursuits.

This was the case with Suzanne. When she was promoted to merchandising manager in her firm, Suzanne found herself with very little free time. As her unit was expanding, a heavy burden of reports fell to her, along with the continuing demands of supervision, budgeting, and planning. After several months of operating at a whirlwind pace, Suzanne began to feel depressed. When her co-workers started noticing, she decided to begin therapy.

In talking to Suzanne, it immediately became clear that she had three Drivers constantly in operation — Be Perfect, Hurry Up, and Try Hard. Her Try Hard Driver, in particular, led her to keep her hands in every facet of her unit's activities. Suzanne could not set priorities because to her Judge everything in her unit was top priority. She had to meet each demand (Try Hard), to meet it at once (Hurry Up), and to maintain a top level of performance (Be Perfect). The result was long hours under high stress.

When Suzanne came home, frequently with unfinished paperwork in her briefcase, she was too tired to go for a walk, to experiment with a new recipe, to do her needlepoint, or to write or telephone friends. Her lunches with fellow professional women, once a major source of enjoyment and support, had dwindled to once or twice each month. In fact, one by one, Suzanne's sources of reinforcement and self-nurturing were set aside.

Fortunately, Suzanne was able to look at what was happening objectively enough to decide to arrange her life in a different way. As she realized how stagnant her life had become, she immediately made plans to have dinner with several friends whom she had not seen during the previous months. Purposefully, she arranged these meetings early enough to force her to leave work at a regular time. She stopped carrying any paperwork home. "I never do the work anyway," she explained, "but I tend to feel so guilty about it that I don't listen to music or read a novel or do something that I might actually want to do."

As Suzanne began to treat herself better, her depression began to lift. Moreover, the fulfillment of her actual job requirements did not suffer. The ever-so-exact reports weren't missed. She still conveyed the information needed, but with much less time and energy spent on making them perfect. She learned to delegate and found that letting go of some of her control did not lead to total collapse. Her staff's morale actually improved. In short, Suzanne developed a Guide who considered self-nurturing a very necessary ingredient in fulfilling her long-range goals.

Self-reward based on increased positive behavior

When any behavior is followed by a positive consequence, that behavior is strengthened. Rewards, even small ones, are very important motivators for habit change. I can well remember how effectively my piano teacher used rewards during my first year of lessons. Upon the successful completion of a piece of music, I received an animal sticker to place in a paper circus car. For my 9-year-old self, this was an important positive consequence.

The same motivating effect will occur when you reward yourself. When Gail followed her thirty-minute walk with lunch, she walked much more frequently than when she moved to an office with no lunch facilities nearby. When Jimmy allowed himself to have a beer with his friends after studying for two hours, he found himself ready to hit his books soon after dinner. When Betty gave herself a point every time she avoided the impulse to smoke and cashed her points in for small articles of jewelry, clothing, and cosmetics, she found that her withdrawal didn't feel so bad.

The more a habit change involves some kind of deprivation, the more vital is ample reward. In her book *I'll Never Be*

Fat Again, Eda LeShan writes, "Nothing turned out to be more important while dieting than learning to comfort and reward myself with gifts other than food. Here's (my) journal entry: No weight loss for two days, and I'm feeling discouraged and sorry for myself. I stopped at the drugstore and bought myself an assortment of makeup I certainly don't need. I felt like an idiot until I realized I had made a sensational shift. Ordinarily, feeling discouraged or depressed would have driven me to a bakery or a candy counter. Good for me!"

Perhaps the most important reward of all is simple self-acknowledgement, like LeShan's "Good for me!" I know that for myself, the acknowledgment "Hey, you finished that section," or "That's five chapters, now. You're almost halfway through" is very important. I'm sure that for runners, seeing the steady progression from half mile, to a mile, to two miles, to five miles has a tremendous reinforcing effect. Accomplishment, achievement — growth, if you will — is intrinsically rewarding when one is proceeding from a Driver-free standpoint, that is, when there are no Hurry Ups, Be Perfects, or Try Hards to ruin the feeling.

To discover unrecognized ways of rewarding yourself, you may want to write for yourself a description of a perfect day. When I asked class members in one "Talking to Yourself" group to do this, a surprising similarity emerged. The typical "perfect" day involved getting up late, eating out, and having leisure time, free from the demands of housework or study or what should be done. The uniformity of the responses probably related to the homogeneity of this all-woman group, where most members were in their late thirties, their forties, or their fifties. For these women, the gift of free time was an extremely important form of self-nurturing.

Allowing yourself what you need to nurture yourself, simple as it may seem, is not necessarily easy. As one woman commented, "I let myself attend a two-month class related to my business, but I wouldn't give myself permission to take a writing workshop for even one night a week." Another agreed, "I'll give myself time to jog, because that's productive and it's good for my health, but I won't allow myself leisure time to sit and contemplate."

Part of nurturing yourself, however, involves just this — expanding through permission the boundaries set by your Self 2 Judge. Instead of confining your self-nurturing to eating out, for example, would you allow yourself a massage or a bouquet of flowers? What about hiring someone to clean the house? Even for women and men who can afford it, paying to have the house cleaned is often not permitted by the Self 2 Judge. How about your perfect day? What new rewards or old favorite ones will you give yourself?

Self-Assertion

Since so many conflicts can be resolved through self-assertion, it is important that you develop assertive skills to the highest degree possible. A thorough understanding of the principles of self-assertion is the fifth prerequisite of an effective Guide. In *Self-Assertion for Women,* I discuss eight techniques that aid in the successful resolution of interpersonal difficulties. Three of the most important, the *"I" Message, Muscle,* and *Fogging,* I would like to detail here.

"I" messages

Skill in asserting positive and negative feelings, in saying no, and in initiating contact with others is necessary for an effective Guide. Learning to use "I" Messages, rather than "You" Messages, is a basic part of this skill. In chapter 5, the distinction between "I" Messages and "You" Messages was briefly discussed. To review, an "I" Message expresses a feeling or states an opinion. It communicates without blaming. A "You" Message, on the other hand, resorts to the use of negative labels. "You" Messages judge another person. In contrast to the "You" Message "You're insensitive," the "I" Message "I get annoyed when you forget to introduce me to your friends" relays information in a manner that is both more precise and less threatening. The future-oriented "I" Message "Next time, I'd like you to introduce me to your friends" elicits even less defensiveness.

The main strength of the "I" Message rests in the two characteristics just mentioned — high precision and low threat. An incident was described in one group that illustrates how "You" Messages fail in both of these regards. While in a public area, Shawn overheard two people talking. The first person began with the classic "You" Message "You're wrong," which led immediately to the defensive reply "Well, you're stupid." To quote Shawn, "It got worse from there." The interesting aspect of this interchange is that in the two or three minutes that Shawn listened, there was no mention of who, what, where, why, or how. In other words, very little actual information was relayed.

"You" Messages may be great vehicles for punishment, but they simply don't communicate very effectively. Moreover, "You" Messages are almost always aggressive, provoking the person on the receiving end to strike back ("Well, you're stupid"), to withdraw ("Then there's no use talking to you"), or to become defensive ("I don't know about that"). In the "I" and "You" Messages that follow, examine your own reactions. Which do you prefer?

Muscle

In my experience, most people assert themselves with more Muscle than is needed. As George Bach, one of the authors of *The Intimate Enemy*, says, they drop the atomic bomb on Luxembourg. I can best show the importance of Muscle by sharing a story told to me by an acquaintance whom I'll call Karen. After an exhausting trip, Karen flew back to San Francisco from the East Coast. On this five-hour

Situation	"You" Message	"I" Message
Jane's secretary neglects to write the time that a message arrived, information that Jane would like to have.	"You're not being careful enough in taking messages."	"I'd appreciate your making sure that the time is listed on each message."
Bob is annoyed to find Jill has made plans to get together with another couple without checking with him first.	"You're inconsiderate as hell. Don't you think I have any say in what we do?"	"Jill, I really feel annoyed when you make plans for me without asking me first."
Jenny comes home late from school, leaving the other members of her family without transportation.	"Don't you ever think of anyone but yourself? You're becoming totally insensitive to the rest of this family."	"I don't want you to be late with the car again. I feel edgy wondering where you are and angry at being left hanging."
The waitress brings Don a meal he didn't order.	"You messed up my order."	"I think there's been a mistake. I ordered the eggplant, not the fettuccine."

flight, she planned to spend her time sleeping or, at the very most, reading a book. However, Karen sat next to someone who wanted to talk.

Rather than assert herself at this point by saying, "I've had such an exhausting trip that I don't feel much like talking today. I'm sure that another time I would have enjoyed chatting with you," Karen decided to do what many of us would probably do — hint. Her hint was to give a one-word reply to each question. As with most hints, there was no effect, and as the flight progressed, Karen felt more and more irritated. Finally, she erupted, exclaiming, "I don't want to talk!"

Her traveling companion, who had been chatting merrily along, got a stricken look and said nothing more. However, rather than being pleased with the result of her expression, Karen felt guilty. She couldn't sleep, and she didn't feel like reading her book. Worse yet, she no longer had anyone with whom to talk. The net effect of the interchange between Karen and her fellow passenger was the lose-lose outcome that so often occurs with beginning assertive attempts.

Karen's assertion *was* an "I" Message. However, she had hit her traveling companion over the head with a club when a feather would have sufficed. Karen had simply used too much Muscle. Her difficulty came not from what she said, but from how she said it.

I find that one of the most difficult assertive skills to master is the use of what I call Level One Muscle. Most people remain passive, come across aggressively, or use a very high level of Muscle in their communication. The effectiveness of the soft yet clear assertion that is Level One Muscle is completely neglected. If need be, there are higher levels that can be employed. Ironically, however, Level One Muscle is the most powerful because it prevents a power struggle. In other words, Level One Muscle is easy to respond to without a loss of face.

Fogging

Whereas "I" Messages and Muscle enable us to send an assertive message, Fogging, a technique developed by Manuel Smith, prepares us to be an assertive receiver. All too often, other people send judgmental "You" Messages to us. They add to our own Drivers with Be Perfect, Hurry Up, or Try Hard commands of their own. Fogging allows us to walk past these negative messages without getting hooked by them.

When you fog, you briefly acknowledge what has been said, without agreeing or disagreeing. By remaining neutral, you steer clear of the other person's judgments. You do not have to defend or to acquiesce, nor do you get hooked into the other person's agenda. Instead, you remain free to reassert your own message. Thus, if Mark has decided to forego a business trip to Europe because his feelings tell him that such a trip, great as it sounds, is unappealing at this time, he may have to contend with various judgmental comments from others. The responses that follow demonstrate two possible reactions to such comments — Fogging and Getting Hooked:

Judgmental Comment	Fogging Response	Hooked-In Response
Mark, you shouldn't miss this opportunity. You may never get another.	That may be true, but I don't feel like making this one.	Well, this isn't that good an opportunity. After all, I'd be working late. There wouldn't be much time for me to sightsee.
Anyone in his right mind would go on a free trip to Europe.	It may seem that way; however, I feel comfortable with my decision.	What are you doing? Calling me crazy? What makes you think you know everything?
Surely your wife doesn't mind your going?	She may or may not mind, but I don't feel that the trip fits me right now.	What makes you think that my wife controls me?
I bet your boss is really upset that you're saying no to the trip.	Well, she may be upset, but I have to make my decisions reflect what's best for me.	Do you think so? Well, maybe I should go.
You're being silly. You should go.	Maybe so, but I'd rather sit this one out.	I'd be silly if I go over there and have a miserable time. I don't like to travel alone.

Notice that Fogging alone allows Mark to maintain his own agenda without becoming defensive and without attacking the other person. The key words *may, sometimes,* and *seem* fulfill Fogging's requirement that Mark neither agree nor disagree with his opponent. For those of you who would like more information about these three assertive techniques, as well as others, I would recommend my book, *Self-Assertion for Women*.

Summing Up

Over conversation one night, John Harrison, a friend of mine, described how he had recently been able to develop a Guide for himself. He did this, however, only after an important learning experience from which he had allowed himself to profit.

"About a year ago," John explained, "I decided that Hatha Yoga would be good for me. I set the goal of practicing the various yoga positions an hour each day, four days a week. The first week I accomplished my goal. The next week, I was busy and pressured with work deadlines, so I only got in three days. At that point, instead of just letting it go, I told myself that I would have to make up for the day I missed and practice five days the coming week. Well, that week was busy also, and I again found time for only three days of exercise. At that point, I thought, 'Oh, to hell with it!'"

Several months later, John began experimenting with a new approach. After his negative experience with yoga, he consciously decided to reorient his Self 2 away from arbitrary goals and judgments toward a sensitivity to his feelings. His Self 2 shifted from Judge to Guide. In other words, John's Self 2 began functioning as a good parent or a good friend, allowing him to make mistakes, to fail, in short to Be Human. John made this transition around another goal—running. This time, he gave himself permission *not* to run every day, *not* to go farther than he felt comfortable, *not* to compete with other joggers on the track.

"Sure, I sometimes feel competitive," John continued. "A guy passes me, and I have the urge to speed up. I admit to myself that it bothers me, but I also tell myself that it's okay to run at my own speed. I remind myself that I want my running to suit me."

"You know something," John continued. "I've been running now for six months, and I'm still enjoying it. I'm up to three miles a day, and I have no intention of stopping."

The bottom line is this: A Guide works. By considering your environment and your feelings, by utilizing the principles of small steps and ample reward, and by operating within an assertive framework, you maximize your positive feelings and your ability to fulfill your own potential. In contrast to the empty orders of a Judge, your Guide offers you a plan of action. It replaces a tension-filled tightrope with a workable sidewalk. You're almost home free. Almost. For some of you, however, there will be obstacles to your new supportive position.

9
■ ■ ■ ■ ■ ■ ■

Obstacles to
Self-Support

HAVING begun to replace your negative tapes with positive ones, it is time to recognize that a number of obstacles may now surface to prevent you from maintaining your new self-talk at a high level. While any new habit is vulnerable, the factors working against self-support are considerable. These factors include (1) a Negative Belief System embedded within the judgmental framework, (2) a Second Line of Defense that squelches supportive self-talk, (3) Driver Interference in the learning of self-support, and (4) False Pride associated with negative self-messages.

A Negative Belief System

The most fundamental obstacle working against self-support is a Negative Belief System, the set of important convictions about yourself and about your world that you formed from your past experiences. If these experiences were negative and you had little support in handling or overcoming them, then your view of yourself and of your world will also tend to be negative. If your Negative Beliefs were established at an early age, at a time when you could not critically evaluate your surroundings and take action to change them, these beliefs are likely to be very strong — so strong, in fact, that any discrepant information relative to them will be ignored, misperceived, or devalued.

Negative Beliefs like "I'm worthless," "I'm inadequate," or "I can't change" can be so tenacious, in fact, that they cast a shadow over startlingly obvious examples to the contrary. Lisa, for instance, held so tightly to the view "I'm not attractive" that she ignored considerable contradictory evidence. Specifically, she dated on a weekly basis and was frequently approached at parties by men who wanted to dance or to talk with her. All current information signaled, "You *are* attractive," but she continued to base her self-image on certain negative experiences from her past. Lisa had developed a self-definition that, once formed, left little room for change. Similarly, George maintained the belief "I'm not accomplishing anything" despite the article he had published and the graduate credits that he had obtained during the past year. His self-definition "I'm a failure" was formed at an early age.

"Why are such positive contradictions to negative beliefs ignored?" you might ask. One reason is that Negative Beliefs are invariably embedded within a judgmental structure. Such a structure blocks incoming information that does not fit its stringent requirements. To use a rather farfetched analogy, imagine a "help wanted" advertisement placed in a newspaper with the requirement "Only those over six-foot-five need apply." When no women and very few men show up to be interviewed, the employer affirms the conviction "It just goes to show, people don't want to work these days."

As you can imagine, based on this framework, a positive event must be dramatic indeed to be counted by the Self 2 Judge. Thus, to feel attractive, Lisa would need constant and dramatic recognition and approval from men. To see himself as a success, George would require strong external acclaim.

Anna, an artist who was depressed about the loss of an important relationship, began after six months of virtual inactivity to work again, painting three or four hours a day.

"Not much," she said, comparing herself to the person who used to paint eight or nine hours without a break. According to her former standard, in fact, three hours was just more fuel for her belief "I can't function alone." Anna forgot to notice that, in the face of a loss, she had overcome her grief enough to begin working again. Compared with six months previously, she had gone far in regaining her former productivity.

When our perspective comes from what should be — the judgmental standard — we lose sight of what is. We neglect to acknowledge what has been accomplished or what has been improved. In the example above, a positive change in the amount of time spent working was not great enough to meet the standard set by Anna's Self 2 Judge. Three hours didn't count when the standard was "as much as before." Thus Anna's improvement proved to be of no value in countering her negative belief "I'm useless without my lover." The arbitrary standards of Anna's Imposed Self led to the rejection of most of the incoming information that would contradict her basic belief. This standard and the self-talk deriving from it also augmented her depression and slowed her continued recovery. Such standards must be rejected if supportive self-talk is to achieve its full promise.

If you recognize any of your own Negative Beliefs or self-definitions that culminate in the judgment "I'm not okay," it is important that you become aware that you may not be perceiving important contradictory information. If this is true, now is the time for you to begin challenging these beliefs one by one. As you do, using the five-step method, you may find these old convictions collapsing under the weight of your current realistic evaluation.

Thus Sandi's self-definition "I'm a quitter" dissolved when examined from her new growth perspective. Sandi realized that much of her "quitting" has been a positive "letting go" of pursuits that did not suit her. Further, she acknowledged the tremendous opposition from her husband and from her own

Judge whenever she attempted to follow her own growth pulse. As she removed her internal Drivers, Stoppers, and Confusers and began asserting herself, Sandi found that her old tag-along definition fit her not at all. "Far from wanting to quit," Sandi asserted, "I find that I'm having a great time working toward my new goals. I know that it might sound hard to believe, but preparing for my Graduate Record Exams feels great. It's like I'm doing mental exercises. I'm having the time of my life!"

A great deal of what I do as a therapist is to help people reevaluate old, worn-out self-definitions and beliefs. Some of these definitions were learned in childhood (You're sloppy. You're selfish. You're stupid. You'll never amount to anything. You're just like your father. You'll only end up in trouble). Others are learned within a marriage (You're a failure. You're impotent. You couldn't support yourself. You're socially inept). Some are learned in therapy (You're neurotic. You don't want to be happy. You don't really want to change).

Yet these definitions are all inferences — conclusions drawn from a limited amount of information. Moreover, they are often formulated by the critical Self 2 Judge of someone else. These worn-out definitions do not have to dominate and control your life. It is indeed possible to look beyond these boundaries and allow information that might change them to filter in. Try it out. List one of your own Negative Beliefs or self-definitions. Now whenever anything happens that might possibly contradict this belief, write it down. Give yourself the chance to form a more positive self-image.

The Second Line of Defense

A second impediment to the development of supportive self-talk comes from what we might call the judgmental position's Second Line of Defense. Having finally arrived at the point of permitting yourself to be human, to have feelings, and to take your own time, you may find that the forces you fought so hard to overcome are not yet defeated. A new set of obstacles must now be faced. This is what I have termed the Second Line of Defense. The beginning shift to positive self-talk almost invariably triggers a number of Stoppers and Confusers, intent on squelching your newly emerging self-support.

The transition from living your life according to *shoulds* and *don'ts* to relying on the messages of your feelings is a very difficult one. When you break through the judgmental barrier to more congruent behavior, when you begin to crack the rigid structure by which you have lived your life, you may find yourself confronting Self 2 warnings and criticisms as never before. This negative self-talk was kept at bay only through your obedience to the commands and prohibitions of your Judge. Now that you have decided to operate in a different way, you become a target of assault. Thus, when Sally does not rescue her friend by trying to solve her problems, she may find herself immersed in a fearful preoccupation with "What will happen now?" She may have nagging doubts about being "insensitive" or "selfish." Likewise, when Bob gives himself permission to relax outdoors in the lounge chair, he may be faced with every judgment that in the past prevented him from doing so ("You're lazy. You're nonproductive. Why aren't you doing something?").

Only by seeing these old messages for what they are (powerful internal mechanisms of control) can you allow them to pass by without getting hooked. And if you are hooked, and return again to your old behavior, you will do so with the added ingredient of awareness. This alone (this awareness of what you are doing and what it costs) will allow you to change. Thus Sally found herself again doing what someone else wanted and going against her own feelings. Only now she was exquisitely aware of the cost and aware that she had a choice. Even if Sally repeats this process several more times, or even many more times, she is building brick by brick her conviction that she must operate in her own behalf.

Not only new behavior, but new attitudes and self-messages can provoke the Second Line of Defense. When Lisa, the woman with the belief "I'm unattractive," first acknowledged to herself that many men actually seemed to like her and that one man in particular appeared quite taken with her, she immediately retreated, saying, "Oh, I'm just selling myself a bill of goods. This attention doesn't mean a thing. I'm being foolish to think otherwise. I can't take the risk."

A host of negative self-labels were provoked by Lisa's Self-Affirmation. She was "foolish" to feel positive and only "selling herself a bill of goods." The attention from her male suitor was "meaningless." Lisa's positive affirmation also elicited the catastrophic thought, "If you let yourself believe this heady stuff, you're going to be hurt and disappointed." The anxiety created by this negative barrage effectively blocked Lisa's escape from her depressing belief "I'm not attractive."

Our culture has no shortage of Stoppers that work against self-support. Labels like "conceited" and "immodest" punish our Self-Affirmations. We pride ourselves on being too "realistic" or "intellectually honest" to accept and enjoy positive information. We give "luck" the credit for any positive achievement ("It was sure a lucky break that I was hired for my new job"). Negative occurrences rest, of course, solely upon our own backs. We fail to give them comparable, critical scrutiny.

Combatting the Second Line of Defense takes almost as much work as repudiating the first. The process, however, is the same. The negative labels and catastrophes that punish your new self-message must be challenged. The questions "What am I telling myself?" "Is this helpful?" and so on allow you to walk past these second obstacles just as you negotiated the first. The examples that follow spotlight the operation of the Second Line of Defense and suggest the supportive alternatives that can neutralize its influence.

Why not consider a positive self-message that you wish to assert. As you do, be aware of any "second thoughts" that

Supportive Self-Talk	Second Line of Defense	Supportive Alternative
I don't like this area of study. I've given it a fair chance and my feelings tell me that it doesn't fit. It's okay for me to let it go and explore something new.	You're just a quitter. You never finish anything.	Wait a minute. I tried out that area and didn't like it. I haven't quit anything. I have learned something about myself and can now move on and explore other alternatives. I'm not putting a time limit on myself.
It's okay to consider myself a competent writer, whether or not I get the grant I've applied for.	It's the bottom line that counts.	No. My self-worth doesn't have to rest on the opinion of others. There are many reasons why grants aren't awarded. These days only one person in ten is funded. I will not buy the bottom-line notion when it relates to my own self-worth.
I met someone at the ballet yesterday who wants to get together with me again. I guess I'm more attractive than I thought.	But then, that's a common occurrence for most people.	Wait. I don't know that. Even if it's common for some people, it's new to me. I'm going to enjoy the feeling and let it soak in.
There were a lot of positive things that I did for my husband. I wasn't a complete failure as a wife.	Those things were trivial. They don't count.	Just a minute. It's okay for me to acknowledge the positive. I'm going to be fair to myself, just as I would be to another person.

dampen your original statement. If this occurs, write down these thoughts as well. Now, examine them and determine your supportive alternative. For some people, several reconsiderations will be necessary before your Self 2 Judge submits to your new internal position.

Perhaps the biggest obstacle of all when it comes to altering your own self-talk comes from an old enemy — the Confuser "It's hopeless." Even when you have experienced the changed emotions that come from a supportive dialogue with yourself, you may be tempted to give up the process as "too difficult" or "too complex." For some of us, trapped in the judgmental position, admitting that we have been "wrong" about our past beliefs seems worse than continuing to be unhappy because of them. For others, change seems like a rejection of a loved person. A mother's Please Others injunction or a father's Be Strong pronouncement is not easily overthrown. Rather than face the sadness of letting go, the escape "It's hopeless" offers a way out.

Driver Interference

Paradoxically, even as you are creating your new supportive tapes, the Drivers Be Perfect, Hurry Up, Please Others, Be Strong, and Try Hard may exert their negative influences. It is not uncommon, for example, to see people become depressed when their beginning attempts at being supportive are not perfect or when negative self-talk does not go away quickly. I've even heard people attack themselves for reverting again to their old habits of self-punishment: "You'll never learn. You're stupid to keep berating yourself all the time. You deserve to feel bad. You know what to do, why don't you do it?" While the content is different (the focus is now on new behaviors), the process has remained the same.

This was true for Jill, who described to one class how she criticized herself for not being a perfect Permitter for her young son. As the class progressed, Jill had realized that she was still viewing herself in terms of the judgmental "should" system, even though her "shoulds" had come to include such growth-oriented behaviors as accepting her son's feelings and allowing him as much independence as possible. Whenever Jill failed in her resolve to respond in a supportive way to her son, she criticized herself severely. Her negative self-talk had not really lessened. She had simply learned a different set of *shoulds* with which to fill her self-judgments.

When we criticize or judge ourselves from the old Be Perfect, Hurry Up perspective, positive changes may not occur. Instead, we will depress ourselves to the point that no change is possible. Such criticism interferes with the learning process by producing a heavy load of self-induced pain that must first be dealt with. The judgmental position slows down growth.

When Liz began telling me all the supportive things that she had done for herself the previous week, she seemed quite excited. However, she also related that she felt very stressed. Although part of this stress seemed connected to old patterns that she had not changed, Liz admitted that her new awareness and the necessity to make new decisions were also factors.

When I asked Liz to imagine herself sitting in the empty chair in front of her and to show both of us (herself and me) how she had been stressing Liz, she slowly began to formulate the negative message: "You aren't going fast enough. There are still times when you know what to do and you don't do it. You've got to try harder." Liz and I both saw immediately one source of her stress. Three Drivers (Hurry Up, Be Perfect, and Try Hard) had taken control of her new decision to support herself. As she moved into the empty chair, Liz answered her Imposed Self: "Let me go at my own pace. You're tiring me out with all this pressure. I'll get there, just leave me alone." As an aside to me, Liz said, "That's my mother. Nothing I ever did was enough to please her."

I'm sharing this example because it is very easy to try to fit a new decision to grow and to support yourself into an old judgmental framework. This is simply not possible. The two frameworks are incompatible. Our feelings require complete respect and trust if they are to direct us in the best possible way.

False Pride

The final obstacle to the development of self-support is what analyst Karen Horney refers to as "False Pride," the deliberate refusal to let go of the demands and expectations of the Imposed Self because these expectations alone seem capable of rescuing us from our own self-hate. Horney describes how early circumstances turn us away from our genuine desires and potentials toward a grim determination to become an ideal person — famous, successful, wealthy, acclaimed. The extent to which we feel worthless, inadequate, and unloved gives some measure of our need to recreate ourselves into an ideal image.

The basic belief here is "If only I can become, accomplish, or achieve such and such, then I will be okay." Such and such can vary from getting a Ph.D. to making $150,000 a year, from marrying a wealthy man to being in the "right" social group. Unfortunately, individuals who base their self-worth on externals never quite make it. Something always falls short. Nonetheless, the pride in these externals can be intense. Karen Horney uses the term "false" to indicate that this pride is not in the service of the Intrinsic Self, that is, keeping up with the "right" social group is boring and stressful, and making $150,000 a year may lead to poor health.

The tenacity of False Pride derives from the conviction that the standards of the Imposed Self should be upheld and that we will be punished if they are not. It also rests upon the idea that these internal demands can be met and that when they are, great rewards and personal vindication will be forthcoming. If we Try Hard enough, we tell ourselves, it is indeed possible to become the ideal person we desire to be. Then other people will be sorry; life will treat us differently. Any suggestion to the contrary—that perhaps the requirements of the Imposed Self are impossible to attain—is met with rage: "I should be above needing anyone, and I will be!" or "I must accomplish something important! The things that I'm doing now aren't enough!" To give up the idea of being above criticism or hurt and to face our genuine limitations and vulnerabilities is very difficult. Yet as long as we cling to the demands of the Imposed Self, we can never really know self-support.

Unless you let go of the desire to recreate yourself in a new image, you can never appreciate or love or respect the person you really are. To say to yourself "That was a job well done" will not be possible, because something about the job will inevitably fall short of your Self 2 standards. The observation "I was really successful today" will be dampened by the concern "Can I do it again tomorrow?" Genuine growth steps will be snubbed with the comment "Everyone else has already done that."

In short, False Pride is simply another element of the judgmental framework. Representing the sum total of your perfectionist goals, it provokes constant negative comparisons with other people and with your own past performance. Such comparisons have nothing in common with self-support.

Practicing Your New Language

As you push past the obstacles of the judgmental position, you will find that your proficiency in creating a positive internal environment for yourself now depends upon you—upon your willingness to practice the five-step program for changing your tapes. Practice will result in your positive self-talk becoming automatic, a high probability approach for dealing with yourself and with your world.

At times, I have been concerned that the information provided in this book, which is basically the same as that available in my "Talking to Yourself" classes, might not prove sufficient for a person to begin making the shift from self-punishment to self-support. Therefore, I was especially pleased when someone wrote to me several days after her class: "I had an experience Sunday evening when I felt my mood drop. I became confused and, sensing the sudden change, I decided that some negative self-talk was on the scene. It was so helpful to be able to get out my notes and settle in to figure out what was going on. I was able to sort it out and then let go of it in a much easier fashion than before."

I had the same feedback from a client who for several sessions had worked on turning off her Be Perfect Driver. While her difficulty in completing her Master's thesis had been the focus of her three therapy meetings, she had, on her own, used the five-step method to decrease her anxiety in several totally different situations. For example, at a company party, she told herself, "You don't have to mingle with the people you think you should impress. Just let yourself talk to anyone who is close by." With her new self-message, she had more fun and made the acquaintance of more new people as well.

In a similar vein, she was able to demagnify the importance of a class presentation by telling herself, "It's okay if you're not the best speaker in the class. Just present the information that you've been asked to present. It doesn't have to sound perfect." Surprisingly, the feedback was the best she had ever received.

As you begin applying the five-step method to issues of your own, you may find it helpful, at least the first few times, to write it all down. Time and practice are needed to develop your new language. You would spend one or two years learning to speak French or German, wouldn't you? Why not make the same kind of commitment to the language of self-support? The next few chapters will help you deal with topics that prove especially difficult for many people: anger, guilt, taking too much responsibility for others, sex, and male/female sex-role messages.

10
·······
Talking Yourself into Anger

THERE'S a joke that has been around for a long time about a man driving through the desert who finds himself with a flat tire, and unfortunately no jack. Having just passed a farmhouse, however, he confidently assures himself, "Oh, no sweat. I'll go back to that old farmhouse. I'm sure the people there will be happy to lend me a jack." With that thought, he starts his walk.

After going a short distance, the traveler begins to reconsider. "I wonder just how generous those people are going to be. After all, I'm at their mercy. I've got to have a jack, and no one else is around." He walks a bit further and adds, "I'll bet that jack is going to cost me a pretty penny. Here, I am a stranger. They'll try to get every bit of mileage that they can from my problem." As he approaches the house and knocks on the door, he adds the final insult, "I bet they're rude to boot."

About this time, a man leans out of the upper window and, in a not unfriendly way asks, "What can I do for you, stranger?"

"Not a damn thing," the man replies. "I wouldn't take any help from you if my life depended on it."

The humor of this joke, of course, lies in the farmer's innocence in provoking the traveler. The traveler's anger springs totally from his own internal dialogue. The realization that this curious process is far from unusual allows us to laugh not only at the traveler but at ourselves as well. It seems that anger, just like depression, is often self-generated. And although, as I affirm with my clients, anger may feel better than depression, it is not an emotion to cultivate.

For one thing, anger results in a massive physiological preparation for action. Friedman and Rosenman, authors of *Type A Behavior and Your Heart*, describe the exact process:

> If you become intensely angered by some phenomenon, your hypothalamus will almost instantaneously send signals to all or almost all the nerve endings of your sympathetic nervous system (that portion of your nervous system not directly under your control), causing them to secrete relatively large amounts of epinephrine and norepinephrine. . . . In addition, this same fit of anger will probably also induce the hypothalamus to send additional messages to the pituitary gland, the master of all endocrine glands, urging it to discharge some of its own exclusively manufactured hormones (such as growth hormone) and also to send out chemical signals to the adrenal, sex, and thyroid glands and the pancreas as well, so that they in turn may secrete excess amounts of their exclusively manufactured hormones.

This extremely physiological activation, particularly if it is a chronic occurrence, has as one consequence internal changes that have been associated with coronary heart disease. The key word here is *chronic*, describing a frequent or an unremitting process. This chronic anger is one of the striking features of Type A behavior. Interestingly, such anger often derives from Self 2 Drivers, Stoppers, and Confusers.

Driver-Generated Anger

Analyst Karen Horney employed the term "neurotic claims" to describe one anger-generating mechanism. A Claim is a

Self 2 *should* placed on someone else. Demands like Hurry Up, Be Perfect, Be Strong, Please Others, and Try Hard can be applied to other people as well as to ourselves. When this occurs, we have begun making Claims. Those of us who are "externalizers" are by definition very much inclined to put Claims onto other people. We direct our judgments outwardly toward others even more often than we direct them inwardly toward ourselves. The question that Jesus asked in the Sermon on the Mount speaks eloquently to this process: "Why do you see the speck that is in your brother's eye, but do not notice the log that is in your own eye?"

Quite often, the most severe Claims are placed on those who are closest to us — our husbands, wives, children, in short, those people whom we view as extensions of ourselves. Because we believe that the behavior of these close ones reflects upon us and upon our own self-worth, we apply our *shoulds* to them. The critical eye cast upon these intimates by the Self 2 Judge paradoxically leads us many times to treat those we love far worse than we would treat anyone else — even complete strangers.

Because of such Claims, our expectations are frequently higher for these intimates than for anyone else. For years, many business executives have demanded that their wives become Please Others adjuncts, putting on the "correct" face for their corporate colleagues. Ministers' wives have likewise found themselves cast in a Be Perfect facade for their husbands' congregations. Of course, a minister is usually in the position where incredible Be Perfect, Please Others Claims are placed on him as well. Now that women are entering the ministry and taking on positions of authority in business and government, it will be interesting to see if they make the same kind of Claims upon their husbands.

Role-related Claims — "You're my wife, and I expect you to act that way," "I don't want any child of mine wearing his hair like that," or "I expect more of you than I do of anyone else because I love you" — rest on this tendency to incorporate those close to us into our own judgmental systems. In *Open Marriage,* George and Nena O'Neil attack one structure that makes such role-related Claims possible — the traditional marriage contract. This contract with its rules and obligations is not flexible in considering the needs of any one couple. Instead, it is based upon a rigid set of *shoulds,* that delimit and make uniform the conduct of many different people.

One effect of these *shoulds* (which in our terminology are really Claims of one person upon the other) is negative feelings. The O'Neils predict that "resentments will be small at first: a few complaints, a little nagging here and there. But as frustration mounts, the resentment will grow, and eventually it will explode. Sooner or later, she will scream, 'I'm sick and tired of doing all the housework myself and working too,' and (he) will yell, 'For Christ's sake, can't you see I need some time to myself?'"

The critical overseeing of the behavior of an intimate, whether due to marital expectations or simply to an internal "should" system projected outward, can lead eventually to the destruction of a relationship. A Be Perfect Claim, for example, applied to one's partner will result in constant fault-finding and a belittling attitude toward that person: "Why did you tell me you were going to be home all day? When I called, you weren't." "You shouldn't have bought that kind of salad oil. You're wasting money." Or, "You embarrassed me by what you said at the party. You don't know anything about economics."

Such statements are not made lightly. They rest upon a mountain of righteous indignation. Beneath their seemingly innocuous exterior lies the Judgmental Claim "You should be perfect," which translates, "You should do everything the way I want it done." As you can see, the outstanding characteristic of Claims is the small tolerance or room for error they give another person. The recipient of a Claim is expected to walk the familiar tightrope. There is no room for changes in plans, for spontaneity, or even for simple feelings.

After a time, the victim of these inordinate demands may rebel, may break the too-tight leash, may fight back, or may even leave the relationship. Or again, the victim may simply acquiesce, giving up the freedom to operate by his or her own Self 1 signals. Of course, this last solution occurs only amid great inner turmoil. The Intrinsic Self is not deserted without protest. Yet, having no assistance, many people fail to extricate themselves from the destructive Claims of another person.

It should be noted here that we are talking about the acceptance of Claims in a relationship where supposedly each individual has the external freedom not to accept them. Thus one individual is not imprisoned by another. This issue, however, is not so simple or straightforward. Many women, for example, feel trapped within a marriage for economic reasons. To fight against their husband's Claims is to combat also the fear of divorce and the very real possibility of a marginal economic existence. Many men and women are imprisoned by low self-esteem. They believe that they must accept the conditions imposed upon them by another person or be completely alone, which within the judgmental framework means without self-worth.

Perhaps most frequently of all, we buy into the Claims of another person because that person's rigid demands are not all that different from the messages of our own Imposed Self. Persons who internalize are often all too willing to accept the blame or shortcomings placed on them by persons who externalize. Criticism is swallowed whole without regard to its factual base. In short, the strength of our internal Drivers provides a good measure of our vulnerability to other persons' Claims. In therapy, one good measure of a person's progress is the ability to evaluate critically the negative judgments of another person. As one of my clients revealed, "I no longer soak up everything James says to me. I don't see him as the ultimate authority anymore. Consequently, I don't feel as bad during our arguments."

Claims, of course, can be placed upon strangers, upon business associates, upon public figures, and as Horney notes, even upon life itself. They are not confined to family members or intimate relationships. Just as one has rigid expectations of one's partner within the "closed" marriage contract, so do many of us have expectations of the world that lead to anger and disappointment.

The idea that everything should go our way is one such expectation. When the toast burns, or the operator cuts off our call, or we miss the bus, we get furious, angry far beyond what an objective observer might consider an appropriate response to the external provocation. This anger derives from our belief that the world is not treating us properly, that we are being dealt a faulty hand.

Moreover, even as the self-evaluative consequences of a loss or a rejection can be much greater than the realistic consequences, so anger generated on the basis of Self 2 Claims can add significantly to the impact of everyday hassles. In an interview in *Psychology Today*, stress researcher R. S. Lazarus confirms, "When people get upset over what seem to be trivialities, it's because the trivial symbolizes for them something of tremendous import. When a shoelace breaks, the psychological stress is from the implication that you cannot control your own life, that you're helpless in the face of the most stupid trivialities — or even worse, that such things happen because of your own inadequacies in the first place." The stress also comes from the realization that our Claims have been thwarted and that we have been denied what we feel entitled to.

The key word here is "entitled." It is important to realize that a Claim differs from a wish or a desire. While a person may wish that everything will go smoothly and feel disappointed when it does not, individuals who have a Claim *demand* that things go their way and feel furious when they do not. The following list of Self 2 Claims gives us some sense of this. Notice how each Claim takes no notice of other people's rights, feelings, and limitations.

I am entitled to first-class treatment.

I shouldn't have to make any major changes in my life in order to lose weight.

I have the right to expect that you will call me back immediately.

I shouldn't have to bother with sexual precautions.

I should have gotten that raise or promotion.

I should have the benefits of a relationship with no restrictions.

My children should do as I say.

My spouse should have the same priorities as I do.

My spouse should know what I want without my saying.

I am entitled to your time and money.

I should never have to wait.

Because I have suffered, things should go my way.

Because I have suffered, I should be immune.

Because I am a man, I shouldn't wash dishes.

Because I am a woman, I shouldn't have to drive.

I shouldn't have to work on changing myself.

Because I am your parent, I should be able to act aggressively toward you.

If I need something from you, you must comply.

Other cars should get out of my way.

You should do what I want you to do.

You should solve my problems.

My spouse should pay attention exclusively to me.

Everything should operate perfectly.

I should be above criticism.

The weather should suit my preferences.

My relatives should give me financial support.

I shouldn't have to assert myself to get what I want.

If I have a need, I'm entitled to the best.

Other people should do things the way I want them done.

I should be treated as someone who is special.

You shouldn't hold me responsible for my bad moods or my hostile behavior.

Whether or not I can afford it, I should have what other people have.

You should ignore anything that happens when I'm drinking.

I shouldn't have to work at a job that doesn't fulfill me.

I shouldn't have to pay interest on this bill. I paid it only a few days late.

Other people should support me until I find myself.

The pervasiveness of Claims in our society today is such that experts have begun to speak of a "psychology of entitlement." In a *U.S. News & World Report* article, "The New Breed of Workers," Jerome Rosow, president of the Work in America Institute, was quoted as saying, "The new generation of workers and their children were conditioned by a boom economy. They have perceived these advantages as normal. Now these expectations have become entitlements." Moreover, according to the *U.S. News* article, "Never in history have American workers been so well paid, so privileged and yet so discontent in their jobs as they are today."

The same psychology of entitlement frequently occurs with students. One college freshman with whom I worked, for example, was on the verge of failing in biology, his one required college course in natural science. He was failing because he wasn't studying. His refusal to study rested on his Self 2 Claims.

"I can't stand the teacher" was Bill's first explanation of his approaching failure. "He talks to us like we're idiots and requires too much work each night. Then he checks — can you believe it? — checks to see if we have done our homework. That's why I'm failing. I don't like to be regimented. I'm in college. I should be treated like an adult. It's none of his business what I do every night. He shouldn't act so much like a grade school teacher."

As you can see, all of Bill's energy is directed at what *should* be. He has angered and frustrated himself and is bound not to give in to what he views as an unfair, outmoded method of teaching. Bill's Claim is that he is entitled to have an interesting teacher who teaches in the way in which he believes he should be instructed. Yet Bill, not the teacher, is suffering the consequences of this expectation.

When I asked Bill if he wanted to alter his tape, he agreed that at least he would consider it, since he needed to make a passing grade in his course. Bill's self-talk reversal progressed in the following manner:

STEP 1: What am I telling myself?

When I sit down to do one of Brown's assignments, I immediately get ticked off. I'm saying to myself, "This is ridiculous. This assignment is not going to teach me anything. Brown is just an eccentric, rigid, mediocre teacher. Why do I have to put up with this trivia!" This is usually where I shut my book and turn on the radio or grumble to my roommate.

STEP 2: Is what I'm telling myself useful?

It's not getting my homework done, that's for sure, and I'm not going to get a very good grade in the course unless something changes. No. I suppose it's not useful.

STEP 3: What are my Drivers, Stoppers, or Confusers?

I'm using a lot of labels. If I used an "I" Message, I would say, "I don't like doing the assignments that Brown is giving me." I suppose I have a Claim that my schoolwork should always be interesting and that my teachers should be more than mediocre. There's another label. I guess I'm cutting off my nose to spite my face where Brown's concerned.

STEP 4: What Permission and Self-Affirmation can I give myself?

I can say, "It's okay to have my negative feelings, but I still need to do the work. I'm a good student, and I'm capable of getting a good grade in this class. It's okay for me to do some things that I would rather not do. The world doesn't have to treat me perfectly."

STEP 5: What would my Guide say?

Just what I said before. "It's okay not to like Brown or the assignments, but I still need to do the work. If I stop making myself so angry, I'll have an easier time getting it done."

The above dialogue shows that Bill was harboring not only a Self 2 Claim (I'm entitled to an interesting teacher) but also a large number of negative labels (rigid, eccentric, mediocre) directed against his instructor. Such labels also produce hostility and animosity. They are what we call Anger-Generating Stoppers.

Anger-Generated Stoppers

There are two basic ways in which Self 2 Stoppers can fuel feelings of anger and resentment. Although these two processes seem on the surface to be at opposite poles, they are very much alike in that both derive from a judgmental Self 2 position. The negative labeling of someone else is the first source of anger. The second is the negative *self*-labeling of one's own impulses to be assertive, a process that inevitably leads to gunnysacking. External labeling or internal labeling, the anger-generating effect is the same.

The power of external labels

Many of us do not realize the power of the external labels that are so much a part of our daily lives. Labels provide a compelling, but at the same time, a dangerous simplicity. One label can determine how we will respond to literally millions of people, so that the complexity of human life and the reality of marked individual differences are blotted out. Negative labels generate feelings of resentment, envy, and hate, all major emotional components of prejudice. Directed toward minorities, toward other nationalities, toward women, or other specific groups, such labels serve the delusion that all members of a group are alike, and that all can be defined through some negative characteristic.

Propagandists take full advantage of the power of negative labels to distance and degrade. I once spent several hours on a plane sitting next to a guy who could not wait to return to Vietnam and kill some more "gooks." I am certain that this young man was not the norm in terms of his desires, but I believe that the label "gook," one used often in military slang, enabled him to justify and even enjoy his grim pursuit, as he described it to me.

When we use negative labels in our day-to-day encounters, the same effect—the distancing and degrading of another individual—occurs. Whether these labels are applied in overt communication or in our thoughts, they lead us to encapsulate another person in harsh judgmental terms. A person becomes lazy, inconsiderate, a slob, or a bitch, rather than someone who has just done something specific that we do not like.

In one class, we turned our attention to dealing with this form of anger-producing self-talk. Ginger, describing herself as having great resentment toward her roommate Trudy, was the first to volunteer. "Specifically," Ginger related, "Trudy copped out on me when I was expecting her to baby-sit."

"What happened," she continued, "was that I was going out for a special date, and I assumed that Trudy would sit for me. We have an arrangement where I keep her child one weekend night, and she keeps mine another. Since she wanted me to sit for her on Friday, I expected her to sit for me on Saturday. On Saturday morning, however, she told me that she wouldn't be able to stay with my daughter, and I had a lot of trouble trying to find someone else. Since then I've been really angry with her, even though it's been a couple of weeks."

After Ginger had described her situation, I asked her if she wanted to change her anger-generating self-talk.

"Yes," Ginger agreed, "I'd like to get past these feelings."

"What am I telling myself" she slowly began. "I'm saying that Trudy shouldn't have changed our routine. How can she be so insensitive? She's flaky and irresponsible. I went out of my way the other day to pick her up at work when her car was in the shop, and this is how she pays me back." As an aside, Ginger added, "Now I'm feeling guilty and criticizing myself, 'How can you be so unloving!'"

You may remember from an earlier example how easily blame can shift from oneself to another person. Here the shift is in the reverse direction, from Trudy back to Ginger. Moving from one pole of blame to another is the only alternative possible within the judgmental position.

"Anyway," Ginger continued, "to go on, I want to ask myself if what I'm telling myself is helpful. I don't think it is. I'm walking around the house with my teeth clenched. I don't feel like speaking to Trudy. I'm so angry that I don't even feel like telling her what's bothering me. I just want her to leave.

What are my Drivers, Stoppers, or Confusers? I know one thing I'm doing. I'm telling myself that because I picked Trudy up at work, she owed it to me to baby-sit on Saturday night. I'm saying she shouldn't have changed her mind. I guess I'm putting a Be Perfect Claim on Trudy. I just thought of something else. I'm telling myself that even if I assert myself with her and tell her my feelings, it won't help. She's too insensitive, flaky, and irresponsible. I can see that I'm labeling my assertion as useless because of my negative view of Trudy. I also feel that if I say something, I'll make things worse. Who knows? Maybe she would respond.

"Now for the fourth step. I'm supposed to look at Permission and Affirmation and direct it toward Trudy this time. I can say that Trudy doesn't have to be perfect anymore than I do. She didn't know how important Saturday night was to me. She didn't have the full picture. I need to let her know what I expect. That's what I'll do. That's step five — the action that I plan to take. Maybe the end result will be that Trudy isn't the roommate for me. On the other hand, maybe this is a misunderstanding that we can clear up."

In this example, Ginger demonstrates the anger-producing consequences of the negative external labels (insensitive, flaky, and irresponsible) that she had directed toward Trudy. She also shows how a critical view of another person can combine with any Self 2 Stoppers already present to block assertive action. This inhibition activates the process of gunnysacking.

The effect of internal labels

As mentioned previously, gunnysacking, author George Bach's term for the holding back of negative feelings, leads to the buildup of high levels of tension and hostility. With gunnysacking, each anger-producing incident is stored away to be reviewed again and again, each new look fueling the smoldering fires of resentment. When someone annoys you, if you have a gunnysack, the annoying incident will not be considered for itself alone. Instead, it will be examined in conjunction with the other negative items that you have stored up.

When Candice shows up late for her tennis date with Marie, for example, Marie is furious. Candice's lateness brings up for Marie the ten other occasions when she has waited, racket in hand, for Candice to breeze onto the court. Marie has fumed about these prior times to her husband and to her friends. She has not, however, told Candice about her feelings. Afraid to risk appearing bitchy or too demanding, internal negative labels, Marie has gunnysacked her resentment. So now Candice cannot understand Marie's grim silence as she gives a perfectly good explanation of her delay.

As you might imagine, gunnysacking is a very common process. When I have introduced the concept in groups, most people have immediately been able to identify situations where gunnysacking occurs in their own lives. In one group, for example, a man described himself as having gunnysacks against so many people that he didn't know where to begin in getting rid of them. "By the way," he questioned, "can I get rid of a gunnysack once it is formed?" A woman confessed that she had the world's largest gunnysack, and the world's best memory. She could recall every hurt and every resentment that she had thrown into it.

To review for a moment, a gunnysack forms when issues are not dealt with at the moment. Because of Self 2 Stoppers (Negative Self-labels, Catastrophes, Rigid Requirements, and Witch Messages), feelings are frequently not expressed spontaneously. Sometimes, they are not even asserted at all. Yet unexpressed feelings do not simply go away. We may think that we are leaving them behind us as we throw them over our shoulders with an "It's not all that important anyway" disclaimer. Instead of hitting the sidewalk, however, they fall snugly into the ever-present gunnysack. There these feelings sit until we are sufficiently angry or tired or fed up not to care any longer, and then they come pouring out. For men, the gunnysack explosion is typically through anger. For women, the eruption may result in tears — tears of rage. The effect is generally the same — embarrassment, guilt, and self-punishment.

To prevent gunnysacking, we need only remove our Self 2 Stoppers so that the natural process of self-expression is permitted. Of course, we need not respond so quickly that we ignore the parameters of a situation or fail to consider good timing. We must realize, however, that three days or three months or three years are not required to find a "right time" to assert ourselves. Here, the Rigid Requirement "If the time is right" supports the process of gunnysacking.

When we deal with the internal obstacles that interfere with self-assertion, our feelings and attitudes will change, even when no change occurs externally. Thus one of my clients described how much more enjoyable his work had become since he had removed some of the internal Stoppers that were preventing him from voicing his negative feelings. "I'm under much less stress," he told me, "and I don't have that heavy resentment bearing down on me all the time." Then, upon a moment's reflection, he added, "You know, I just realized. The people I work with haven't really changed at all. It's just that I am no longer taking care of them at my own expense. I now speak up when something bothers me. It's me who has changed."

The removal of a gunnysack reduces anger by allowing us to see each situation as it is, uncontaminated by past feelings of resentment. We do ourselves and others a favor when we avoid gunnysacking and keep our slates clear.

Letting go

Unfortunately, there are times when assertion isn't possible. Perhaps the person with whom we need to speak is not available; perhaps our experience has told us that the person is unwilling to receive an assertive message; perhaps the assertion we have made does not affect a change. Do we continue to beat our heads against an unfeeling wall? No. There is a second choice. It is within our power to let go of our anger and resentment. The task of letting go is not an easy one. Propped up as it is on one side by the conviction that the other person is "wrong" or "unfair" and on the other by the judgment that letting go means "failing" or "giving up," the process involves more than a passive decision. It requires a full realization of the cost of chronic, sustained anger and an active combatting of the Stoppers that prevent one from letting go.

Sandra found herself in this position in regard to her next door neighbor. For the umpteenth time, her neighbor's dog had dug up some of her flowers. As usual, Sandra had asserted herself. Once again, however, her straightforward, honest approach had not led to a positive response on her neighbor's part.

Sandra now feels furious that her well-intentioned efforts with this neighbor have come to naught. She does not want to go as far as to call the police, as most of the problems have been minor annoyances. Yet she experiences a mounting rage as her assertion is again and again ignored. Most of Sandra's anger, in fact, rests upon her belief that with a little cooperation things could have been easily resolved. She has spent a great deal of energy talking to her husband and her friends about this neighbor. She even catches herself at odd times reviewing to herself what has happened over the past couple of years. A hot flush of hostility comes just from thinking about the "numbskull," a label that has settled into Sandra's vocabulary.

Sandra is in a situation where she has been assertive but to no avail. She must now "raise her muscle" and take some action other than discussion, or she must let go of her anger-producing thoughts. Since Sandra has decided that she doesn't want to go any further in her action, she agrees that it might be wise to look at changing her internal dialogue. In working on this problem, we examined Sandra's own self-talk.

The first question, "What am I telling myself?" Sandra immediately answered. "I'm saying that my neighbor isn't treating me right. I've been as considerate and as nice as I could be, and she doesn't do anything to help ease the situation. Her dog runs rampant; he's always in my flowers; he barks at night; and . . ."

At this point, I interrupted Sandra. "You could go on and on, couldn't you? Why not consider the cost here? Right now, even, what are you feeling?"

"You're right," Sandra agreed. "It's amazing to see how easy it is to get right back into those feelings of anger, even when that's not the purpose here. Well, one cost is that I feel very angry, and there's nothing that I can do with that anger. If I were a violent person, I'd wring her neck. But that would get me into trouble, wouldn't it? I know that other people are tired of hearing me bitch about my neighbor's latest idiocy. Something in me, though, doesn't want to let go of it. I feel justified in being angry."

At this point I interjected, "Sandra, who is suffering whenever you review all these annoyances in your mind? Is it your neighbor, or is it you? You know, during our last few meetings, you've talked more about this neighbor than anyone else. Is she really someone you want to keep carrying around in your head?"

"No, she isn't. Let me see if I can finish this process. I need to consider if there are any Drivers, Stoppers, or Confusers operating. I know. I think that I have a Claim that I put on other people. I really do believe that if I behave fairly toward someone else, that person should also behave fairly with me. I get furious when that doesn't happen. It's as if someone is not playing the game the way it's supposed to be played. I guess I'm also into a Try Hard Driver. I'm trying hard to make my neighbor see it my way. But it seems I'm beating my head against a stone wall. I realize that the person suffering right now is me and that I need to let go of my anger and my Claim that my neighbor should treat me fairly. How do I do it?"

"Why don't you just continue?" I suggested. "Give yourself permission to let your anger go."

"Okay," Sandra replied, while leaning back in her chair for the first time. "I do give myself permission to stop struggling with this. I've had enough. It's simply costing me and everyone around me too much. It's okay to let go of my anger and my struggle. I'm not going to try hard anymore to make it right."

"Good. What about your Guide?" I asked.

"I don't know," Sandra replied. "I think I've taken all the action relative to my neighbor that I want to take. That's part of letting go, isn't it? I guess that I will affirm to my husband and the people I've talked to about her that I'm going to stop concerning myself with the things my neighbor does. And if she ever does anything extreme, I will call the authorities. If not, I'll accept the irritations as part of living."

Before she lets go completely, Sandra may have to go through this tape change process several times. She may have to repeat to herself more than once the reminder "Unfortunately, people don't always treat others fairly. But I don't have to carry the person I dislike most around in my thoughts. Perhaps I learned something from this experience, perhaps not. But I can let go of my anger."

Anger-Generating Confusers

A final source of self-generated anger derives from Self 2 Confusers. Each Confuser (The Arbitrary Inference, Misattribution, Cognitive Deficiency, Overgeneralization, Magnification, Vague Language, and Either/Or Thinking) has the potential for triggering feelings of anger and resentment. The joke about the traveler at the beginning of this chapter, for example, is based on the Confuser Arbitrary Inference. Just as we direct Confusers against ourselves, we can and do use them against other people, proving once more our basic belief—you can't trust anyone; people are undependable; or everyone's out for number one.

The tendency of the Self 2 Judge to perceive what's lacking rather than what's present can distort our evaluations of other people just as it can lead to confusion about ourselves. Thus Keith walks into the house and notices everything that Betsy hasn't done—the kids' toys are scattered around the room, the beds are unmade, the dinner not cooked. He is immediately annoyed. For one thing, Keith has a Claim that if he works outside the home, Betsy should do all of the housework. The decision that Betsy would not pursue her career until the kids were all in school, but instead be a full-time mother, has been gradually amended by Keith to include the clause full-time housekeeper as well. Moreover, Keith ignores what Betsy *has* done all day — baked cookies with the kids, paid the bills, cleaned the oven.

Operating in Keith's self-talk are, in fact, a number of Confusers. Let's identify them as we examine in detail his inner speech, murmured as it is under his breath, through clenched teeth: "This is too much! Don't I have the right to expect a clean house when I come home from a hard day's work? (Self 2 Claim) I guess Betsy feels that she can just laze around all day (Arbitrary Inference, Cognitive Deficiency). Other men don't face this (Overgeneralization, Vague Language). This house is a mess (Magnification)." Unless Keith is willing to examine what he is telling himself, his Confusers will, in all likelihood, continue to provoke his anger and impair his relationship with Betsy.

If his sullenness triggers the same process in Betsy, an increasing distance will develop which in time may lead to a complete communications breakdown. The monthly series "Can This Marriage Be Saved" which appears in the *Ladies' Home Journal* is replete with similar examples of Confusers and their repercussions. For those of you who want to become skilled in recognizing anger-generating Claims, Stoppers, and Confusers, I can think of no richer source of raw material.

A Final Word

The intent of this chapter has not been to convey the idea that anger is basically a "bad" emotion or that a person should never feel angry. Your internal signals of anger are very important. Like a pain warning that tells you to remove your hand from a hot surface, anger can give you the emotional momentum to make necessary external changes.

It is important, however, that your acceptance of your anger and your assertive expression of it be tempered by the recognition that anger can be internally generated — through Claims, Confusers, and Stoppers. Moreover, when your anger is chronic, when other people are frequently viewed as "wrong," as "jerks," or with other epithets I won't mention, when negative characteristics suddenly spring up in other people overnight (such as "I never realized how inconsiderate, obnoxious, and insensitive So-and-so really is"), when you suffer from the negative effects of your anger (tension, interpersonal difficulties, psychosomatic problems), you have a strong indication that your self-talk is dosing you with more anger than is necessary. In all likelihood, this is anger generated by the judgmental messages of your Imposed Self, not an Intrinsic Self 1 response.

Why not examine your own anger-generating self-talk? If you truly want to, you can free your internal environment from the extra stress of living with chronic resentment.

11
· · · · · · ·
Self-Talk and the Rescue Process

A repetitive, destructive interaction that perhaps a majority of people engage in, often with extremely negative consequences to themselves and to others, is the Rescue Process. This destructive interaction is quite separate from its extremely positive look-alikes — Love/Loyalty/Support. After describing the Rescue Process to members of my seminars, person after person has admitted in relief or exasperation, "That's me!" validating my belief that many people struggle with this issue. These people are not just therapists, nurses, and teachers, or others in the "helping" professions, nor are they just the spouses or parents or children of alcoholics who have recognized and begun dealing with this process under the term *codependence* or *co-addiction*. The deeply personal stories I have heard along the way have convinced me that Rescuing is an unnecessary and painful detour. It is also a useless one. In fact, Rescuing inevitably leads to self-victimization. Corresponding to the age-old adage, it is a road to hell paved with good intentions.

Whether operating in a one-to-one relationship, in a family, or, for that matter, in the political and social arena, Rescuing simply does not work. This chapter will present Rescuing for what it really is, describe how it is created, how it is maintained, and how you can put an end to it, by changing your self-talk and challenging your early decisions.

The Chrysalis and the Butterfly

A little boy finds a butterfly still in its chrysalis, struggling to remove itself from the outgrown prison which had been its home and protection a short time earlier. The little boy wanting badly to help, takes out his pen knife and carefully cuts the threads that bind the seams of the chrysalis. As he accomplishes this most delicate task, the butterfly emerges. However, it is a butterfly whose wings have no strength, who cannot take off in flight. The little boy has unknowingly deprived the butterfly of a necessary and important struggle. In trying to save it from pain, he has taken away its birthright — the ability to fly.

This story symbolizes for me the tragic paradox of the Rescue Process, the well-intentioned desire to help, which actually results in substantial harm to the growth of another individual. As a veteran Rescuer myself, someone who has spent most of my life first in the process and later making the slow, frequently painful changes required to emerge from it, I feel qualified to present to you what I have learned over the years. Beyond my own personal experience, I have had the privilege of working with hundreds of other people, themselves at different stages in recovery from Rescuing.

Rescuing, as I have already noted, is similar, if not identical, to the concept of codependence that developed in Alcoholics Anonymous and Al Anon. Within my groups on the Rescue Process, there are always a large number of adults who have had an alcoholic parent. Anywhere from one-third to one-half of the group members began their life as the child of an alcoholic. As we will see, given the circumstances that lead a person to make Rescue decisions, it is no surprise that these conditions are invariably present within the alcoholic family. However, one does not need to have had an alcoholic parent to become emmeshed in Rescuing. Clearly, inadequate parenting of any sort, as well as early negative environmental conditions, lead a child into the Rescue Process. And to be sure, Rescuing begins early.

I know, personally, that I was a Rescuer by the age of five. I remember at that time telling two of my father's friends how mean my father was to my mother. The principle "meanness" involved his smoking while my mother and I rode in the car with him. My earnestness in making the complaint and in attempting to Rescue my mother was not diminished by the perhaps innocuous crime that my father was committing.

Another childhood example of Rescuing, shared by a woman now in her fifties, occurred at an even earlier age. This woman remembered her three-year-old self in a circumstance in which she and her mother had moved in with her grandmother to get away from an abusive father. When the father came to the door, the grandmother picked up a knife to keep him from entering into the house. She recalled moving in front of her mother, thinking to herself, "If he gets past Grandma, I'll stop him!"

As well-intentioned as Rescuing is for a child, it is misguided, based on illusions of omnipotence and power that the child in actuality does not have. These illusions, if not confronted and changed, lead to behaviors that, at their best, do not work and, at their worst, can have tragic consequences for everyone involved.

Rescuing Defined

The Heroic Impulse lies deep within most of us. We all long to be the knight on the white charger. We want others to see us as the "good guy." Our religions, our national myths, our fairy tales, and our afternoon soap operas assure us that Rescuing is the righteous way. This is the foundation, the core, of all high drama. But what is the reality here? Just what is the Rescue Process?

Rescuing means taking responsibility for the happiness, health, or well-being of another person. Rescuing does not confine itself to other people. One can attempt to Rescue a job, a business, a marriage, or any of a number of abstractions. Furthermore, we may be asked to assume this burden, or we may not, but, a Rescuer — with a capital R — will take on the job anyway, and with it the responsibility for correcting a situation, invariably making adjustments at his own expense. As Rescuers, we become a kind of shock absorber, attempting to soften everyone else's blows with our own time, money, and energy. What is worse, we frequently Rescue without even knowing we are doing so. Thinking that we are helping, we maintain or worsen the status quo.

And why are we doing this? It certainly has nothing to do with our intelligence or our intent. Quite simply, we are following a set of decisions that we made years before when we were children. As Rescuers, we cut into ourselves quite automatically. Our self-talk programs us to Rescue. This programming tells us that we don't count, that our feelings and needs are less important than someone else's. It also tells us that we can handle it because we are stronger than they are. Given these inner directives, it is not surprising that when someone has a problem, we are more than just there; we make the problem ours.

The diagram that follows demonstrates this predicament. The Rescuer (Person A) has assumed the burden of Person B. The shaded area in the Figure (Person B's problem) has become Person A's focus. She must solve her husband's alcohol addiction or her friend's heartbreak before she can focus on herself. He must fix his wife's depression or remedy his company's financial woes before he can relax and enjoy himself.

When I began as a therapist, I can recall thinking to myself, "If I could just make all my clients well, I'd have no problems — I'd be completely happy." Internally, I was parroting the old song, "I want to be happy, but I can't be happy, 'til I make you happy too." Little did I realize that my focus on

The Rescue Position

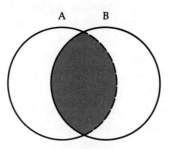

The No Contact Position

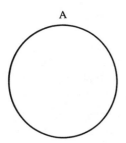

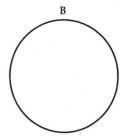

The Supportive Position

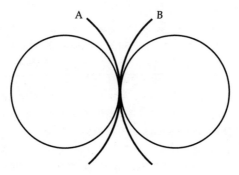

my client's problems was a total distraction from issues of my own that, given half a chance, would be clamoring for my attention. This is typical of the Rescue Process. In fact, one of the major payoffs of Rescuing is that, just like alcohol or drugs or overwork, it effectively distracts us from our own pain.

Looking again at the diagram, notice that Person A has also caved in and repudiated his own boundaries and feelings (as represented by the dotted line). He is trapped in a symbiotic relationship, which over time can feel more and more like the proverbial tar baby. Every move he makes will ensnare him more. He begins to feel resentful and guilty as his time and energy is increasingly funneled toward Person B. At home, in the shower, in the check-out line, Person B's problem occupies most of his time and energy.

At this point, the classic Rescuer will shift to the second position — No Contact. Somehow he will manage to extricate himself from the magnetlike attraction that has kept him hooked to the other person. A growing mixture of resentment, guilt, and depression expedites this shift, which is likely to be sudden and dramatic. Perhaps he will drop-kick himself three thousand miles across the country to get away from his never satisfied, always demanding mother. Or, he will simply forget to call the friend he has talked to every day for the past six months. At some point, our survival instincts turn on Red Alert, and we have to get away. Cutting loose may be messy, but there will come a point where it has to be done. The job will be left, the lover dumped, the calls ignored.

Having disentangled, the Rescuer may think his problem solved. He no longer allows himself to get close enough to anyone to Rescue them. He may have no interest in a relationship, seeing it as one more person to take care of. He may describe himself as having difficulty making commitments and internally vow never to date someone more than a month at a time. Perhaps his walls are so high that no one will ever get in again. Yet he is lonely and depressed.

Some Rescuers even manage within the context of a relationship to maintain this No Contact Position. As Karen explained, "I make my own plans. If he wants to come along, fine. If not, that's okay too. I take care of myself." Karen thinks she is involved, but she isn't, not in a way that allows for the development and unfolding of intimacy. For Karen, as for many Rescuers, closeness or dependence of any kind looks far too much like the old Rescue connection. Like many of the men and women who have Rescued their parents, their brothers and sisters, and their former spouses, she simply does not want to take another chance. Karen, like all of us in this No Contact Position, is still a victim of the Rescue Process.

The good news is that there is another way of relating. There is a third option. I call it the Supportive Position. Although superficially resembling Rescuing, in the Supportive Position the other person's problem remains clearly where it should be — in the person's own territory. The shoe remains on the right foot. Yet, in contrast to the withdrawal, burnout, and explosiveness that characterize the other two positions, here we are actually able to offer love, support, nurturing, and genuine help. We are able to be there in a way that does not cut into ourselves.

The Supportive Position demands only that we set precise limits. Our boundaries have to be solid. Notice the contrast in the figure between Person A's boundaries in the Rescue and in the Supportive positions. Admittedly, limit setting is one of the most difficult tasks facing someone who has learned to Rescue, for that person was not encouraged to have boundaries or even to be in contact with the personal feelings from which boundaries are defined. His Judge will have numerous negative labels (selfish, self-centered, noncaring) with which to punish his limit setting. It is a task, however, well worth confronting, for the alternatives of self-victimization or isolation are even costlier.

The Drama Triangle

Dr. Steven Karpman, psychiatrist and colleague of Eric Berne, the brilliant originator of Transactional Analysis, sat in front of his television set doodling football plays. As he drew lines of players moving from one position to another, a second image began to superimpose itself. Players in real-life dramas move from one place to another. Rescuers switch into Victims, even as Victims become Persecutors. Dr. Karpman, in the serendipitous fashion of many great creators, had just fashioned the Drama Triangle.

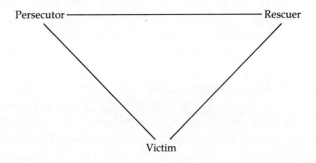

Here, in a simple triangle, is an explanation for drama on stage and, all too often, in real-life Rescue Games. Enter the triangle as Rescuer, and before the ride is over you will have spun around to Victim and Persecutor as well. Want another spin? The stakes get larger. Loan a friend some money. He may pay it back, but quite possibly your "down-and-out" friend (Victim) will suddenly, and with seeming unpredictability, switch from Victim to Persecutor, failing to answer your phone calls and forgetting to mention the loan whenever you see him. Now, you get to play Victim on your way to Persecutor, as you stoke your resentment, telling first this person and then another.

The first go-around is often brief, somewhat inconsequential, each player unconsciously testing the water. Often a person can pinpoint that first trip around. Bob, a sales manager in a high tech corporation, recalled it clearly, "I remember the exact day I began to rescue Sally, one of my office program-mers who was a thorn in my side for the next three years. I was giving her some negative feedback about her perfor-mance, and she began to cry. I was completely undone. I started listening to her problems and totally forgot the feed-back. I wish now that I had handed her the box of Kleenex and walked out."

Different people bail out of the ride at different times, some immediately, others only at points of tragedy. It took Bob three years. It is not at all uncommon to find people taking the destructive ride again and again, hoping against hope that this time the other person's problem will finally dissolve.

Freida, a thoughtful woman in her early fifties, described her attempt to rescue her mother over the course of over forty years, "I was the youngest child and, for some reason, I was the one who always tried to make Mother happy. We were very, very close, and I never did anything to anger her. When I reached adolescence, on rare occasions, I would stand up to her, or fight back, or let her know that I had some need. Then my father would say, 'Make up to your mother. We don't want her to feel bad.' So I would give in. She decided that my other brothers and sisters were against her, so that left only me. I had to do everything. Even today on the lunch break, I not only bought something for me, but I also bought something for my mother."

Most people, like Freida, enter the triangle first as a child. And what Freida learned in childhood — and the decisions she made in this most powerful environment — tend to stick. These decisions (carried out through the controlling self-talk of the Judge) will be acted on in the future with the same person, or with substitutes that we meet along life's way.

By returning to the triangle, we can examine this phenom-enon more precisely. For every Rescuer (R), there are two additional players, the Victim (V) and the Persecutor (P). The Drama Triangle demonstrates their relationship perfectly. Pic-ture a solid triangle with a pin in the center anchoring it to a board. The positions R, V, and P are fixed on the board. The triangle, itself, spins around and around. Like a ride at the carnival, you may get on at point R, as Rescuer, but as the ride goes on you will have experienced all the other positions. What most of us do not realize when we don our white hats and set off on a grand Rescue pursuit is that we will bite the dust as Victim, and then emerge later as a full-fledged Persecutor.

Rachel, like so many women who are Rescuers, started her love affair with Charles thinking that he would get his life together and become the man she wanted him to be if only he had a little help and support from a loving woman. After a year of Charles not changing, Rachel found herself more and more often feeling like a Victim. Then she began to Persecute Charles, a role she consciously abhorred. She began to nag, to call him names, and to talk about him behind his back to both his and her friends. But still lurking in the background was her basic Rescuer's belief, "If only I try hard enough, he'll change."

Most of us identify with the Rescuer position; we have a more difficult time owning up to the Victim or Persecutor within us. Yet these are equally important, though often hidden, aspects of the Rescue Process. Rescuing is not easy.

The Price You Pay

The price you pay is high. In fact, Rescuing costs many people their entire lives. In order to understand how this can be true, let us examine this proposition within the framework of Transactional Analysis. In Transactional Analysis, people are described in terms of their Parent, Adult, or Child parts (Ego States). An effective person has a Parent part, to nurture and take care of himself and to utilize good judgment about the world at large; an Adult part, to sort out current incoming information; and a Child part, to experience feelings and creativity. When two people are in a Rescue mode of interaction, important parts of both people get cut off, so that only one whole person is left intact.

Transactional Analysis

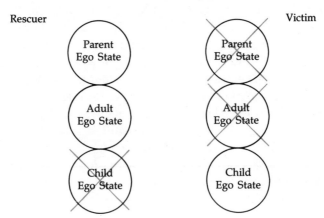

As you can see in the Transactional Analysis diagram, the Child Ego State is crossed out. Many Rescuers recall very little about being a child. They were the little adults of the family, the confidants of a parent, or the parent of younger brothers and sisters. When I ask members of my classes to draw a picture of their early families, a clear distinction between the Rescuers in the group and the non-Rescuers is immediately apparent. The Rescuers do not play in their drawings. Their drawings do not portray family scenes of happy interaction. Instead, isolation is the norm. When there is contact, the Rescuer is more likely to portray herself as comforting a crying mother.

The result of a child's focus on another is that there is very little energy left to explore one's own self. Rescuers, in truth, often have a diminished sense of who they are. Moreover, any message from their Child part is frequently ignored, discounted, overridden, or ridiculed. The Child part of the Rescuer gets very little attention, just as the real child of the past was, in truth, neglected. It is not surprising that the Child inside the Rescuer is often depressed, or that certain pseudo-nurturing activities such as overeating replace genuine self-nurturing.

The loss of one's own Child, of one's unique and special quality of aliveness, life interest, and enthusiasm is the biggest tragedy of the Rescue Process. The road to reclaiming that Child, which I call the passage through the Void, is one of the most frightening and rewarding aspects of healing.

As we can see from the preceding diagram, the adult Rescuer is allowed to function only within a Parent or an Adult mode. As Rescuers, we basically ignore our own feelings, needs, ideas, and hopes in the totality of our focus on the other person. As a simple example, I recall a day I spent skiing, while in the throes of an active Rescue Process. While I was aware of the beauty of the surroundings — snow, bright blue sky, warm sunshine — as I waited in the ski lift line, I was not really present in the sense of having fun or enjoying the experience. Instead, my thoughts were back in my office, trying hard to solve the crisis of a couple with whom I was working. As I look back, I hate to consider how many hours I have spent in such misdirected thought — not engaging in the essential clarifying or analyzing role of a therapist, but in the frantic Try Hard of the Rescuer.

Such lost hours expand for many into lost months, lost years, and lost lives. Imagine the child of the alcoholic who marries an alcoholic and spends his life struggling to resolve that drama of promises and betrayals. Or, the woman who came into therapy to deal with the depression and emotional depletion resulting from years spent trying to Rescue a friend. Or, Charlene, an attractive attorney, who described herself as "adopting" difficult men, men with potential, who need to change just this or that. "The cost," Charlene reflected, "is that I'm 36 years old, and I don't have the child that I desperately want."

The Price They Pay

When you Rescue someone, you may save that person from her momentary pain, yet sentence her in the long run to a life without competency, self-sufficiency, or wholeness. Like the little boy who tries to help the butterfly, an act of supposed kindness can lead to unforeseen and grave consequences. Take for example the common admonition "Don't cry." While frequently used as a well-intentioned palliative, this injunction actually prevents another person from using her own feelings to emerge stronger from a painful situation. Crying is one of the body's best tranquilizers. It is the best, if not the only, way to emerge from a loss into a new place of acceptance and even transcendence. Physiologically, crying has been found to release toxic chemicals from a person's body. Anyone who has had a "good cry" knows the relief that is provided. Those who seek to suppress the symptoms of loss, like physicians who too quickly prescribe tranquilizers or give a grieving person a sedative, inadvertently make the healing process harder. The wisdom of generations has supported the confrontation of loss through the rituals of grief. Only our Rescue culture seeks to limit this healing confrontation. This, in turn, puts us in a reality built upon avoidance. The child raised on the "Don't cry" injunction may as an adult shut off his own tears with self-talk like "Don't wallow in self-pity" or "Don't be such a baby" and instead have a drink or take a drug.

If we look again at the Transactional Analysis diagram of Parent, Adult, and Child, we see that for the Victim, the Parent and the Adult parts are crossed out. An implicit assumption is made that these parts are either absent or useless. The Victim is seen as lacking. This subtle, but powerful, negative view of the Victim, even if it agrees with the Victim's own assessment of herself, demonstrates the persecuting flavor of the Rescue Process. As in the case of those Rescuers of primitive peoples, who could not see or appreciate the strength and adaptiveness of another culture, so the Rescuer denies the capabilities of the supposed Victim. Thus, a parent who does a child's homework for him or oversupervises the child's effort underestimates the child's ability to perform on his own and seriously hinders the development of that child's Adult and Parent parts. The grown-up child of such a parent may end up doubting his own ability to do anything without assistance.

By Rescuing children, we train them to feel helpless and to have low self-esteem. Certainly a child needs support. But when a child can do something on her own, she should be allowed to do it, even if it is not perfect, and even if it is easier for the parent to do. So many adult men and women learn "I can't" because a parent did not allow an imperfect "I can" — in cooking, in painting, in writing, or in any new pursuit.

Moreover, a parent who Rescues a child from the natural consequences of his actions, sets up a circumstance where harsher consequences will be subsequently forthcoming. Again, the distinction between Support and Rescue is very relevant here, because children absolutely need support in dealing with the problems they face. But the child needs also to be involved in the resolution. He does not need to be Rescued.

The movie, *Dance with a Stranger*, about the life of the last woman in England to be sentenced to death and executed, exemplifies this, only with adult players. One of the main characters, a playboy, frequently acts out, "misbehaves," in bars and social company, and is Rescued from the consequences of his actions by a close male friend. His bad treatment of the main character and her becoming Victim to his Persecutor makes up the bulk of this story. As this drama escalates and the stakes get higher, this man and his friend are accosted at gunpoint by the woman. As she aims the gun at the playboy, his friend again attempts to Rescue. In this most gripping scene, the woman tells the playboy's friend to get out of the way, or she'll shoot him. The friend quickly moves, leaving the playboy to face a consequence far greater than the bloodied nose that might have been his rightful due at an earlier time had his friend not been so quick to intervene. In short, Rescuing prevented the playboy from coming to terms with the consequences of his own be- havior. His Parent (self-protective) and his Adult (accurate computing) parts were seriously hindered in their necessary development.

In Alcoholics Anonymous, the phrase "hitting the bottom" means allowing someone to face the consequences of his behavior. It means pulling out the safety nets. Hitting the bottom may involve a parent stopping any financial assistance, or a spouse no longer accepting excuses for broken agreements. It may mean that a secretary stops doing the boss's work. For many people it is only when consequences are experienced, when the bottom is hit, that a decision to change — to stop taking drugs, to get psychological help — will occur.

The recent idea of "bringing the bottom up" through confrontation *before* the job has been lost, the marriage dissolved, or the money spent, has worked in programs such as the Betty Ford model of intervention. Here, the family begins the painful process of confrontation while at the same time letting go of Rescuing and protecting the alcoholic or the drug abuser from the consequences of his behavior.

True Victims

Before going much further, it is important to make a distinction between a True Victim and a Self-Victimizer, or a Professional Victim. This distinction will in turn help us establish when rescuing (with a small "r") is vital and when it is merely part of the Rescue (with a big "R") Process. The issue is not as simple as it might appear. If someone were to have a heart attack in front of me, I would obviously want to do something to help. The person in crisis would be a true victim, and I would be a true rescuer. I might spend a great deal of time and effort to rescue, but I would most likely feel no resentment toward the victim. In fact, I might feel a sense of self-empowerment from having had the opportunity to be of real value in the life of another. But it is important to note that this rescue is time limited, that it is unlikely to occur again, and that the person suffering at the time is truly unable to take care of himself.

There could be a tendency at this point to think of the simple physical/emotional division as a convenient dividing line. However, as one physical therapist put it, "I deal with people all the time who are true victims — of accidents and disease. But I still find that I have to be aware of the Rescue Process. It is very easy in such a circumstance to also become a Professional Victim — to have people do for you what you can do for yourself — because it is more difficult for you than for them. I have to challenge people to stay out of the role of Victim even if it means their experiencing a lot of pain while they are in the process of doing something for themselves. If I Rescue them and make it easier in the short run, I can destroy them in the long run."

Alcoholism generates a similar dilemma. The alcoholic may present himself as a true victim of alcohol, and indeed in part he is. Alcohol will not only kill, but it will also interfere with a person's capacity to take care of himself in a clear, logical manner. However, failing to realize that the alcoholic is also playing out a Victim role is the surest way to find yourself tolerating behaviors that you would not tolerate in another person, such as excusing broken agreements, or accepting missed appointments, or allowing abusive verbal and physical behavior. Rescuing the alcoholic by tolerating such behavior or by shutting yourself down to prevent its occurrence, (that is, being extra careful not to trigger an outburst) will only preserve the status quo. Thus, the excuse "He only hit me because he was drunk" may allow a woman to tolerate abusive behavior for years. In actuality, the truth might be "He only drinks in order to hit me, without having to face any real consequences."

Children can be and often are True Victims. They lack one of the major freedoms that adults, at least theoretically, have — the freedom to leave a bad situation. A large number of my adult clients who as children lived in abusive situations have confirmed that attempts to run away from home were usually not successful. Children cannot simply go to another home, knock on the door, and say "May I join your family?" As our willingness to accept the reality of child abuse increases, there will be more genuine rescues (in the best sense) available for the true child victims in our society.

When someone grows up, the distinction between true victim and Professional Victim blurs. It blurs for the therapist as well as for the person in the throes of his/her own Victim position. Many people who now function as Professional Victims were true victims as children. The Victim role was learned and, like a weed, which has many roots and branches, continues to exert its effect through the decisions made in childhood.

The person operating in the Victim position has usually not realized that she is no longer living within in the confines of her childhood situation and that she no longer has to live by the decisions necessary at that time. Not having the option to leave creates for a child circumstances where less-than-desirable decisions have to be made in order to survive. These decisions frequently involve major harm to an individual's true self. The child, trapped in an abusive family, will cut off major parts of herself, so as to function within that environment. She may limit or completely block her spontaneity, her assertiveness, her sadness, or her anger.

Without access to these important, sometimes vital, parts of herself, she may tolerate abusive situations in the present, even though in reality she now has the option to leave. She is no longer a *true* victim, but that fact may make little difference if she does not know it. Like the person who drowns within three feet of shore because it is dark and she does not know where she is, so the Professional Victim relies on old information about herself and others and remains limited by inadequate options. Moreover, the Professional Victim is more familiar with a world in which she is mistreated. Thus, she will feel safer with an abusive person, in the sense that she knows what to expect, than with someone who treats her well. If she is with a positive other, she will continue to test that person's limits, even behaving in abusive ways herself to elicit the abuse she expects. Like the child who carefully searches the house for a monster, rather than be taken by surprise, so the fearful Child within the Victim is determined to ferret out the danger, which her background has convinced her must be there.

If as therapist or friend or spouse or parent, we collude in the current self-victimization of the now adult individual, we do him great harm. Often in the guise of sympathy, we agree with the Victim's life view, again reinforcing his old beliefs and self-talk. Confrontation, gentle if possible, is an important alternative.

I'm reminded of Claire, a former client, who had been a true victim as a child. As an adult, she perpetuated this position in several ways, one of which was to fantasize a disastrous future for herself. In one session, she scared herself by imagining that she would end up as a bag lady in San Francisco if her parents didn't help her financially. When we scare ourselves, our Child part takes the information as true, and corresponding feelings of sadness or panic are immediately generated. As Claire began to cry, I might have said something like "Oh, it will be okay," or "Maybe we can find a way to get your folks to help out." Instead I said, "You sure like to show yourself horror movies!" This was not what Claire had expected to hear. Startled, she stopped crying, and half laughing, half angrily, threw her Kleenex in my direction. As she promptly emerged out of her Victim position, she began considering real options for making money, so that she would not in fact end up in the situation that she was fantasizing. And she carried these new options out by applying for and getting a better job with good retirement benefits.

The Rescue Beliefs

BELIEF #1: Rescuing helps.

FACT: Rescuing harms.

Rescuing is a harmful process. What it helps in the short run, it hinders in the long. Both people are always diminished in some way by Rescuing. If this is true, why do we cling so tenaciously to the idea that we can Rescue another person? First, as we just noted, Rescuing gives the momentary illusion of helping. A distressed friend seems to feel better after we have talked to her for several hours. We forget that the same conversation may take place another thousand times, and that by talking to our friend, we may actually prevent her from confronting her problem directly by facing the actual situation or person, or by getting some professional help. As one woman shared, "My daughter went back to Al Anon, only after I went on a week-long vacation and wasn't there to drain off her emotion."

In the workplace, the individual who Rescues on his job can see concretely how this or that fire gets put out, one more time. He does this by overextending, by working all weekend, or by not taking legitimate time for himself. The corporate world actually encourages this kind of self-sacrifice (self-victimization). However, the source of the problem (poor planning, unrealistic deadlines, short staffing) is not confronted in a way that could generate long-term benefit. In the end, the corporation itself suffers by worker turnover, burnout, inefficiency, increased health care costs, and, in the extreme, premature death from heart attacks and other physical ailments aggravated by the toxin of stress.

Unfortunately, our persistent hope that Rescuing will work, coupled with our misunderstanding of certain basic aspects of human behavior, maintains us so persistently in the Rescue trap. This sense of hope, this loadstar we follow, tells us that with just a little more effort or a little more money or a little more love, the other person's life *will* get better. We forget that the Victimizing process is self-generating, and that even as we are struggling to put out a fire in one area, the Victim is fanning one in yet another. As Rescuers, we ignore our own pain by focusing our attention on this illusion of future resolution. Yet we are as likely to solve the Victim's unhappiness as we are to light up a black hole by reversing the gravitational field. While bad situations do in fact change, and people indeed can get their acts together, I would venture to say that this is never the consequence of Rescuing. If anything, Rescuing leads to just the opposite result.

The reason for this is extremely simple. When we Rescue, we reinforce or reward the other person for screwing up. We do not reward his efforts to succeed. Nor do we allow the negative consequences of a particular action to speak to the person. Thus, whenever Sally loses a job, her mother rushes in with extra money to bail her out. Not only does Sally not need to face the consequences of showing up late for work, but she also gets extra strokes in the form of money and attention from her mother. Someone from outer space, looking at this situation, might deduce that Sally gets paid by her mother for getting herself fired. And while this is not her mother's intent, it is, in fact, the case.

In romantic relationships, Rescuing likewise retards the process of obtaining reality feedback. Concerns about "hurting the other's feelings" inhibits honest and direct communication. Dissatisfactions are often obscured until the distance between partners is too great to bridge. Legitimate complaints are not voiced, but are instead "gunnysacked," thrown into that invisible garbage receptacle we all carry. As resentment builds, one person may even begin an affair. This action paradoxically serves to Rescue the original relationship, by distracting the straying partner from her anger and dissatisfaction, as well as by meeting some of the unmet needs in the relationship. Yet as Diane Vaughan recounts in an article "The Long Goodbye":

By the time the other partner realizes the relationship is going down the drain, the initiator is already so far gone that efforts to save the relationship are futile.

How many "sudden" breakups of marriages of twenty or more years' duration are actually the result of stifling legitimate assertion and confrontation, caused by the Rescue Process?

BELIEF #2: If I'm _____ , you'll change.

FACT: Another person's changing has nothing to do with your effort, goodness, intelligence, or intrinsic self-worth.

One day, as I cried about one of my clients for the hundredth time, I remembered a fairy tale that my mother used to read me. It had been my favorite fairy tale—Rapunzel. Retold with the appropriate labels, the story goes like this:

Once upon a time there was a woman who begged her husband to pick some rare and highly desired herbs for her from the garden of a wicked witch. *(Notice that from the story's beginning we have a perfect drama triangle in operation. The original set-up involves the wife as the Victim, her husband as the Rescuer, and the witch as the Persecutor.)* In the gathering of herbs, the husband gets caught, thereby making himself the new Victim and his wife, for getting him into this predicament, the new Persecutor. The witch steps in to Rescue him under the condition that he promise to give her his firstborn child *(the new Victim)*.

After a time, the child Rapunzel is born and is taken to the witch's tower. Rapunzel is a beautiful child with extremely long hair. "Rapunzel, Rapunzel, let down your hair," the witch calls out, whenever she wants to climb up to see her young captive.

One day, a handsome prince traveling through the countryside sees this strange occurrence and falls in love with Rapunzel. He decides to Rescue her by helping her to escape. However, the witch finds out about the young lovers' plot and cuts off Rapunzel's long braids. She then lowers them to the unsuspecting prince, and as he ascends to save Rapunzel, the witch lets go of the braids. The prince falls into a thicket of thorns at the tower's base, piercing his eyes. Thus, the prince who set out to Rescue the Victim Beauty from her Witch Persecutor (and thereby persecute or victimize the Witch) becomes the Victim himself.

Rapunzel, now thrown out by the witch, encounters the prince in the forest. As she sees him, she cries, and her tears fall into his eyes, which are then healed. She now truly rescues the prince, and they live happily ever after.

As strange as it may seem, I had embedded deep within the Child part of me the belief that I, like Rapunzel, had the power to heal with my tears. I believed that if I was sad enough, someone else would change. The little girl inside me had continued to heed this belief—unconscious to the Adult part of me—and was attempting to resolve through the magic of tears the problems of my clients, whom I felt obligated to Rescue. This realization allowed me to decide at an emotional level that my sadness had nothing to do with another person's changing.

Other people fill the "If I only . . . , you'll change" blank with other adjectives. The Rescuer/Persecutor combination is often "If I'm angry enough, you'll change." Intellectuals believe, "If I figure out the perfect thing to say, you'll change." Others believe, "If I'm good enough, you'll change." A common reason people enter therapy is to discover some sort of modern-day magic to create change in another person. Again, such magic simply does not exist.

BELIEF #3: I'm the only one.

FACT: There are many alternative sources of support for someone who assumes self-responsibility.

Another Rescue belief, leading to negative self-talk, is the notion "I'm the only one." Often, the source of this erroneous belief is a parent's dysfunctional bonding with a child. That child, out of her vulnerability, tolerates being used by the adult as the adult's only confidant, confessor, comforter, or friend. Later, when the child grows up, he will argue, "I 'have to' talk to so-and-so each day. I'm the only one she will talk to."

"Of course, that is her choice," I reply, "but she has, in fact, many more alternatives than you. As long as you meet all her needs, however, she probably will not seek those options out." Sometimes, the Rescuer is shocked at how quickly another Rescuer (or even a vehicle of genuine support such as therapy, or Alcoholics Anonymous) is found if he decides to step out of the role of one and only.

BELIEF #4: I'm stronger. I can handle it.

FACT: You have limitations and needs that are just as important and essential as the person playing Victim.

Within every Rescuer I have met has been a neglected, deprived, or abused inner Child who is just as vulnerable as any person whose principal role is that of Victim. I am confinced, in fact, that as we let go of the Rescue position, the memory and experience of early victimization by a parent, teacher, or other adult never fails to emerge and must be dealt with. Each Rescuer must ultimately confront her own inner victim, grieve the past deprivation and abuse that was her lot, and move on. This grief will arise only when Rescuing is terminated and empty space is created for recognizing and mourning the past. Rescuing is based on an omnipotence that is an illusion. Letting go of the illusion of strength uncovers the vulnerable child inside.

BELIEF #5: I'll have a life once so-and-so is okay.

FACT: Until you make the decision to stop rescuing, you will continue to replicate your early environment and deprive yourself of a life of your own.

Victims don't get better unless they themselves take responsibility for their lives. Parents and friends can remain in the Victim position for a lifetime. You, as Rescuer, can easily use up fifty years of your life attempting to change another person and still find that other person to be a bottomless pit of difficulties. Since one of the intentions of Rescuing is to distract yourself from your own pain, once a Victim does, by chance, grow into self-responsibility, you'll simply find another in short order. To have the life you deserve, you must first and foremost stop Rescuing. When you stop, like the alcoholic who takes his final drink, you will face a scenario that may seem empty and meaningless. In short, you will face your Void.

Anti-Rescue Self-Talk

1. The other person is totally capable of changing his life situation even if that person perceives himself to be a Victim.
2. I do not need to convince someone that she is capable of change.
3. I do not have the power to change anyone but myself.
4. I am not responsible for the health or happiness of any adult person.
5. My primary responsibility is to the Child within me — to be supportive to that Child.
6. I'm okay if I never help anyone else.
7. It's okay to pursue things just for me.
8. It's okay to let go of relationships that are not nurturing to me.
9. I can feel good about myself.
10. I deserve a life too.
11. My needs are as important as anyone's else's.
12. Even if someone is helped temporarily by Rescuing, the benefit won't last.
13. I support others best by keeping my own house in order and correcting my own flaws.

The Recovery: Facing the Void

When the Rescuer's role is discarded, most people experience a gaping void, a terrifying sense of being alone in the world. There is an immediate loss of identity. The distraction of organizing one's life around another person is suddenly gone. In one sense, the letting go of this predictable life role is no different than giving up any addiction. Jamie said it best, "When I stopped Rescuing, the Grand Canyon seemed to open up inside me."

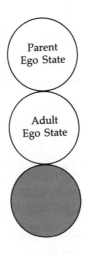

I experienced this Void quite intensely, when I gave up a substantial piece of my own Rescue Process. Suddenly, I had a tremendous amount of time on my hands and free energy that I didn't know how to use. I did not welcome this change, because my previous time-structuring activities were all connected with actual Rescuing (talking to clients on the telephone for hours at a time) or with silent Rescuing (worrying). So when I was no longer spending my minutes and hours in this way, I was at a loss.

As Eric Berne tells us in his book *What Do You Say After You Say Hello?*, time structuring is one of the most important activities in which we engage. According to Berne, "Most people become very uneasy when they are faced with a period of unstructured time." For me, that sense of unease was more like absolute panic, best described by the image of being in the middle of the ocean with no one around, treading water. I felt totally anchorless. A second image was that I had just arrived from outer space and had no connection with anyone. No Rescue connection felt like no connection at all.

Penny Marston, a patient advocate and one of my clients, described her experience of the Void in very similar terms. After stopping her attempts to Rescue her sister, she wrote, "Like an addict facing a cold turkey withdrawal, I entered the period after my escape from my own personal triangle. I *had* been an addict and the 'substance' with which I had been abusing myself was other people.

"As long as there had been one other human being around, I had focused on him or her. Now, I was suddenly and unexpectedly alone. I had expected peace; instead I found myself close to panic. I had thought that she would not be able to get along without me, but she went spinning off without a backward glance. She never even said goodbye.

"My friends, who had been so warm and supportive during the crisis, sighed 'Thank God, it's over,' and went on about their business. My husband was tired of the whole thing. Everyone expected me to get on with my life; no one realized that I did not know how.

"So, backed into a corner with no one to talk to but myself, I faced the only person left: Me. Gradually, I heard a strange sound. It was my own heart beating.

"Now, I know that the challenge is just beginning. But a curious thing has happened. The panic is gone."

Facing the Void is a terrifying experience for anyone. This is not really surprising when we recall that Rescuers initially survived, or at least made their lives better, by shifting their

focus from self to other. A child closes off her own unman-
ageable pain and anxiety and instead puts her energy into
trying to better the situation. Frequently, the child's effort
does have a positive effect — temporarily. The depressed parent is comforted; the chaotic and disordered house is cleaned;
the neglected and abused younger children are protected.
The cost to the Rescuing child is frequently unseen. Yet important energy is taken from self-exploration, from play, and
from creativity, and given into service to the family. In the
isolated and deprived early families of most Rescuers, the
child was forced prematurely into adulthood.

The extent of this loss is acknowledged only when we
realize how much a child experiments with the different parts
of himself through play. Here, interests develop, and the
knowledge of who one is and what one likes is born. For the
child who is serving the needs of a parent, either in actuality
or by worrying, this incredibly important process is greatly
retarded.

Stan, for example, became his mother's companion when
she made herself the Victim of a bad marriage. Stan offered
her the companionship that her husband did not provide. The
cost for Stan was that he had no playmates of his own, nor
any sense that he needed them. Only years later did he realize
that he lacked the experiences of socializing, leadership, and
cooperation that were crucial in his adult life.

The Necessity of Grief

Facing our own emptiness and the true deprivation of the
Rescuer's early life leads us to feelings that have been buried
for many years. These feelings of anger, sadness, and grief
involved the loss of many things: the loss of a childhood, the
loss of parents who were functioning adults themselves, the
loss of opportunities for play and exploration, the loss of trust,
the loss of access to your own sadness. If you had to play the
role of the strong one in the family, you lost the opportunity

to be needy and to receive care and nurturing. You may have hidden your pain behind an automatic smile, and convinced even yourself through denial that "It wasn't that bad" or that "Other people had it worse." When you let the smile go, you may find what seems like mountains of pain underneath. You may find yourself grieving childhood hurts that were long ago forgotten or minimized.

Only when I stopped Rescuing did I begin to grieve the loss of my father. He was the typical absent father, which so many of the family drawings by Rescuers show. Many times, he was gone on Rescue missions of his own, visiting this or that down-and-out person. When my grief began, I was shocked at its intensity. I was amazed to be crying (sobbing really) about incidents I had remembered only as humorous anecdotes.

As I grieved, a new voice began to emerge. "What about me? I deserve a life too." The self-preoccupation of my parents became clearer, and the causes of it, the deprivations in their early lives. I began wanting to focus on healing myself. I dreamed of a newborn horse, still wet from its own amniotic fluid, who was being packed into a wooden crate. The crate was too small, and someone began to break the young horse's legs to force it into the box.

Clearly, my own Rescue structure was destroying me. I began to break out. Each time I allowed myself to grieve over an early loss, some new aspect of myself was reowned. Grieving served to dissolve the old Rescue beliefs and connections. It created the space for something new.

Self-Renewal

An image appears. A field cleared of all weeds and briers now lies fallow, seemingly naked, yet pregnant with the possibilities of new growth. The impulse for this new growth comes from your Real Self. The free spirit inside you can now creatively add to your life. There is now space and time to pick up the threads of arrested development, to return in memory to childhood, to those activities and interests that were set aside, because Rescuing took precedence.

For me, that interest turned out to be horses. Perhaps sharing with you my own discovery will show one way in which the Intrinsic Self creates joy and wonder.

It began as a flicker of attraction when I saw an *Arabian Horse* magazine in a snack shop next to a class I was teaching. My instantaneous counterreaction was pure Judge (and a replica of my mother's voice), "You don't need that." The power of the Judge, as we all know, is not to be underestimated, and I was sufficiently stymied so that I left the shop without the magazine. Another Stopper "It cost too much" (yeah, $3), never ceases to amaze me. I can spend a great deal on a fancy restaurant meal (for my Adult part), but invariably I have a difficult time spending money on my inner Child. It is as if buying for this part brings up greatly outdated financial information, while my Adult transactions are more or less up to date.

In any case, before leaving for the day I had bought the magazine and found a world of excitement and beauty that was clearly connected to very deep feelings. This discovery led me to begin riding lessons, driving an hour each way to a riding facility. I later found a stable five minutes away from where I lived. This amazing "coincidence" is something I have seen over and over. When one creates the interest and space for something to occur on the inside, it frequently manifests itself on the outside. Perhaps it is a function of attention. As we have noted in the concept of the Confuser, we "see" only small pieces of the world. Someone has gone so far as to describe the "small worlds" most of us inhabit. I drove the same road to a trampoline teacher (another new interest) time after time without ever noting the presence of a gas station. It was only when I needed gasoline, that the station, which had naturally been there the whole time, suddenly materialized.

From riding lessons, I proceeded to sponsor a horse, and then to buy my very own Arabian, Bey Shar, "Bennie," who has given me more real joy than I can possibly convey. Upon telling my father that I was planning to buy a horse, he offered me one word of advice, "Don't!" Thankfully, I was able to look beyond his well-intentioned, yet limited notions, and listen to my own self.

My time-structuring dilemma was solved but with an activity and relationship that gave me joy, excitement, exercise, and adventure, all the things that we know are healthy and life-preserving. What I had previously spent my time doing (Rescuing) had been anxiety-provoking, depressing, and unhealthy. I invite you to find those threads of past and current interest and excitement in your life. Whether it be learning a new sport, developing an artistic talent or taking long leisurely walks, there are activities uniquely yours if you take time to stop, look, and listen. Stop judging. Look around. And listen to yourself.

One final Permission is required. Rescuers did not as children receive the support that they needed, so most of us now have a hard time asking for or receiving any help. In this regard, don't be afraid to find a teacher or a coach. Get as much help and assistance as you need. Stop being a loner. Allow the Child inside you to receive. Without my trainer, I doubt that I ever would have had the freedom or confidence to take long rides in the hills. You now have the resources to re-parent the neglected child inside you, to allow your Real Self to emerge. You can now be for yourself the supportive and interested parent that you never had. Like someone in a workshop once said, "It's great being my own Parent, now that I have both money and car keys."

12
·······
Sex and Self-Talk

WILL I get an erection? Can I keep it? Am I going to be able to satisfy my partner?

Will I have an orgasm? Do I want to have sex? Will my partner get mad if I don't?

Is there something wrong with me? Am I normal?

Perhaps by now it is not surprising that the same critical focus that permeates every other aspect of our lives affects our sexuality as well. Displeased with our natural responses, we push for better, longer-lasting, more intense reactions, paradoxically interfering with our inherent capacity to respond sexually. Society itself places an incredible burden of *shoulds* and *don'ts* upon this natural function. Again we are walking a tightrope. One step off this perilous course plummets us into a chasm of self-contempt.

Neither men nor women are exempt from the realization that sex is not always the blissful experience that it's supposed to be. In *The Hite Report,* for example, Shere Hite established that only 30 percent of the women surveyed regularly had an orgasm through sexual intercourse. Similarly, a *Psychology Today* survey of over 52,000 people revealed that 55 percent of the men responding were not satisfied with their sex lives. While there are many reasons for this dissatisfaction, none has a greater influence than our attitudes toward ourselves and toward our partners. When these attitudes are based on Self 2 Drivers, Stoppers, and Confusers, we are directed away from our own sexual centers, pushed from pleasure into performance.

Sex and *Shoulds*

The greatest known deterrent to effective sexual functioning, according to Masters and Johnson, is performance anxiety. Much of this anxiety is generated by Be Perfect, Hurry Up, Be Strong, Please Others, and Try Hard commands. With such Drivers in operation, a sexual relationship becomes a proving ground for an individual's masculinity or femininity or even the person's own self-worth, leaving little room for feelings of arousal and desire. All five Drivers can and do interfere with the open and spontaneous expression of sexual feelings. The Driver that stands out, however, in its capacity to undermine sexual arousal is the self- or partner-inflicted demand to Be Perfect.

The Be Perfect Driver may require that sexual contact always involve intercourse. ("What's wrong with me? Why can't I make it?") It may demand a hundred percent orgasm. ("Did you come? Why not? Did I do something wrong?") There may even be the expectation of simultaneous or multiple orgasms. ("Why couldn't I last longer? I'm depriving you.") It is through such internal pressure that the Be Perfect Driver turns a sexual experience into a performance, an achievement to be met, an obstacle to be overcome.

The examples above illustrate the intrusive self-talk that results from an individual's own Be Perfect command. The same pressure, in the form of Be Perfect Claims, can be brought to an interaction by one's partner. Bill, for example, wants Sara to have an orgasm with each sexual encounter. When she doesn't, he feels inadequate and angry, mad at himself, and mad at her. Yet the more Sara tries to have an orgasm, and the harder Bill works to give her one, the more difficult it becomes.

Sara's self-talk gives us some sense of her inner turmoil: "Am I going to get aroused? What's wrong with me? Why do I have to have this problem? It's hopeless. I'll never be able to come. Maybe I should just fake it. Bill's trying hard. I shouldn't make him feel bad." The anxiety generated by Sara's own self-talk makes it impossible for her to relax and tune into her own sexual feelings. Instead, she becomes a spectator, monitoring her own arousal or lack thereof. Through Bill's pressure and her own, she has created for herself a negative internal environment where sexual arousal does not occur.

Are you aware of the Drivers, Stoppers, and Confusers in Sara's inner message? Triggered though they are by Bill's Be Perfect Claim, Sara's inner speech rests upon her own Please Others constellation. She would be less affected by Bill's Be Perfect ideal and freer to speak up for herself if she were not basing her own self-worth on pleasing him.

Many of us are like Sara. In trying to please our partners and protect them from any feelings of inadequacy, we dampen our own sexual enjoyment. Commonly, a woman tries to hurry up her sexual response; a man struggles to slow down. Each attempt, well-intentioned though it may be, exacerbates rather than resolves the arousal problem. This is true because the tremendous pressure that exists concomitant with these demands seriously interferes with sexual arousal. Moreover, each difficulty in becoming aroused adds additional performance pressure. A vicious downward spiral is established, where anxiety leads to nonperformance, which leads to even more anxiety.

It is no accident that a standard action of most sex therapy programs is to forbid sexual intercourse to a dysfunctional couple. The sensate focus exercises developed by Masters and Johnson actually go as far as to forbid any genital stimulation during initial touch sessions. By removing the couple's focus from success or achievement or the endpoint goal of orgasm, an opportunity for a leisurely, nondemand pleasuring is provided. The power of the Be Perfect Driver is reduced.

The structure of these exercises (one person gives while the other receives) aids in turning off the Hurry Up, Try Hard, and Please Others Drivers as well. Some programs assign a time period (twenty minutes, for example) for nongenital pleasuring. This time interval in the beginning may seem extraordinarily long for two people who both have incessant Hurry Up demands. Yet, as Masters and Johnson note in *Human Sexuality Inadequacy*, "For most women, and for many men, the sensate focus sessions represent the first opportunity they have ever had to 'think and feel' sensuously and at leisure without intrusion upon the experience by the demand for endpoint release (own or partner's), without the need to explain their sensate preferences, without the demand for personal reassurance, or without a sense of need to 'return the favor.'"

Such "new rules" existing in the therapy process are necessary to break the stranglehold of the judgmental *should* system. As we have seen repeatedly, the *shoulds* and *should nots* of this system have little relevance to reality. This is particularly true for sexual *shoulds*, based as they are on misinformation that has been passed on in the context of shame, bravado, and fear. The damage of this misdirection is noted in *Male Sexuality*, where Bernie Zilbergeld describes how basically normal, healthy men "rigidly cling to certain rules as to how sex should be and how a man should act in sex." Zilbergeld goes further to acknowledge that men have accepted "unrealistic and, in fact, superhuman standards by which to measure their equipment, performance, and satisfaction, thus insuring a perpetual no-win situation. Whatever men do, it's somehow not enough, when compared to the standards they learned."

Women have incorporated equally damaging judgments, although at least until recently, the focus of these standards and *shoulds* has been different. For men, abiding by the judgmental position has meant a continuation of the Be Perfect, Be Strong achievement demands that are part of the traditional masculine role in other areas. Stopper labels like "weak, inept, and unmasculine" have kept at bay any soft feelings that might spontaneously arise. For women, the Please Others Driver has dominated, leading to a focus on male pleasure and satisfaction at the expense of their own. Labels like "castrating," "pushy," and "loose" have effectively squelched the more assertive, demanding aspects of female sexuality.

The myths that Bernie Zilbergeld describes in *Male Sexuality* highlight the judgmental position's influence on the sexual behavior of men. As we shall see, these myths include a large number of Drivers, Stoppers, and Confusers.

MYTH 1: *Men should not have, or at least not express, certain feelings — feelings of weakness, confusion, fear, vulnerability, tenderness, compassion, and sensuality.* The Driver involved is, of course, the old bastion of the masculine role, Be Strong. If you doubt this, ask yourself the question I asked one class. Can you imagine any macho movie hero suggesting to his costar, "I need to be held," or "Let's cuddle"? The very word "cuddle" seems incongruous with the traditional masculine image. Yet the need for touch, for affection, and for nurturing is an important *human* need. Naturally, this Be Strong Driver leaves many women feeling deprived. Throughout *The Hite Report*, women state that they do not get enough touching, hugging, and caressing. They complain that touch is considered by men as a prelude to sexual intercourse, not important in and of itself.

MYTH 2: *In sex, as elsewhere, it's performance that counts.* Here again, sex is seen in terms of achievement, rather than pleasure. The Drivers Try Hard and Be Perfect turn sex into work. I can still remember the instruction of one sex therapist to a male client who was very concerned with such performance issues as how often and how long: "Let's focus on your becoming less of a bookkeeper and more of a lover."

MYTH 3: *The man must take charge and orchestrate sex.* According to this myth, there is no room for a man to be passive, only the demand to Try Hard and Be Strong. This is another way of stating that sex is work and that a man has to remain in control. He himself is deprived of the opportunity to be taken care of and nurtured. Of course, the female partner is also denied. If the man is always to be in charge, she in turn must always be on *his* sexual agenda. Her own assertion is not permitted. Is there any doubt that power struggles develop over this inflexible rule?

MYTH 4: *A man always wants and is always ready to have sex.* The Drivers are Be Perfect and Be Strong. This myth ignores the great number of external and internal factors that can and do influence human sexual performance. It is responsible for the many cases of impotence that derive from one negative experience, an experience based on nothing more than the fact that the necessary conditions for sexual arousal were not met. These conditions for men and for women generally include an interested and interesting partner, a safe setting, an atmosphere of acceptance, and a freedom from external preoccupations and worries. The Be Perfect tightrope does not allow a man to assert, "I don't feel like sex tonight," or "I'd rather just be close." Its "you should" demand must be met or the self-punishment "You're impotent" or "You're not normal" ensues. The anxiety resulting from this self-punishment can create a self-fulfilling prophecy of dysfunction.

MYTH 5: *All physical contact must lead to sex.*

MYTH 6: *Sex equals intercourse.*

MYTH 7: *Sex requires an erection.*

MYTH 8: *Good sex is a linear progression of increased excitement terminated only by orgasm.*

Myths 5, 6, 7, and 8 are all based on the Be Perfect Driver with the familiar correlate of Either/Or Thinking. Sex is defined as one hundred percent sexual intercourse (or for some, one hundred percent simultaneous orgasm through intercourse) and anything else constitutes a failure. The term "foreplay" is an interesting by-product of these myths. Meaning *what comes before,* this term reinforces the idea that any sexual activity other than intercourse is incomplete. As Shere

Hite comments on the sexual conditioning of women, "But especially we learn that, no matter what else, intercourse and male orgasm *must* take place." Previously, she had noted, "Sex is defined as a certain pattern — foreplay, penetration, intercourse, and ejaculation — and intercourse *is* the pattern."

These myths, of course, turn sex into a proving ground rather than an encounter that can nurture and regenerate. It is unfortunate that men, so concerned about having an erection and completing the obstacle course that culminates in satisfying their partners through sexual intercourse, do not realize that most women value communication and warmth over performance. Most women would like less Be Perfect, Be Strong, and Try Hard demands from their partners and more loving intimacy. For most women, penis in vagina is not the only, or even the optimal, means of achieving sexual satisfaction. A man does not have to have an erection for his partner or to prove something to himself. Yet within the judgmental structure, no erection, no sex.

Women collude in the myth that their partners' erections are necessary for sexual satisfaction. In Lillian Rubin's *Women of a Certain Age: The Midlife Search for Self,* for example, several of the women interviewed expressed how they were holding back their own emerging midlife sexuality out of the fear that their husbands could not meet their needs. In each case, sex was defined solely as sexual intercourse. These women were walking on eggs around their partners' inability to get or to maintain an erection. Yet with such a demand placed upon an involuntary function, it is no wonder that sexual avoidance and impotence occur.

Equally destructive as the male belief in the absolute necessity that sexual activity culminate in intercourse is the female myth that a woman should be able to have an orgasm through sexual intercourse alone. As in most situations, what we have been taught *should* be (our Self 2 Judge's notion) is not necessarily what is. Lonnie Garfield Barbach in her book *For Yourself* corrects this myth: "The physiological fact is that intercourse alone just doesn't seem to provide enough of the right kind of stimulation to the right area to permit many women to become aroused to the point of orgasm."

So, too, the belief that a woman must have sex based on her partner's need rather than upon her own has had a negative influence. The Driver Please Others pushes many women to override their own feelings and submit to the demands of their partners. Fear of rejection and a concern that they will be seen as prudes or as teases or as frigid pushes many women, even very young women, into sexual activity before they are ready for it.

Along these same lines, Barbach notes the erroneous beliefs held by many that "sex is not as necessary for women as it is for men" and that "a man's sexual release is more important than a woman's." These beliefs again lead a woman to overvalue her partner's sexual feelings and undervalue her own. They reinforce the Please Others stance inherent already within the traditional feminine role.

Sex and Stoppers

Existing side by side with society's push toward ever more intense sexual performance are a number of strong prohibitions against sexual enjoyment. Years of messages say "don't": don't enjoy; don't be sexual; don't initiate; don't communicate; don't show your feelings; don't be vulnerable. As Barbach notes in speaking to her female readers, "We may have been taught that a nice girl wasn't even supposed to know that such a thing as sex existed, at least not until after she was married. Then, miraculously, sex was supposed to lose all its nasty connotations and become a joyful experience." And even those men and women who were fortunate enough to escape with few internal prohibitions against sexual enjoyment frequently have barriers to communication about sex.

Needless to say, the negative self-talk deriving from these "don't" messages interferes with sexual arousal. There are three primary areas where this Stopper intrusion occurs: (1) in sexual assertion; (2) in the appreciation of one's own sexuality, and (3) in the evaluation of sexual behavior itself.

Sex and self-assertion

If Stoppers interfere with assertion in general — and we have seen that they do — you can be certain that for most people they are present to an even greater degree when it comes to sexual communication. Fears of rejection, criticism, and disapproval usually increase with the degree of sexual intimacy. Yet if you are not free to share your feelings during sex, especially your questioning and anxious feelings, they stay with you, growing larger, even as you fight to push them aside. Unexpressed, these negative and anxious feelings can become major obstacles to sexual arousal.

Therapists Bernard Apfelbaum and Martin Williams of the Berkeley Sex Therapy Group have recognized the difficulty that many people have in owning and voicing the feelings that arise during a sexual encounter, especially feelings that differ from society's "this is all so wonderful" ideal. In their work with individuals and couples, they help people to decipher feelings that a person does not have the space or the time to put into words because of the pressure of internal and external sexual demands. Under these circumstances, a set of "script lines" is developed with each individual. These "script lines" are direct statements describing the emotions that were experienced during a specific sexual encounter. Once articulated, they are written down so that when similar feelings arise again, they can be voiced.

Within the protective framework of sexual therapy, people often find that the honest assertion of heretofore unspoken feelings can lead to an intimacy and subsequent arousal impossible to attain when energy is spent trying to deny negative emotions and capture a perfect sexual interlude.

Statements like "I'm feeling really hopeless about ever getting turned on" or "I'm embarrassed" make room for closeness and arousal where distance and alienation have been before. In a therapy context, an environment is created where this negative expression can be viewed as a positive desire for intimacy rather than as an attack or as a punishment. Listed below are some of the "script lines" that the Berkeley Sex Therapy Group has employed in working with sexual difficulties. Notice the level of intimacy involved in these assertions. Notice further how they go against our standard notions of what should be communicated during sex:

> I'm wondering how you're feeling.
> I feel out of touch, cut off from my feelings.
> I feel alone.
> I wish you could help me to get out of this mold.
> I feel embarrassed.
> These feelings seem so irrational. They're almost ridiculous.
> I'm afraid that I will do something wrong.
> I'm afraid you might be bored.
> I feel like I've got to do something.
> I'm worried that you might be getting impatient.
> I want to touch you while you're stroking me.
> I want to kiss you.
> I feel so desperate.

A second element of the Berkeley Sex Therapy Group program is the establishment of a framework where negative feelings can be asserted at the exact moment when they are experienced. This kind of assertion naturally requires the overriding of any rigid requirements against interrupting one's partner. Thus if Maureen is feeling left out as Charles is moving to higher levels of excitement, it is important that she voice her sense of isolation at that moment, not later over dinner, when there is nothing that can be done to alter her feelings of estrangement.

Why, we might ask, is it necessary to go through such an elaborate procedure? Why write out "script lines"? Why take care to insure through mutual agreement or by means of a therapeutic framework that the communication is safe? Why assert negative feelings as soon as they arise? Why express them at all? The answers to these questions lie in the recognition of just how surely the judgmental system squelches honest communication and distances people from their immediate experience. Accepting and sharing this experience is an important basis for sexual intimacy and arousal.

It is not uncommon for a person to be at one level sexually and at another level emotionally. In our society, sexual barriers are often broken more easily than emotional ones. Not infrequently, for example, a woman who has spent the night with a man will feel awkward about telephoning him the next day. The standard Stoppers—Catastrophizing ("Maybe he doesn't like me"), Negative Self-Labels ("I don't want to seem pushy"), or Rigid Requirements ("I'll call *if* he has indicated that he wants to see me again")—can inhibit even minimum assertion. A woman in this position finds that she is at a superficial level emotionally while at a very intimate level sexually.

Even with committed couples, intimate communication is frequently nonexistent where sex is concerned. The fact that so many women (and men) fake orgasm is one indication that intimate assertion is blocked during what is considered by most people to be the most intimate sexual act. *The Hite Report* found that over a third of the women responding to the question, "Do you ever fake orgasm?" answered yes, and that an additional one-fifth of the respondents admitted that they had misled their partners about their sexual responses at one time in their lives. Bernie Zilbergeld explains male faking in this way, "They can't fake erections, but we know of more than a few who fake orgasms. But the main things they fake are their feelings. They pretend to be confident when they're not, to know when they don't, to be comfortable when they're uneasy, to be interested when they couldn't care less, and to enjoy when they feel otherwise."

Such deception, whether it involves orgasms or feelings, is motivated by many Self 2 *shoulds* and *don'ts* — by the desire to avoid punishment or rejection, by the need to please, by the fear of hurting one's partner's feelings, or by the hope of getting the sexual encounter over with more quickly. Of course, the false information conveyed by such deception leads the partner to assume that everything is okay, thus decreasing the chance of achieving the conditions necessary for adequate arousal. Many of the pleasuring exercises that form the basis of sex therapy provide a framework that says, "It's okay to be honest. It's okay to communicate your likes and dislikes. It's okay to assert your feelings. It's okay not to know everything." It is interesting that such an explicit mechanism needs to exist in order for such basic permissions to be felt. Such is the strength of the judgmental position.

The appreciation of your own sexuality

An important ingredient of sexual arousal is the appreciation of your own body and the acceptance of yourself as a sexual being. Yet because of negative conditioning experiences, many of us have little delight in our bodies. Instead we worry about our sexual selves. The picture-perfect Playboy centerfold and the media image of the sexual stud have sharpened our Be Perfect focus to a highly critical edge. Our anxiety/punishment tapes, with their negative labels and catastrophes, are ever-present. Lynette, for example, considered herself as no longer a "real" woman after her menopause. She viewed her sexual self as "incomplete."

When through our discussions she realized the negative viewpoint that she was bringing to every sexual encounter, she chose to let go of these negative labels. She also found herself orgasmic again for the first time in several years.

In *For Yourself,* one of the first exercises that Barbach suggests for the preorgasmic woman is the examining of her body in front of a full-length mirror. Once this is accomplished, the further suggestion that she explore her body with her hands is given. These first steps form the beginning of a detailed program whose purpose is to make a woman and her partner knowledgeable about and comfortable with her individual sexual response.

This same kind of permission is important for men as well. While men have generally had fewer sexual roadblocks, they have frequently had *more* sensual ones. Consider, for example, how many men would feel comfortable about taking a bubble bath or sleeping on satin sheets without a partner. Again, it frequently takes an authoritative program to give such permission. The Masters and Johnson sensate focus exercises clearly assert that it's okay to enjoy and spend time on nongenital pleasure. It becomes, in fact, a demand of their program. This is a new experience to the man for whom touch has simply been a signal to rush into sexual intercourse. Of course, this kind of sensual focus and permission enhances rather than replaces sexual arousal.

The negative evaluation of sexual behavior

This brings us immediately to what has been for many women and men a strong Stopper focus — masturbation. According to Kinsey, masturbation may be defined as "deliberate self-stimulation which affects sexual arousal." Here for many people a critical Self 2 Judge heaps abuse upon this sexual act. As Barbach describes, masturbation is "an intimate and very personal experience which we have been taught is dirty, sinful, shameful, and even physically debilitating. The guilt, fear, anxiety, and repulsion that surrounds masturbation is astounding, especially when one realizes not only how pervasive it is among human beings, but how beneficial, pleasurable, and relaxing an experience it can be." Shere Hite found in her survey of the sexual behavior of women that 82 percent of women reported that they masturbated and 95 percent of them could achieve orgasm easily and regularly through masturbation. Statistics reported for men are similar.

According to Kinsey and his associates, 92 percent of the total male population has engaged in masturbation.

As a matter of fact, critical judgments have been associated with most forms of sexual expression. The number of rigid requirements associated with sexual expression is truly astounding. This has been particularly true in our society in regard to female sexuality, where the "double standard" continues to apply its distorted judgments. As one woman writes in the Hite Report, "A man who has many lovers is 'sowing his oats'; a woman . . . is a 'prostitute' or a 'nymphomaniac.'"

The result is, of course, an impossible bind. Pushed to be sexual by a culture that considers sexual allure all-important, a woman is at the same time castigated for her sexuality. She finds herself in a lose-lose situation, going along with her partner's sexual demands without any real pleasure of her own.

You may want to evaluate the kinds of negative labels that you have applied to yourself in regard to your own sexuality or to your own sexual assertion. These judgments are learned and as such they can be changed. Perhaps the best guideline that we can follow is the concern that any sexual expression honors both our own feelings and the feelings of our partners. This involves a recognition that all individuals have the right to assert their genuine desires, including at any point in a sexual encounter the basic right to say no to actions that do not fit or feel good. It also involves the obligation to be honest with one's partner so as not to mislead or take advantage.

There are always those who believe that moving off the tightrope means "everything goes" — that being sexually free means having no sensitivity or concern for society or for the other person involved. The information conveyed by pornography is of this sort. In her article "Erotica and Pornography: A Clear and Present Difference," Gloria Steinem noted that erotica is the "mutually pleasurable, sexual expression between people who have enough power to be there by positive choice." In contrast, pornography's message is "violence, dominance, and conquest. It is sex being used to reinforce some inequality or to create one, or to tell us the lie that pain and humiliation (ours or someone else's) are really the same as pleasure." Pornography is full of such Confusers — assumptions that are simply not true. The message that women like pain during sex or that "no" really means "yes" are blatantly false. Yet through pornography these assumptions become part of our sexual folklore.

Following are examples of the five-step method applied to two common sexual concerns:

Situation: Pressure for orgasm

Sara feels pressured by Bill to have an orgasm. In her desire to meet his expectations, she finds her own sexual arousal decreasing. Sara goes through the five-step process as a way of clarifying her feelings.

STEP 1: What am I telling myself?
I'm saying that something is wrong with me. Bill is only trying to help. I can't say anything negative to him. I don't want him to feel bad. I'll just try harder.

STEP 2: Is my self-talk helpful?
Well, I guess not. I'm feeling tense, and Bill seems to be getting even more upset with me. I could fake an orgasm, but I've never done that with Bill before. I don't want to do that. Maybe I don't have to see what's happening as all my fault. I felt okay about my response before Bill got so upset.

STEP 3: Is there a Driver, Stopper, or Confuser in operation?
I'm trying hard to please Bill. He's trying hard to please me. I'd feel better if there wasn't so much fuss about my having an orgasm.

STEP 4: What Permitter and Self-Affirmation can I use to support myself?
I can say that it's okay for me to stop taking care of Bill's feelings and to tell him what I want. It's okay for me to stop trying to have an orgasm and let it happen.

STEP 5: What kind of action can I take?

Well, first, I'll talk to Bill. I'll see how he reacts. If there's still a problem between us, then perhaps we need to consult a sex therapist.

Situation: Performance pressure

Michael is very anxious about his ability to perform sexually. Because of his concern, he has withdrawn from almost all interaction with women.

STEP 1: What am I telling myself?

I'm saying that I can't let on that I am anxious about getting an erection, because if I do, the woman I'm with will reject me. I'm saying that I won't date anyone until I can get over this problem. I'm saying that I'm not much of a man.

STEP 2: Is my self-talk helping?

Well, I'm isolated and depressed and feel like hell. I still can't get it up. I guess it isn't helping much.

STEP 3: What are the Drivers, Stoppers, or Confusers in operation?

Be Strong. I don't want to have any problems, especially sexual ones. I guess I'm catastrophizing that a woman wouldn't understand, and I haven't even shared my feelings with a woman. I'm labeling myself "not a man."

STEP 4: What Permission or Self-Affirmation can I give myself?

I can tell myself that it's okay to have feelings and to express them. My feelings are there whether I like them or not. Maybe a woman will like me even if I'm not great in bed. Hell, maybe if I weren't keeping all this junk to myself, I could function. I'm in therapy. Maybe a woman would be willing to work with me.

STEP 5: What action can I take?

I think I'll let myself start dating, and forget about having intercourse for a while. If I meet someone I really like, I'll tell her what my problem is and see how she reacts. It's not hopeless. I've simply got to stop pressuring myself and let myself do what I feel like doing, even if it's nothing.

You may wish to put your own negative self-talk concerning sex into this framework. Shifting from self-punishment to self-support is not any easier with sexual issues than with other concerns. In fact, it may be more difficult. The contrasting premises of the judgmental and growth positions will let you see at what stage you are in this transition process. Which alternatives do you now accept?

Judgmental Position	Growth Position
Sex must have a goal: tension reduction, procreation, the affirmation of sexual prowess, and so on. Therefore, sex should always result in intercourse and orgasm.	Sexual feelings are valid experiences in and of themselves. They don't have to lead to anything to be enjoyed.
A sexual experience shouldn't cause negative feelings. If it does, don't let on. Suppress feelings of loneliness, sadness, or vulnerability.	Unless you are free to accept and express whatever you feel, a sexual encounter becomes an alienating rather than a nurturing experience.
You should be able to put aside any problems and become aroused regardless of what's going on within your relationship.	For some people, bypassing problems is not possible. Sexual feelings do not exist in isolation. It's okay to honor your feelings and refuse to push them aside.
You should know in advance whether or not you're interested in sexual intercourse, so that you don't mislead your partner. Otherwise, it's justified for your partner to call you a tease. Be sure you want to go the full distance before you buy your ticket.	It's okay to let your experience determine whether you want to stop or continue. You are not on a train to a particular destination. You're expressing yourself sexually with another person.

Judgmental Position	Growth Position
You should always be ready for sex and always be able to perform.	Both men and women have the right to say no.
You should never interfere with your partner's arousal, regardless of how you feel.	Sex involves communication. It's okay to express your feelings during sex.
You should not need to tell your partner what pleases you. Likewise, you should know the "right" way to please your partner.	Communication of likes and dislikes is essential for both men and women. There is no "right" way. People differ in what is pleasuring to them. You are the only expert about your sexuality.

13

· · · · · · ·

Male Self-Talk—Female Self-Talk

"**I**F you can't say something nice, don't say anything at all." "Act like a lady!" "Don't be too smart." Or did you grow up on "Don't be a sissy!" "Take it like a man!" and "Big boys don't cry!" Whichever set of messages you heard as a child, the basic effect was the same. You were being guided, shaped, molded — your behavior channeled into actions and attitudes that were considered appropriate for your own sex. You were, without knowing it, buying into an intricate structure with rules applicable to almost every area of your life — how you walk, how you talk, what you wear, what you feel, where you work, how you play, how you love. Within the nooks and crannies of this structure, pieces of individual identity may find a space, but the structure is adamant in terms of its requirements. Just as blue is for boy babies and pink for girls, so certain feelings, attitudes, and activities *are* masculine or feminine.

The encouragement of "sugar and spice" for little girls, and toughness for little boys continues to be a serious proposition, one all too often oblivious to the person underneath. "Act like a lady" and "Take it like a man" are general dictates, not advice tailored to the specific, concrete, day-to-day circumstances that each of us (female or male) faces. These dictates are soaked up by developing children to become basic rules about how they should behave. Thus, many women learn to deal with their worlds — even with the hostile provocations in their worlds — through friendliness. So much so that when confronted with danger, women tend to think that "being nice" to their attackers will save their lives. So much so that in one psychological experiment, women who were electrically shocked and then permitted to react to the person who had shocked them relaxed only when their counter responses were of the friendly variety. Men, on the other hand, learn never to back down, to face each hostile encounter with aggression or risk a loss in self-esteem.

Of all the artificial boundaries upheld by the Imposed Self, those based on society's outworn beliefs about masculinity and femininity are perhaps the most severe. Setting out on a highly specific sex-role path, people often find themselves propelled into behaviors that have little connection to the feelings and needs of the Intrinsic Self. The woman who because of her sex-role training has left behind the power of her anger and the man who for similar reasons cannot tap the healing tears of his grief are both operating at a loss. Yet only now, as the definitions themselves become looser, have we begun to question heretofore "right" (that is, culturally expected) ways of being a man or a woman.

One of the recent shifts in the belief system that defines masculinity and femininity has been manifested in the recognition of psychological androgyny — the simultaneous occurrence in one individual of both "masculine" and "feminine" qualities. Thus, a woman can be gentle and understanding, traditional feminine virtues, and also self-reliant and strong, traditional masculine characteristics. A man can be assertive and analytic, and at the same time compassionate and sensitive. Having one set of characteristics does not diminish or take away from the other.

As strange as it may sound, this is a relatively new idea, a permission born in the seventies. Within the standard framework, the more masculine characteristics a woman owned, the less feminine she was considered. She was not allowed to have both. The same either-or viewpoint was applied to men as well. A man was either strong or gentle. He wore the standard masculine attachments like a badge or risked being considered effeminate or not a "real" man.

The feminist movement of the seventies put stress upon this massive sex-role structure. Women sought to redivide the sex-role pie, taking for themselves the right to equal access to the professional world, equal pay, equal free time. And among the feminine shouts of discontent were also male voices daring to redefine what being a man really means. Poet Rod McKuen wrote the song "I'm Strong But I Like Roses." Books like *The Hazards of Being Male* and *The Male Machine* attacked the concept of masculine privileges and presented the costs inherent in the traditional masculine role.

Sex-Role Messages

When one begins to look closely, it is truly astounding to realize the extent to which sex-role dictates have been incorporated even in our most liberated selves. To quote just one example, Phil Donahue, in his autobiography, writes about his discomfort in finding himself alone in the backseat of a car while Marlo Thomas is sitting in the front seat with the driver. In his own words, "There was Marlo in an animated conversation with the driver, and there I was — America's number one syndicated talk-show host — in the backseat, for Chrissake. . . . I was embarrassed to say, even to Marlo, that it caused me suffering."

Breaking the subtle rules and expectations and privileges of traditional masculinity and femininity does indeed cause alarm. Without the rules to rely on, each man and each woman is left to his or her own insides for guidance. Assertion becomes more than a drill, it becomes a necessity. Yet even here, perhaps especially here, the old framework tangles with the new. As one of my clients said in speaking to the part of herself who constantly reminded her of "feminine" *shoulds* and *supposed tos,* "Stop tripping me up. Whenever I start to move, you're there to stop me, to redirect me, to make me question my own instincts. No wonder I always stumble and look clumsy."

My own initial recognition of the power of sex-role obstacles occurred during one early self-assertion workshop. A member of this workshop—a woman—was practicing the assertion, "This is a line. Would you please go to the back." Because her first practice attempt was rather feeble, the other participants urged her to repeat her statement again, only a bit more forcefully. Her next try was clear, direct, and assertive. Struck by the contrast between this latest effort and the one that had come before, the group spontaneously broke into applause. In the presence of overwhelmingly positive external feedback, however, she questioned, "But didn't I sound like a bitch?"

Operating here, of course, was the old Stopper process of Negative Self-Labeling. The label, however, was feminine specific. (Men do not squelch their assertion by calling themselves "bitches.") Moreover, the action this label punished was also sex-role determined. (I have never heard a man castigate himself for being a "bastard" under similar circumstances, say, for upholding his place in line.)

This observation concerning the gender bias inherent in many negative judgments is crucial to an understanding of how sex-role beliefs and the self-talk they generate affect a person's moment-to-moment reactions. For women, acting forcefully, taking charge of a situation, and disagreeing with another person's opinion are actions that are especially vulnerable to negative self-talk. These actions have been traditionally masculine, in responsibility and in privilege.

For men, the Negative Labels that most frequently appear are associated with the heretofore feminine domain of sensitivity. Herb Goldberg, author of *The Hazards of Being Male,* comments, "The autonomous male, the independent strong achiever who can be counted on to be always in control is still essentially the preferred male image." This image precludes such emotions as fear or sadness or dependence. The negative labels "sissy," "cry baby," or "chicken" punish the expression of such emotions. In my work with men, I have seen them most avoid the self-message "weak." Rather than face this dread epithet, many men choose to squash their feelings of sadness or need. Of course, blocking such feelings does not mean that they disappear. They simply surface in disguised form (the fist shoved into the wall to override the experience of emotional pain) or go underground to wreak havoc in unseen places.

Beyond the punishment of certain avenues of expression (tough feelings for women, soft feelings for men), there is a second sex-role difference that ultimately relates to self-talk. Consider the following situation: A man walks into a room and trips over a chair. His first reaction — anger. His first expression — "Who left that *?!@! chair out!"

In the same situation, a woman is likely to respond in a different way. When she walks into a room and trips over the chair, her feeling response is more probably anxiety. Her self-talk — "My, you're getting clumsy. You'd better look where you're going next time." If she is hurt, she may cry.

These differing reactions can be explained as the result of two important processes: externalization and internalization. In my experience, these processes are sex-related. The man more typically directs blame outward; the woman focuses inward. If this perception is indeed accurate, the differing reactions of men and women to external stress become more understandable.

Moreover, each process results in profound differences in self-esteem. People who direct blame outward are much more likely to keep their self-esteem intact even in the face of difficult circumstances than the self-blamer who will frequently experience low self-worth. Perhaps the reason that more women than men come into therapy on a voluntary basis has something to do with this perceptual/attributional difference.

Whichever process you see in yourself, it is important to realize that both internalization and externalization lead to the distortion of incoming information. Both lead to unpleasant feelings and disturbed interpersonal relationships because both ultimately rest upon the judgmental view "someone must pay (be blamed) for any mistake." Neither allow the straightforward, nonjudgmental reaction "Ouch! I'd better move that chair," a simple, practical response with no component of *self*-evaluative pain.

Sex-Role Costs

"I have always felt that a wife's job shouldn't be more important than her husband's," Joyce tells me, a not uncommon statement, even now. Yet this self-definition, related as it is to Joyce's sense of her own femininity, is the kind of arbitrary boundary that leads people to close the door on large parts of themselves. Joyce had given up a promising job in the fashion industry in order for her husband to relocate. The ensuing depression that she felt was debilitating and painful. Yet it was also a warning—something like the discomfort that comes from putting on a shoe that doesn't fit—that her sex-role definition was too tight.

For many women, depression is the consequence of such sex-role limitations. As painful as depression is, it frequently represents an assertion of the Intrinsic Self, making the heretofore forbidden statement "I won't." Put another way, depression is for many the only acceptable way of saying no to the commands and pressures of the Imposed Self. This is particularly true for the woman whose principal problem results from doing what the traditional feminine role has told her to do—Please Others.

As with any imposed message, those inherent in the traditional feminine role may operate in such a subtle way that a woman does not even know that she is caught in its demands. She may simply go along with its basic prescriptions without being aware that she is following a script that has been supported and reinforced for many years. This script, according to Suzanne Keller, includes the following tenets:

1. A concentration on marriage, home, and children as the primary focus of feminine concern;
2. A reliance on a male provider for sustenance and status;
3. An expectation that women will emphasize nurturing and life-preserving activities;
4. An injunction that women live through and for others rather than for themselves;
5. A stress on beauty, personal adornment, and eroticism; and
6. A ban on the expression of direct assertion, aggression, and power strivings.

These feminine prescriptions, described by Keller in 1974, are surprisingly similar to those Virginia Woolf described many years earlier under the title "The Angel of the House." Woolf's angel "must charm . . . sympathize . . . flatter . . . conciliate . . . be extremely sensitive to the needs and moods and wishes of others before her own." This angel, Woolf confesses, "used to come between me and my paper . . . bothered me and wasted my time and so tormented me that at last I killed her . . . or she would have plucked out my heart as a writer."

Because of her automatic acceptance of this feminine role, it did not occur to Elizabeth to question that her very real need to gain a sense of order and control in her own life by finishing her graduate school application, paying her own bills, and sorting out her mail was thrust aside for four days while she took care of everyone else. Yet each day, she grew more irritable and depressed.

While it is frequently enjoyable to support and assist other people, all too often helping someone else involves cutting into one's own self. This was true for Elizabeth. Helping had become Rescuing. In obeying the dictates of traditional femininity, she had shoved her own needs into last place.

In altering her own self-talk, Elizabeth was able to affirm, "It's okay to please myself." She found, however, that this Permission had to be backed up with a specific daily plan in order to be actualized during her day. Elizabeth's plan was to list each morning two things that she wanted to do for herself. At the head of her list was getting a medical checkup. Her constant internal drive to take care of others had led her to neglect her own physical well-being.

Men, too, pay a high price for conforming to the traditional masculine sex-role. While a woman is prohibited from pursuing fully and completely her own talents and abilities, a man is denied access to his innermost being. Herb Goldberg goes so far as to describe men as zombies and daytime sleepwalkers. "Our culture is saturated with successful male zombies," he states, "businessmen zombies, sports car zombies, playboy zombies, etcetera. They are playing by the rules of the male game plan. They have lost touch with or are running away from their feelings and awareness of themselves as people. They have confused their social masks for their essence, and they are destroying themselves while fulfilling the traditional definitions of masculine-appropriate behavior."

Basic to society's description of masculinity has been an emphasis on doing as opposed to being — work, accomplishment, success, that uninterrupted run to the goal line. Evidence, accumulating along the way in the form of houses, cars, bank accounts, investments, degrees, and honors, states, "You are okay; you are doing what you are supposed to do." Once the script is accomplished, the possessions accumulated, what then?

With all of one's self-worth eggs in the masculine basket, is there any wonder that when the basket breaks the results can be devastating, and for most men, break it will through retirement or impaired health. It will break because the complete turning away from one's own inner experience is impossible. If a man denies his own Intrinsic Self long enough, suppresses his physical and emotional signals, he places himself at jeopardy for great risks — from heart attacks that occur "out of the blue," to alcoholism, criminal activities, or suicide.

In *Heartsounds*, Martha Weinman Lear recounts her husband's heart attack and subsequent coronary illness. Much of the book is told in Dr. Harold Lear's own words. In speaking of his illness-forced retirement, Dr. Lear observed, "You take someone like myself who was taught that you are what you achieve, you are what marks you get, you are what society says you are. I had been an 'A,' a *macher,* a leader in my profession, running around giving papers, getting kudos and green stamps. And suddenly your public persona is wiped off the board. And then who are you?"

In a previous section, Dr. Lear had described the experience of worthlessness that ensued when these masculine props were removed, worthlessness that "had not been *caused* by the heart attack but had been *released* by the heart attack, a dam broken and the torrents of self-loathing rushing through; and he knew finally that he had better do something about it, or all this rage turned inside out and all this self-abuse would get him nothing more or less than another heart attack." This, perhaps most common of male scripts, which says that an individual's self-worth is no more nor less than the sum of his accomplishments, is one increasingly taken on by women as well.

Breaking Out

Breaking out of a lifelong script that defines self-worth in terms of either the masculine or the feminine sex role is not easy. In many ways, the male-female structure has supported both men and women, made interaction safer, more predictable. Yet this structure has also impaired, and impaired severely. When we recognize the extent of the psychological and physical damage that derives from obeying the rules of this structure, we have met a vital prerequisite for change, for beginning to alter our sex-role boundaries.

Intellectual awareness is not enough. It is only a first step, a necessary but not sufficient condition. The gut-level experience of the physical and psychological costs takes longer. When they have been bludgeoned and bypassed for so long, signals of hurt or pain or sadness must be great indeed before they are noticed. To give a simple personal example, in the throes of my own Rescue Process I have experienced myself talking to a client on the telephone for thirty minutes or more, quite oblivious to the tension and mounting pain in my arm, until the conversation was over. Now, I am allowing myself to see how I harm myself in my preoccupation with helping someone else. As I permit myself to be aware of how deeply my Rescuing cuts into me, I am letting go of this way of being in the world.

Certainly, the man who has learned as a little boy to shut off his experience of sadness will not find it easy to cry. The woman who has not been encouraged to listen to her anger will need permission and practice before the negative roadblocks to her Intrinsic Self are removed. Yet, for people who want to expand the boundaries of their own sex roles, there are ample opportunities for risk-taking. For a woman, the road to increased freedom usually leads outward — going back to school, acknowledging her own competence, speaking out as an authority. It means following, for perhaps the first time ever, her own agenda.

For a man, the same risk-taking must occur in confronting new territory. Here, however, the key is often the permission *not* to venture forth into the very areas that women need permission to enter. As Herb Goldberg says, "The male's inherent survival instincts have been stunted by the seemingly more powerful drive to maintain his masculine image." The permission here is to listen to and honor one's own feelings of pain, of fear, and of need.

Stan first gave himself this kind of permission on the ski slope. It seemed to him a simple enough place to start — doing an activity that he enjoyed yet that had a curious driven quality to it, in a place where he had no responsibility to anyone else. As he examined his feelings instead of simply obeying the automatic requirements of his Self 2 Judge, Stan began to question why he needed to ski the toughest runs with his friends at the fastest possible rate. He realized that if he were absolutely honest with himself and acknowledged what he actually felt as opposed to what he was supposed to feel, he had to admit that he experienced the most exhilaration and felt most in tune with himself on the intermediate slopes.

In order to get in touch with the seeming split between his feelings and his behavior Stan began asking and answering the standard questions

"What have *I been telling myself?"*

"I've been saying that I should push myself, that skiing means confronting challenges. I tell myself that I should give myself a workout, and that I have to keep up with the other guys."

"What's the cost?"

"I go against my feelings. Just because I can do something (and this is a big one for me) doesn't mean that I have to do it. I wear myself out; I risk injuring myself; I don't improve my form; and most important, I don't have as much fun."

"What's the Driver here?"

"It's Be Strong, Try Hard, and Please Others, in that order."

"What Permission and Self-Affirmation can I give myself?"

"I can follow my feelings. Just because a challenge is there, I don't have to tackle it. I don't have to prove my masculinity to anyone. I don't have to try hard here either. Skiing is for fun. I'm going to give myself that."

"What does my Guide say?"

"From now on, I'll ski by myself even if everyone else is doing something different. I'm going to assert what I want to do."

Stan's new permission may make no sense to his friends. It may make no sense to anyone operating from the judgmental framework. Yet this permission allows Stan, through his action, to support his Intrinsic Self. The decision to follow his genuine feelings narrows to nothing the split between the masculine and the feminine, between his assertion and his intuition. As he backs up his feelings instead of going against them, Stan will experience the rare pleasure of being at one with himself.

And now, what about you? Based upon your sex-role training, what emotions and behaviors do you judge as inappropriate? What did you learn from your father and from your mother about being a man or being a woman? What do you feel compelled to do because of your gender that does not honor your genuine feelings and needs? What impulses from your Intrinsic Self do you squash because they do not fit into the sex-role boundaries of your Judge?

To be more specific, as a man, do you always require yourself to take charge (drive the car, change the tire, and such) without being sensitive to your internal signals of tension or fatigue? As a woman, do you take responsibility for all the housekeeping? Do you, male or female, defer to someone else in certain areas, simply because of that person's sex? If so, and if you experience that there is a cost attached to this behavior, what new permissions will you give yourself? You may want to begin making sex-role changes in a small way. As you discover that you can shape your external environment to achieve a better fit with who you really are, you will find yourself ready to risk a larger step. Examine your male talk or female talk. It is quite possibly obscuring the real person inside.

14

. . . .

The Development
of Negative Self-Talk

I WAS haunted for many years by the question, "How come?" Why do we beat ourselves up? Why do we limit ourselves with prohibitions that seem to have no reason? Why do we talk to ourselves in a manner that we would not use with another person? As a firm believer in the notion that the human organism is oriented toward growth, I experienced this phenomenon of negative self-talk as extremely incongruent with human evolution, especially when it leads to physical disease and psychological unhappiness. To reconcile this seeming contradiction with which I was faced, I put forth the hypothesis that strange and even seemingly destructive ways of operating in the world were at one time necessary adaptations. I believe that behaviors that now hinder us were once necessary to our very survival. The same self-talk that now generates depression (and may even lead to suicide) originated in decisions that may have literally saved our lives at an earlier time.

But how could survival lead us to numb ourselves, to lock feelings away, to forget a part of our experiences? I believe that the answer lies in the fact that the Intrinsic Self operates in the service of the organism *as a whole*. Just as an animal whose paw is caught in a steel-jawed trap will gnaw the paw off in order to escape, so the Real Self will curtail or squelch itself in an attempt to survive in a situation where normality is dangerous.

Moreover, as Alice Miller has emphasized in her books *For Your Own Good* and *Thou Shalt Not Be Aware*, it is not merely the trauma of abuse with which a child must deal, but also the lack of permission to grieve, process, or express the emotion generated by the trauma. A common expression, "If you don't stop crying, I'll give you something to cry about," states this in clear and brutal terms. When the environment is abusive, a child will construct a psychological map to help her minimize the amount of abuse she must face. This painfully drawn map continues to operate *on its own* even when the environment and circumstances of its origination change. All of us, to some extent, operate from such maps, maps that set up unnecessary obstructions (Stoppers) and commands (Drivers), and make no sense in terms of our present-day realities (Confusers). Therefore, we all need help in differentiating or discriminating past from present.

A joke that I frequently tell in my workshops illuminates this point. The joke has to do with a client who perpetually snaps his fingers. The therapist, being nondirective, ignores this behavior for some time, until finally her curiosity gets the best of her, and she asks, "Who do you keep snapping your fingers like that?" The client replies, "Oh, I thought you knew. It's to keep the lions and tigers away." The therapist, incredulous, responds, "But there are no lions and tigers around here." The client, with infinite patience, agrees, "Well, it works quite well, thank you."

How many of us, without even knowing it, act in ways that are no longer necessary? But to stop our own "finger snapping" is to risk that our demons may in fact reappear.

The Judge as Protector

To return to our dilemma, in a more specific frame, how can statements such as "I'm not good enough," "Something's wrong with me," "I can't depend on anyone else," "No one could love me," or "I'm stupid" have served to protect an individual? To answer this question, I propose to demonstrate that the Judge develops originally to protect a child from the adverse elements in his environment, most particularly from a parent, frequently from a teacher, a sibling, or an abusive member of his peer group, and that this protection takes the form of negative self-talk.

Second, I will show that this Judge is no more severe or brutal than the environment necessitates. Third, examining the Judge leads to the discovery of forgotten or hidden elements in an individual's childhood. Fourth, the Judge allows an individual to hold her parents and other caretakers in the best possible light, thereby maintaining hope. Finally, fifth, an individual fails to let go of his Judge because its function has been so necessary and vital in preventing pain.

I first formulated these hypotheses in working with multiple personality issues. An extreme form of the splitting or separating of one self from another occurs in this disorder. Frequently, one self is pure Judge, brutal and vindictive toward the other selves. Often, this self "contains" painful memories from which the other self or selves are protected. In my work with a client whom I'll call Jane, this persecutory self was clearly present, abusing Jane physically as well as emotionally. Whenever Jane felt or attempted to express genuine feelings, she would become extremely anxious, and switch into a second persecutory self, Judy. Judy would do whatever she could to stop these feelings, even hit or bite herself. When I restrained Judy, her anxiety would increase into a full-blown panic reaction. After a point, this anxiety would peak, and Jane would again return and experience her original feelings.

In the process of working with Judy, the persecutory self, I discovered the circumstances in which she became necessary for Jane's survival. Jane's mother would explode and beat Jane unmercifully whenever she expressed feeling or needs. However, when Jane/Judy would hit herself, her mother would often stop her own vastly more threatening abuse. Moreover, when Judy could stop Jane from expressing or even experiencing these normal feelings, there was much less chance of her mother's going "crazy" and brutalizing her. By her abuse, Judy, Jane's developing Judge, was actually attempting to protect Jane, the real child. In all probability, by doing so she saved Jane's life and therefore her own.

In this vivid example, it became clear to me that no matter how bizarre certain behavior appears to be in the present, this behavior had a function in the past and that this function was survival. My respect for this inner protective mechanism increased dramatically as I worked with Jane and her second personality, Judy.

If you examine your own Judge from this perspective, it will give you direct evidence about *your* early environment. Physical punishment, ridicule, withdrawal of love, psychological or physical abandonment, or the threat of abandonment all have great influence upon a child. Rather than risk losing a parent's love, a child will discard valuable parts of himself. Because the Judge develops so early, we may have no memory of what led to its development. This amnesia with regard to childhood is something that affects all of us. Moreover, we all resist painful memories of the feelings we all experienced in being reared by imperfect parents, even those who were doing their best. But beyond the mere forgetting of childhood memories, several other factors help to blur the connection between the Judge and one's early environment. One is the superadaptability of the child; the other is the ability of a child to live in fantasy or denial.

Superadaptability is demonstrated by what has been called the "good child syndrome." Some children are so well-behaved that they receive very little punishment or reproach. These individuals rarely remember as adults any reasons for their severe internal Judges. This was certainly the case with me. I realized a year or so ago that one of the main reasons my parents rarely spanked me when I was young was that they had very little reason to punish me. By the time I was five years old, and within memory's reach, I was, in the negative sense, the perfect child. In other words, my inner Judge was so strict and so severe that I never stepped out of line. I think that had I been a more normal child, my parents would have been much more punishing. I would have stepped outside the line more often and triggered what would have been heavy judgmental consequences.

In other instances, denial operates. Parents are viewed in a falsely positive manner, because for a child to see the harsh reality of his parents' limitations would be too terrifying. Many people who had horrifying childhood experiences have, with the help of amnesia of the past and other cognitive distortions, convinced themselves, "I had a happy childhood." The cost of this common delusion is that the negativity that was a part of the early upbringing is absorbed by the Judge and directed against the Real Self. The child decides "Something's wrong with me," and "I'm not good enough," two of the most common negative decisions. The decisions allow some sense to be made of the toxic environment without having all hope dashed. As the child's reasoning goes, "If the fault is mine, then maybe I can change. If I am just better, smarter, prettier, or, if I stop causing a bother, having needs, or being different, then things will change. The environment isn't awful. It's me." Thus, the Judge transforms a bad situation into one where there is hope. With hope, the child continues, albeit with an increasingly heavy weight of internal Drivers, Stoppers, and Confusers.

In making a simple image of all of this, I sometimes say to my clients, "To keep your Mom and Dad on a pedestal, you had to lie on the floor." In other words, to idealize a parent, you have chosen to denigrate yourself. Accepting your own parents as human beings, often with very real and profound practical and emotional limitations, is very difficult. Often, much grief is required to let go of the illusion of their being or ever becoming the parents that were wanted, needed, or even deserved. But this acceptance is part of the work necessary in dismantling the Judge and getting yourself up off the floor.

The upside-down framework just described creates an interesting paradoxical experience where an individual will fight against receiving positive feedback. I see this frequently when a client refuses to believe anything positive about herself that I might offer. My comments are discounted, "Oh, you have to say that; you're my therapist," implying that I would actually lie in order to try to help. The real reason for clinging to her negative attitudes, however, is that to accept a new view is to risk the lions and tigers returning, in the form of being shamed or tricked or humiliated for believing something positive. "I'd be totally devastated if I believed you liked me and then found out I was a fool and that you didn't. I'd rather not take that risk," one client shared. For someone who was punished for any good feelings ("Don't get a big head," "Who do you think you are?" "You're getting too big for your britches"), or given a slap across the face whenever a spontaneous or genuine feeling was expressed, letting go of the negative squelchers can be experienced as a life-or-death proposition.

In illustrating the dilemma, I sometimes tell the members of my workshops the story of a man who fell off a ship and was struggling to stay afloat. The men on deck threw him a life preserver, but each time he attempted to grab for it, he went under again. It became clear that the man overboard was being pulled down by a sack of rocks that he was holding. One man on board ship cried out to him, "Drop those rocks." The struggling sailor replied, "But they're *my* rocks." I have often wondered how many of us could wholeheartedly and honestly deny having felt, "But they're *my* beliefs. I'm too frightened to let them go."

The question arises at this point, "Why does a child need to protect himself from seeing reality as it is? Why is it preferable to turn against oneself instead of recognizing the truth? Why would we create illusions that turn out to be rocks that hold us down?" The answer lies in the fact that the attachments children form with parents, even bad parents, are necessary for their survival. There may even exist some instinctual basis for this attachment, as has been found in animals (particularly birds) who "imprint" to the first moving object they see upon hatching. A professor of mine, Dr. Kenneth Melvin, actually found that he could imprint baby "Bob White" quail to a sparrow hawk, the quail's natural enemy in the wild. The baby quails followed the hawk even when the hawk made threatening and aggressive movements toward them. Nature, in this case, seemed convinced that attachment serves a higher purpose than avoidance. So the Judge operates to allow a child to hold the parent in the best possible light, so that the child can maintain her attachment to the parent, even when the parent is abusive or unavailable.

There is a further factor that lends support to the notion of putting the parent in the best possible light even at the expense of the child's own self. Recall that the absolute reality for most children is that they cannot leave their family situations, even if they want to. Many of my clients at one time or another attempted to run away. Many others fantasized that their real parents would soon come to find them and take them away from the harmful or non-nurturing environments in which they currently lived. But in the end, almost all had to adjust to a particular family and its dysfunction.

Several years ago, I saw a television program in the *New Twilight Zone* series entitled "The Children's Zoo." In this story, a little girl whose parents are constantly fighting receives an invitation to visit the children's zoo. She convinces her parents to take her. She enters through a separate children's entrance while her parents walk into the zoo through the main door. In the next scene, we see the little girl looking into cages of parents, who try to convince her to take them home and give them another chance to be good. One couple seems to have recognized their wrongs and genuinely to want a second chance. In the final scene, we see the little girl leaving the zoo with this new set of parents, while her original mother and father are in a cage, still fighting, hardly aware of what has transpired.

If such choices were available to us as children, it is possible that the decision to turn against the Intrinsic Self, which so many of us make, would not occur. Nor would we take on negative labels and attitudes about ourselves.

Handing the Labels Back

Thankfully as adults, we can make new choices. We can hand the negative labels and judgments back to the people and to the environment in which they belong. We can get up off the floor, as we take other people off their undeserved pedestals.

This is what Karen, a client of mine, was able to do. Karen went through much of her life in an isolated manner, considering herself a "misfit." When someone makes a decision like this, it is often quite easy to discover where it came from simply by asking, "How does that label fit you as a little kid?" Or one can ask, as I asked Karen, "How old do you feel right now?"

KAREN: I feel like I'm seven.

ME: What's happening to you at seven years old?

KAREN: I'm in school, and I'm seeing all my friends, and they have really nice parents and nice homes, and they fit in, and I don't.

ME: How don't you fit in?

KAREN: Well, I don't fit in with my father. I can never please him.

ME: Do you think that any little girl would fit in with your father? *(Karen's father happened to be an extremely violent and self-centered man.)*

KAREN: Probably not.

ME: Who's the real misfit? Is it you as a little girl, or is it your father?

As my questions began to have an impact, Karen's face lit up and she spontaneously asserted to her father, "Hey, I'm not a misfit! Nobody could fit in with you!"

After all those years the label "misfit" went back to where it belonged. In this case it went back to Karen's father. Karen no longer had to protect her father by believing she was bad. In handing the label back, Karen began to rid herself of a critical basic belief. She no longer needed to walk into a room carrying with her the label "misfit." She can now let go of self-talk such as "You're not going to fit in," "Nobody's going to like you," "There's something wrong with you," or "You might as well not come here."

Because Karen, as an adult, no longer needs her father to be okay at any cost, she can make a new decision and leave this negative attribute where it really belongs — with her father.

Thanking Your Judge

Given that (1) the Judge protects the Child, (2) the Judge is no more brutal than the environment necessitates, (3) the Judge maintains hope of change, and (4) the Judge helps to prevent early childhood pain, it seems important that we give our Judge a proper acknowledgment. As a prelude to letting go of our Judge, an expression of appreciation is often appropriate. I have found that the Judge is usually more willing to retire when this acknowledgment is given.

A clear example of this occurred recently. I was using a two-chair technique with Diane, one of my clients, in order to examine the role her Judge played in keeping her under rigid control. In the two-chair technique, a person alternates between two chairs, talking respectively as her Judge and her Intrinsic Self.

I asked Diane to sit in one chair and to let herself assume the role of her inner controller, or Judge. But instead of confronting her Judge as an enemy, I ventured, "I bet you really had to keep Diane under control as a little girl, so that she would be safe."

Diane's eyes welled up with tears as she replied, "Yes, she would get hit if I didn't."

I then asked Diane's Judge, "Is that what happened when she talked back?"

Diane replied, "There was just one right way to do things."

I said, "Oh, in your family, there must not have been much room to be spontaneous or different."

As we talked further, I acknowledged the importance of Diane's original decision to control herself. To her Judge/Controller, I empathized, "I really know how important you were to Diane. You protected her very well in her family."

Diane, still crying, asked if she could thank her Judge. "I want to thank you for keeping me quiet, because you knew I would be hurt. Thank you." She sobbed quietly for a moment and then added, "But I want you to know that now I'm big, and I won't let anyone hit or yell at me ever again, so you need to stop controlling me. You're no longer needed to protect me, but thank you for being there a long time ago."

Diane cried softly for a few more minutes and then looked up as if to say, "Okay, I'm ready to move on."

Discriminating Past from Present

We all are born with the capacity to generalize. If I touch a hot stove, I'm more careful the next time I approach any stove, not just the one that burned me. This capacity to generalize, particularly around pain, is no doubt a survival ability. Moreover, as thinking organisms, our ability to generalize is far greater than any animal because we can concretize our generalization into a cognition, for example, "Don't trust men," or "Women aren't good at math."

Discrimination learning, in contrast, is about noticing difference and change. The cat who scratched me last year is different from the cat approaching me now. I don't automatically need to be afraid.

The conditioning that occurs in childhood leads to great generalization, particularly when pain is involved. Without knowing it, we frequently overgeneralize, treating *now* as if it were *then*. This overgeneralized way of behaving operates unconsciously, making it even more pernicious. In order to discriminate past from present, an active reevaluation process needs to occur.

This was true for Jim, a two-hundred-pound athlete who felt, "I'm always backed into a corner."

In working with Jim, I suggested, "Would you be willing to walk into the middle of the room and see why it's not safe there for you?" (Jim wanted a 360-degree range of motion.) He agreed and stood in the middle of my office.

I continued, "Will you imagine your mother approaching and see if she interferes with your motion?"

Jim imagined his mother and said, "Oh. I've got to face the same direction that she does."

Jim had made an early decision to protect his mother. Part of this protection meant that he would do things just like she wanted. So Jim told his mother that he was resigning that job and got back his ability to look around the room.

Then I asked him to imagine his father getting up, and Jim responded, "No, with him here, I've got to stand in the corner, because I don't trust him. He might hurt me."

This was absolutely true when Jim was a little boy. He had a father who was abusive and brutal.

At this point I said to Jim, "How tall were you as a little boy, when you were so frightened of your dad?"

And he guessed, "Three feet."

I asked him, "How tall are you now?"

"Six feet."

I followed with the question, "Can your father hurt you now?"

Jim laughed and said, "He can't hurt me now!" and the spell was broken.

An illustrative story comes to mind as I write. It is about my horse, Bennie, and an overnight ride I took several years ago. At that time, he was a young horse and couldn't be tied up with the other horses, so he and one difficult older horse were placed in adjoining squares, contained by a small electric wire. At about two in the morning, I heard hooves galloping past my tent and found that Bennie had broken through the small wire and was feeding on the grass and enjoying his freedom. I wasn't surprised. But the interesting part of the story involves the second older horse. Having experienced the effects of the electric fence, doubtlessly on other occasions, this horse did not attempt to escape. Even though the electrical impulse was thoroughly dismantled, he continued to stand in a small eight-by-eight enclosure while outside a great grassy world beckoned. He stood there that evening and for the better part of the next day. Perhaps he would have stayed even longer — such is the power of generalization. Although everything had changed, nothing in fact had changed for him.

In detailing the early development of negative self-talk, its purpose in survival, and the ubiquitous failure to differentiate *now* from *then*, I hope to give you a more solid intellectual base of understanding that will help you drop the rocks of negative beliefs, which we all carry, and encourage you to stop your automatic finger-snapping. In carrying this information into the final chapter "Listening to Yourself," it is my wish that you will have the courage to wait and find out that the lions and tigers are long gone, and the need for struggle and self-limitation is no longer there.

15

. . . .

Listening to Yourself

JUST as there are great costs to following the judgmental messages of your Imposed Self, so there are great benefits in turning toward the signals of your own genuine feelings. I use the qualifier "genuine" because many of us have directed our lives according to the feelings generated by the Self 2 Judge. We have listened to the warnings of this Judge, have reacted with anxiety to its scary stories, with depression to its criticism, and with bitterness to its recital of shortcomings in others. These self-generated negative feelings (anxiety, bitterness, depression) have obscured and prevented from emerging the delicate, ever-changing impulses of the Intrinsic Self.

Many of us do not know our Intrinsic or Real Self. And quite often, we are afraid, even terrified, of allowing it to emerge. If in early life, our Real Self was greeted with punishment and pain, we decide that we are somehow bad or defective and that we must hide. We see ourselves as monsters, outcasts. We deny the great value of knowing and listening to ourselves. Out of fear, we create what can feel like an insurmountable barrier, a False Self, a Judge, who attempts to offer protection and disguise, to deal with what has been imposed on us.

Typically, the Judge's voice is very loud, whether in Driving or Stopping us. In contrast, the Intrinsic Self usually speaks softly. Unless, of course, we fail to listen; then this voice will ultimately shout to us in dreams, symptoms, images, and illnesses. Yet this is precisely the kind of communication that most of us have been trained to misinterpret or not to take seriously.

Thankfully, there are ways that our Intrinsic Self continues to communicate with us even when we have barricaded it behind our best walls of Drivers, Stoppers, and Confusers. The Real Self communicates through feelings, dreams, images, and symptoms.

Feelings

Discovering the differences between your intrinsic feelings and desires and those that come from the Imposed Self is sometimes difficult. As we have seen, anger, sadness, or fear can be self-generated by the Judge, or they can arise spontaneously out of the wisdom and protective operation of the Intrinsic Self. As I frequently say to people in "Talking to Yourself" workshops, I could ask you now to depress yourself, scare yourself, or make yourself angry, and I am sure that you would be successful in generating these feelings. I sometimes add that I'll refer anyone having difficulty to the daily newspaper. The reader might like to try this exercise. In spite of all the emotions generated, however, there is no positive action or protective outcome. In fact, more than likely, by engaging in this exercise you would be doing yourself damage. Feelings generated by the Judge lead to much inner distress, which has a known negative result on the body and on the immune system. If you find yourself generating emotions that do not lead to positive or protective action of some kind, you are probably operating from your Judge.

After a time you can catch the negative feeling loops that your Judge creates. Depression loops contain self-talk like

"You'll never accomplish anything," "You're just a failure," "You'll never get what you want," or "No one cares about you." Anger loops put the blame on others, but not in a manner that will lead to successful assertion, negotiation, or change. Self-talk such as "He never cares about me," "She's just out for herself," or "Life isn't fair" generate chronic anger. Fear loops such as "Be careful," "You may say the wrong thing," or "No one will like you" can keep us out of commission and out of the game entirely. In short, while the emotions of the Intrinsic Self lead to action, the emotions generated by the Judge are usually experienced in the form of chronic and all-pervasive feeling-attitudes. Instead of assertion motivated by the energy of anger, we get hostility — dry and brittle. Instead of sadness that activates a healing grief process, we see chronic depression and even the inability to cry. Rather than fear that leads to self-protection, we have indiscriminate self-generated anxiety about things over which we have little or no control. The corrosive aspects of these chronic negative emotions, generated by negative self-talk, damage our health, happiness, and relationships with others.

On occasion, these heavyweight emotions reach a critical mass and erupt in a damaging and usually unsatisfying discharge. If any action results, it is action ultimately against the true self — suicide, homicide, or child abuse, explosions of the gunnysack.

In contrast to the festering, chronic, static quality of emotions generated by the Judge, emotions springing from the Real Self are usually vivid, time-limited, and have the possibility of resolution through expression.

In his book *Healing the Shame that Binds You,* John Bradshaw emphasizes the intrinsic action potential in emotions when he breaks down the word into two parts "E-motion" emphasizing the motivation and action to which healthy anger or sadness leads. Learning to distinguish these two forms of emotion is critically important. One path leads to healing; the other keeps you stuck in negative, counterproductive loops that prevent change and damage your life.

Discriminating emotions generated by the Judge from those arising from your Real Self also require you to examine carefully your self-talk. Words like "should," "ought," and "have to" are favored by the Judge. Such words give clues as to where the message is coming from. Listen to Mike's self-talk as he describes a decision he can't seem to make. "I don't want to take this job, but it would do me a lot of good financially. And I should plan for the future. Who knows, I might even like it. I just don't know what to do." In actuality, Mike's feelings have told him what to do. He is simply afraid to follow them. He is not trusting or backing up his own perceptions. Like many of us, his mind dominates. Notice the terms "should" and "might" and the reasonableness of his argument with himself. Yet Mike doesn't move. And it is good that he doesn't! Why? Because any action would have to be forced across the body of his genuine desires.

Contrast Mike's self-talk with that of Karen. Karen found an apartment that by all external standards seemed just right. "I should like this place," she told herself and as quickly replied, "but I don't feel comfortable with it somehow, and I'm not going to take it." Within a brief moment, Karen made the shift from the judgmental position with all its reason and logic to her own intrinsic gut-level response. Later that day, by allowing herself to follow her feelings and walk around a neighborhood where she wanted to live, Karen found her apartment — one that fit just right, inside as well as out.

Karen's adamant refusal to take any action not backed up by her feelings did not occur overnight. She had experienced the tremendous cost of refusing to follow her own Intrinsic Self. Having come face to face with the reality that she had to make room for herself or that she might not survive, Karen began to listen, really listen, to what she told herself. As Karen affirmed, "I came to realize that I don't have to be at the point of collapse before I listen to me. I'm very clear now about what I want to do, even in seemingly inconsequential matters, and I refuse not to treat my feelings with respect."

When through your actions and decisions, you, unlike Karen, choose to discount and ignore your Intrinsic Self, your Self 1 feelings will signal this betrayal. If these feelings are allowed to emerge (not squelched or punished with labels like "self-pity," "unreasonable," or "selfish"), an important lesson will be learned. Your feelings will provide a measure of just how far you have drifted from your own center.

Cynthia made the decision to allow her feelings to speak to her. When faced with an intense version of a familiar stomach pain, she stopped taking her regular painkiller. She knew that her stomach felt as if it were wrenching apart because of the conflict in which she had immersed herself, and she was determined to experience fully the costs of going against herself. She viewed her pain as a message to herself, a demand to achieve a better fit between her inner and outer worlds. The moment Cynthia moved to back up her feelings by asserting herself, by saying no to a number of activities she didn't want to engage in, and by removing herself from a toxic environment, her stomach immediately relaxed and *all* pain stopped. She had allowed her internal teacher to speak to her, and she had chosen to listen and act in congruence with her inner message.

As much as many people distrust and disclaim them, feelings are the most important means for becoming acquainted with the Intrinsic Self. Your emotions give you information about a situation or a person that is simply not available through mere thought. You may tell yourself that you have no good reason to feel as you do, but this thought is based on the fallacy that all of the information available to you emotionally is also available to your intellect. The person who wants to leave emotion out of a discussion is usually choosing to leave out the one most important factor. Whether the decision involves what color to paint the bedroom or what child custody arrangements to make, feelings are paramount.

Along these lines, it is important to realize that the position to which you owe allegiance is not always visible through your behavior. Thus, when Jim asked the various members of one class for feedback about his decision not to date for a while, he received diverse reactions. Some members told him that his decision sounded fine to them; others suggested that perhaps he should push himself a little more to get out and meet someone. One member wondered aloud, "How can you tell when you should push yourself?"

The crucial information to answer that question is, of course, lacking in the material just presented. This information pertains to Jim's feelings. As a matter of fact, Jim was enjoying himself immensely, even though he wasn't dating. He was neither lonely nor depressed, but instead savoring a newfound sense of freedom and allowing himself for the first time to discover what he genuinely liked and disliked. To have placed a *should* upon himself, however much psychological sense it seemed to make, would have interfered, not helped. There is rarely, if ever, a need to push or prod when one is connected to the inner well of energy and aliveness that is the Intrinsic Self. Stoppers have to be removed in order to free that energy, but rarely do we need to push. Aliveness is movement; there is no need to program it.

Dreams

A good friend of mine found herself in a job that did not suit her, leaving her depressed during the day and tearful at night. She dreamed of a great killer whale caught in a tiny pond. One of my clients, a medical doctor, dreamed that she was operating on a patient without anesthesia. As she cut into the patient's flesh, the patient raised up and screamed at her, "You're hurting me!" a shocking and disturbing message that led her to examine how she was treating herself. Another client had a dream in which she was told to treat a large extended family of people in family therapy. The only problem was that everyone was talking at once, and she couldn't get a word in edgewise. She walked outside to get a cup of coffee and when she returned, she was criticized by her boss for leaving the scene. In her nondream life, her Scare Talk, Blame Talk, and Should Talk constantly prevented her from taking any clear direction. She experienced many voices but no one was in charge. As her dream told her, she needed to gain control over her inner voices and decide which voice to listen to and follow. The good inner therapist in her dream needed to take charge.

We are all made up of many voices — Judge, Guide, Real Self, Protective Self, Free Child, Adaptive Child. This inner family may interact to create a toxic environment, in much the same way that real families can be toxic to some or all of its members. The tyrant-ruled family is often replicated on the inside when one part of the self, usually the Judge, rules with a punishing barrage of negative self-talk while the other family members hide in fear or shame and often wage some sort of hidden war against the inner controller.

Liz Walker's dream, which she so beautifully writes about in the passage that follows, shows us how dreams can convey, in a creative story, many important parts of ourselves, including our unclaimed Intrinsic or Real Self.

If we follow the dream interpretation methods of the founder of Gestalt therapy, Fritz Perls, we can see that each aspect of the dream represents some hidden or disowned part of ourselves. Identifying with these diverse characters and voices can give us great insight into the present state of our actual situation and help us clarify the direction in which we need to move. Liz entitled her description "The Session."

The air was warm, the ground churned to dust two and three inches deep by military vehicles. I was attached to a South American army division along with several other United States civilians, and it was moving out. Soldiers were packing, loading trucks, leaving the area.

Word came that the enemy was closing in, so activities speeded up. Men were running about, shouting. I called out directions to my civilian comrades but we had not been organized properly. There was no agreed plan so my efforts were ineffectual.

Across the wide brown river, I saw the enemy army, limbs swinging in proud unison, eight and twelve abreast, moving along the other bank, southward, to where I knew a bridge was located. Each was dressed exactly like the hundreds of others: drab green tunic, black shirt, long straight black native-born hair. It was an army made up entirely of women!

My pulse raced, breath stuck in my throat. I yelled to a colleague but he paid no attention to me. I was on my own, searching frantically for a way out or a place to hide, clambering over containers on the last outbound truck, seeking a niche, a place to wedge my body, and failing to find one, dropped to the ground.

Enemy voices closed in. There was no foliage to hide me. I dived in the dirt, thinking to still my heart and breath, to act like a casualty of war, already dead, not worthy of their attention.

Soldiers entered the clearing. I felt their presence not more than six feet away. I heard a slight metallic sound, sensed the M16 pointing at my back. Dust gritted between tongue and teeth as I melted into its warmth, my body a frozen cage of fear in the hot sun.

I woke from the dream in a panic, hit first by the imminence of death, then by the dream's dire prediction. Was this to be the sum of my life: a hopeless victim?

"Tell me about yourself as the guerilla soldier," Pam said.

"But I'm not the soldier. That's the whole point! I'm the goddamned victim on the ground. The soldier's going to kill me."

I had related the dream to Pam almost without breath, running words together in a way that had become familiar to us both over our relationship as patient and psychotherapist. I first sought her help after my mother died, when I couldn't stop crying and moping about. We met once a week, dissecting every feeling I could muster about the woman who had dominated my life, for whose affection I had yearned and worked, and whom I never pleased nor ever really knew.

As my feelings got rearranged, my growing strength caused other dislocations that called for Pam's guidance and support: the most important one a long, drawn-out, very messy divorce. Pam had seen me through death and taxes, loves and jobs, and several significant personal losses. Through it all she got to know, indeed helped to shape, the inside configuration of my being, and could thus comprehend very readily my words and their meanings in a given situation. In short, we were on the same wavelength.

"You're all the parts of your dream," Pam said. "Now, tell me about yourself as the soldier."

It was quiet in the bright little office as I stilled my breathing. My eyes ran a tiny figure-8 round and round a dirty spot in the carpet. I squeezed them shut as I thought of myself in the soldier's role.

"She is . . . I am . . . committed to a cause. A great cause," I said. "I am very disciplined. And focused. Very clear about the job I have to do. I am defender and protector of my beautiful country. And I'm righteously angry at its invaders. I am dedicated and supremely capable of carrying out my responsibilities and winning our freedom."

"Good. Now, tell me about yourself as the country."

"I've been abused by outsiders for centuries." I was really in it now. "My resources depleted by them for their gain—my own people denigrated, mistreated, denied their rightful stature and position. But I still have valuable natural resources. It is now time for my people to take charge, harness these resources, use them for our common good. . . . My God."

There was silence in the room.

"That is a powerful dream," Pam said.

"God. I'm not just the victim?"

"The victim is your old self. The way you used to be. The way you once had to be to get along. Now you have other choices."

"I'm the soldier. The country. The whole goddamned army of women soldiers."

"Your dream is telling you this."

Silence.

"So I can become a guerilla soldier. Dedicated. Focused. Disciplined. That's my way to go."

"Sounds good."

"I need to preserve my resources . . . energy, talent, money, time. Stop frittering myself away trying to please people. Trying to get approval."

"Yes."

"Christ, it's hard."

"I know it is. But you can do it."

"Yes. If I think like a soldier, it becomes clear. Thank you. Thank you so much." My eyes spilled rivers.

"It's your dream. And your interpretation. No need to thank me."

"Yes. It's my dream. My guerilla warrior. But you gave me the way to understand it. Thank you for that."

"You're welcome," she said, smiling full into my eyes. There was a warm lull between us, then her eyes dropped to the desk pad and a small calendar book. "When would you like to meet again?"

In the following weeks and months, Liz returned to her dream. Anchoring herself as the warrior instead of the victim allowed her to confront and master many difficult situations in new and powerful ways. I particularly enjoy dreams like the one Liz's Real Self wrote for her. In such dreams, hidden powers and capabilities are frequently manifest in disowned and unlikely characters.

Images

On several occasions images have quite possibly saved my life. At least, by listening to their messages I have gone in a different direction. It seems that Images have appeared when my Real Self felt the necessity to send me an important message, or perhaps when my Judge, having failed so miserably to solve the problem, exhausted, quit the center stage for a moment and allowed another part of me to emerge.

A most recent image involved a client whom I had become involved in Rescuing. Her suicidal behavior was both provocative and serious, and I found myself emotionally hooked into

Trying Hard to save her. I felt terribly inadequate because it seemed that whatever I attempted backfired or was "not good enough" — typical Rescuer self-talk. Although I generally avoid getting caught in the Rescue dilemma, her genuine anguish accompanied by suicidal threats and attempts were strong enough to trigger my old reactions. Moreover, I was still hanging tight to certain illusions about myself and had not accepted my own human limitations — that the ultimate responsibility for her life was her own, and that I had, in truth, very little control over what she did.

One day as I pondered my dilemma, an image appeared in my consciousness. It was the image of myself swimming out into the ocean, drifting farther and farther from the shore, attempting to "save" my client, who was headed at an even faster pace into the open sea. Upon "seeing" myself in this motion picture, I had the immediate sense that if I swam any farther, I would not be able to make my own way back to safety and I would drown. This image had particular impact on me for two reasons: first, I had almost drowned in the ocean several years previously and may, in fact, have saved myself only by clear, authoritative positive self-talk, like "Put your mask back on and start swimming toward the shore"; and second, because this very client had previously spoken of drowning herself.

After this image presented itself to me, it became very clear that I was in over my head. As the old cliché goes, "A picture is worth a thousand words." I was able to acknowledge and take responsibility for the seriousness and fragility of my own position and let go of my futile attempts to Rescue this individual, attempts that may even have been reinforcing her suicidal behavior.

Such spontaneous occurrence of imagery is very powerful. I believe that we can supplement this seemingly automatic process by asking ourselves for information and by being receptive to the answer when it occurs, whether in the form of a picture, words, or a dream.

The idea of using imagery to heal ourselves was originated by Dr. Carl Simonton, Stephanie Mathews-Simonton, and James Creighton in their book *Getting Well Again*. These three cancer specialists found that people can contribute to their own healing by the thoughts and images they themselves generate. Imagining, for example, great white sharks eating and destroying cancer cells was one of the exercises found to be useful with cancer patients considered to have severely progressed diseases. Other images presented by the Intrinsic Self are also effective.

In his book *Healing Yourself*, Dr. Martin Rossman describes the use of imagery to get in touch with an Inner Healer (similar to our Guide). This Healer, visualized in pictorial form sometimes as a wise person and sometimes as an animal, can speak to us from the wisdom of our Real Self. We all have the capacity to create this inner resource. If you doubt this, just remember the creativity you express in each of the dreams you compose on each and every night, or in your Scare Talk. Bringing a healing image of an inner healer, or Guide, into your current consciousness is fully possible. You need only to ask for this respectfully and keep your Judge's contempt and cynicism at bay.

Speaking of the Judge, it is interesting to note that images can also be useful in helping you let go of your Judge. I have developed at least three such images that I would like to share with you. These images are based on the information provided in chapter 14, about how negative self-talk actually develops.

The first image to visualize is the puppet that I use in my "Talking to Yourself" workshops to symbolize the Judge. It is the type of puppet that fits over my hand. By moving my fingers, I can cause its mouth to move. The puppet is a soft, cuddly SHARK. It demonstrates aptly the mixed qualities of the Judge, the harm that originates from intended protection. Again, I have found that the Judge is usually more willing to retire when its positive intentions are recognized and acknowledged.

A second image of the Judge is that of the three-stage rocket used in much of the early space program. To get the rocket launched, a huge first stage was necessary in order to lift the payload out of the earth's gravitational field. This accomplished, it was necessary for this first stage to disengage and fall back to earth, allowing the rocket to go farther into space. Without this letting go, the rocket would have been pulled back to earth, constrained by a now unwieldy structure.

Similarly, many of us need our Driver- or Stopper-oriented Judges to survive a toxic early environment; and we need these Judges to remove ourselves from that environment. Yet even when we reach the point where further pushing destroys the good life that we have worked so hard to achieve, when we now have a cushion so that some enjoyment, relaxation, and fun can be ours, the Judge continues to push and prod, the constant cajoler. Many times we remain emotionally in our early environment even though we have physically escaped from it.

A final image is found in a parable from the *Teaching of Buddha*. This parable is about a man who is walking alongside a river. The ground he walks on is difficult, covered with rocks, brush, and trees. He notes that the opposite riverbank appears much easier, and decides to build a raft and cross to the other side. Indeed, he finds this bank to be flat and without the obstacles he had left behind. Feeling relieved, he picks up the wooden raft, which he made to cross the river, hoists it over his back, and proceeds on his journey. The question is asked, "Is this a wise man?"

Symptoms

Symptoms often give us the message that we have failed to listen to our feelings, images, and dreams. Our Judgmental Self has been unwilling to yield the conductor's baton and our Intrinsic Self has been forced, as in the famous line from *The*

Godfather, to give us an offer we can't refuse — can't refuse to listen to, that is.

One of my clients, whom I'll call Bill, was given such a message when he collapsed with back pain. Bill was literally flat on his back, unable to meet what had become a murderous schedule of obligations. Since these were all "good things" he wanted to do and felt he should do, Bill, the "hero" of his family, had not even considered the idea that he had personal, physical, and psychological limitations. He felt pride in the level of his work output and corresponding shame around the idea that he needed to do less.

At first, Bill was furious at his back. "It's not supposed to do that," he complained. Bill thought of his body as a machine and got very angry at the idea that his body had any physical needs or requirements. People with such attitudes are usually mimicking the toxic messages from their early life when parents, in a hurry and under stress, got mad at them for taking too long in the bathroom or for getting sick and missing school.

Given that his back was unwilling to get well just because his Judge commanded it, Bill found himself, for the first time in his life, having to sit still. Unable to run from himself through work and physical activity, he began to get acquainted with himself. Feelings he had never experienced began to emerge as Bill created for himself a second chance of sorts to get his life under control. The benefit of his back pain was that Bill began to relax and experience valuable and pleasurable parts of himself that he had never known. He also began to take seriously the small signals of overstress that precede a major back-related emergency. He began to set limits with others and to give himself time and space. And unexpectedly, by being more selective and making room for his creativity, Bill became even more successful. The Judgmental position, our notions to the contrary, often prevents us from high achievement. It almost certainly prevents us from achieving happiness.

In writing this chapter, I began to think of my grandmother, a woman whom I knew only while she was confined to a wheelchair. She had been severely crippled by rheumatoid arthritis, an autoimmune disorder. She developed this disease at a time of severe personal stress and crisis in her life when my grandfather, to whom she'd been married for seventeen years, decided to become a Baptist minister. His decision would have catapulted her into the demands and expectations of a minister's wife. It was something that she did not want. I recently wrote a poem about her experience and tied it to my own transition at age 34, when I separated from my first husband. I'd like to share it with you as a note on symptoms and on the transmission of Judgmental rules from generation to generation. I also wish to look at the changing of these inner commands.

Prisons

At 34, she sealed her joints
Of knee and arm and hip and leg.
In protest, silent and forlorn,
She hammered shut the opened keg

Of love that until then had flowed
And rapture turned to rage.
She silenced all and shut all down
The option of that Age.

In 1920, Southern time,
The choices were but few.
He chose to be a man of God,
So what was left for you?

But prisons are inside you
Not made of wood or stone.
You locked your joints to keep you there.
You feared too far to roam.

Your love, he chose to follow God,
A Minister to be.

But that for you was such a trap;
Was such a travesty.

A minister's wife, a servant's lot,
A role not to endure
To walk within those judgments
A whited sepulcher.

Not you who loved
Your pretty legs, your independent mind.
You would not be their prisoner,
The good and modest wife.

But prisons are inside you
Not made of wood or stone.
You locked your joints to free yourself
But then, you could not roam.

And I, at 34, did go.
Was I doing it for you?
For forty years you were locked up,
And he imprisoned too.

In 1980, Western time
The choices were a few.
I left instead of squelch myself,
I left without a clue.

I bought myself a horse of red,
But kept him in his stall.
My horse, he longs to ride away
To gallop away from all.

But prisons are inside you
Not made of wood or stone.
And I, I am just like you.
And I, I cannot roam.

And now I look around about
The new prison I have made.
Its bars are made of pity.
Its jailers dig my grave.

And I am still just like you,
In a cage made of rules,
The rules that you handed down,
The rules that crippled you.

The rules that told you not to speak
Not to say "I don't,"
The rules that let you chain yourself
Instead of say, "I won't!"

For prisons are inside you
Not inside of wood or stone
And you and I may ride away,
If we slay the rules, alone.

The rules that are handed down . . .

John Bradshaw has said that what we don't hand back to our parents, we hand down to our children. But in handing back the judgmental rules, we can give ourselves new Permissions, and these too we can pass on to our children.

The Cost of Not Listening

In his excellent book *Anatomy of an Illness,* to which I have alluded before, Norman Cousins devotes an entire chapter to the topic "Pain is not the Ultimate Enemy," a chapter in which he describes the preoccupation of the American public with pain and their misunderstanding of what pain represents. As Cousins states, "The most ignored fact of all about pain is that the best way to eliminate it is to eliminate the abuse. Instead, many people reach almost instinctively for the painkillers — aspirins, barbiturates, codeines, tranquilizers, sleeping pills, and dozens of other analgesics or desensitizing drugs."

Cousins goes on to describe the work of Dr. Paul Brand with the dread disease of leprosy. Dr. Brand discovered that the principal effect of leprosy on tissue was that it killed the nerve endings, and that many of the most debilitating characteristics of leprosy (missing fingers and toes, blindness) were not specific manifestations of the disease process itself, but were instead by-products resulting from the loss of pain receptors. This compelling example of a disease that has as its main symptoms the loss of the ability to experience pain was used by Cousins to reinforce his thesis that pain is not the enemy. In summarizing the work of Paul Brand, Cousins comments, "He is a doctor who, if he could, would move heaven and earth just to return the gift of pain to people who do not have it. For pain is both the warning system and the protective mechanism that enables an individual to defend the integrity of his body. Its signals may not always be readily intelligible but at least they are there. And the individual can mobilize his response."

When I read this account, I was so impressed that the next few weeks afterward I shared it with many of my clients. If the term *anger* or *sadness* were to be substituted for the word *pain*, I believe that the message would still hold true. Feelings are the means by which the Intrinsic Self informs us that we need to alter our current state. Symptoms tell us that the messages of the Imposed Self are too severe or that the external environment in which we find ourselves is toxic and needs changing. If we ignore these messages and do not permit their awareness, we too are like the person with leprosy. Important receptors have been silenced, and we are vulnerable to assault.

Just as patients with leprosy will often injure themselves physically because no pain receptors in their hands signal "too much," so those people who do not listen to and honor feelings of fatigue or sadness or depression injure themselves. The philosophy many carry was summed up by one person's comment, "Well, if I *can* do it, then why not?" The "why not" relates to the cost.

In contrast, if you do begin to listen to your Intrinsic Self, you may find that your real interests have very little to do with your present occupation, or that your current lifestyle does not permit you to spend time doing what you most enjoy. You may find that your relationship with your friends is based on little more than a mutual Rescue Process. You may even discover that your love relationship has little connection to your Real Self.

To open up to this kind of discovery, you must be aware of just how costly it is to deny your Intrinsic Self. For some people, letting go of their imposed paths becomes a question of physical or psychological survival. I have worked with several people for whom the choice was either developing a new way of protecting and nurturing themselves or complete collapse. As one of my clients affirmed, "I had the choice of getting myself an office/retreat in a building at $500 a month or finding myself in a hospital at $2,000 a day." Pushed back against the judgmental wall, other people have broken physically, their life-threatening illnesses (cancer, diabetes, coronary heart disease) telling them to change or die. Not all of us have to get to such a point before we begin to listen to our feelings, but many of us do. As Shirley Luthman notes in *Collection 1979*, "Some people's rigid structures are so powerful that only the threat of physical death would shake them."

Taking the Leap

As you recognize the importance of taking the leap from your judgmental structure to trusting and honoring your own Intrinsic messages, you may initially scare yourself as you look across the chasm to your familiar position. Linda, for example, trusted herself enough to leave a financially secure and socially prestigious marriage because she was not happy. From the very beginning of her divorce, she experienced a newfound sense of comfort and well-being. Yet even with this strong inner confirmation of her decision, she continued to doubt her actions on a moment-to-moment basis.

Linda had made a major step toward leaving her former judgmental restrictions, yet still she frightened herself with her own Self 2 warnings, "You feel good now, but just wait.

You'll be sorry." As Linda discussed her misgivings with one class, she recognized that her warnings to herself were quite similar to those given her by her mother. I suggested to Linda that she consider these warnings to be remnants of her old structure that she now has a choice about listening to or not.

We have referred to these warnings as the Second Line of Defense. Remember that when the entire judgmental structure begins to crack, these remnants will confront you in an intensified form. Your anxiety may actually mount, and if you are not careful, you will scare yourself back into the old framework. Yet if you view these Self 2 messages for what they are — debris from the old structure — you will see, perhaps for the first time, portrayed in front of your eyes, all of the catastrophes and judgments that have prevented you from moving until now. At this point, you have a *clear* choice between listening again to these Self 2 prophecies or deliberately ignoring them.

The Benefits of Listening

Fortunately, interspersed between these periods of fear and doubt will also be the sensation of something totally new — the experience of comfort and well-being emerging from your own insides. This experience provides the necessary and sufficient evidence that you are operating in conjunction with your own Intrinsic Self. As Carolyn told me, "Something new has happened. The other day I found myself smiling, just because I felt so good. Not smiling at anyone, not smiling for any particular reason, but smiling because I like me and I like what I'm doing. I'd never done that before — ever."

Along with feelings of well-being, an increase in energy will occur when you follow your Self 1 signals. When Howard came into my office, he began describing new ideas about what he wanted to do with his life, as if he were dealing a deck of cards in front of us both. "Can you believe how many ideas I had this week?" he exclaimed. "And they just came to me. And I've had so much energy," he continued, "that it's almost like I'm floating. There's no longer any gravity." Howard's energy is reflecting his new decision to stop punishing and depressing himself. Having repudiated his old "That won't work" philosophy, his Intrinsic Self has rewarded him with an abundance of ideas.

In the same way, following your Intrinsic Self will result in lowered stress. By refusing to drive or push beyond your own natural pace, you gear the level of stress in your life to your capability level. Although, as Hans Selye has stated, the complete absence of stress, like the absence of temperature, is not to be desired, you can overstress yourself. By acting according to the dictates of your Imposed Self and ignoring your Self 1 signals, you put yourself emotionally and physically in great jeopardy. By listening to yourself, you can stop this damage. You can become what cancer experts Carl Simonton and Stephanie Mathews-Simonton call "weller than well."

Accepting Others

As you begin to accept and honor your Intrinsic Self, you also tend to give other people this same degree of understanding and permission. You begin to allow them to experience their own emotions and to listen to their internal signals.

Nowhere is this kind of support more important than in dealing with children. Allowing children to walk along the symbolic sidewalk is most important. Forcing a child onto a tightrope creates inhibited or rebellious reactions. Yet without any limits or guidelines whatsoever, there is no protection for the developing child — no guide to support and affirm the child's intrinsic needs and talents.

Jamie was raised on the judgmental tightrope and although now an adult and a parent herself, she continues to react to her mother's Judge as she did when she was small. Half in jest, Jamie shared with me a prototype of her conversation with her mother.

MOTHER: How are you?

JAMIE: Fine.

MOTHER: What's new?

JAMIE: Nothing.

MOTHER: Where are you going?

JAMIE: Out.

I remarked to Jamie, "That's one way to keep her Judge out of commission," and she broke into peals of laughter. "I never quite thought of it like that, but you're right. There's a lot going on right now that I would like to share with my mother, but she would start picking things apart, and I'm not yet strong enough to deal with that, so I shut her out. Knowing my reactions to my own mother, I'm very careful not to respond judgmentally to my own kids. I want them to be there, even if I don't think they're doing everything exactly right."

Certainly, children need guidance, but any true guidance must honor and nurture the child's Intrinsic Self. In *A Private Battle*, Cornelius Ryan tells of his relationship with his son Geoff:

> Geoff wasn't always sullen and withdrawn. When he was four or five there was a constant happiness caught often by my camera, a joy of life and love of people. Did we stamp it out? Did I try too hard to make him a fisherman, a hunter, an athlete? Did Kathryn try too hard to make him a scholar? We wanted only the best for him but on *our* terms; it was always *our* view of what was best. When he tried and failed to manage a task we'd set, we'd put him over the jumps again. Is it any wonder we find him, now just past seventeen, sullen and antagonistic?

Again, it bears mentioning that the decision that a child's feelings do count and that it is important to create a structure in which the child is okay whether or not he/she conforms to parental expectations does not mean that no guidelines are in order. Without a Guide (which is learned, just as is the Judge, through interaction with others), a child can be defenseless against the pressures of peers and the demands of society.

"It would be nice," parents sometimes say, "to let our children take their time, but look at the competition. There isn't time for the luxury of finding oneself. I have to push or they might not get into a good college. This is going to determine the kid's life."

In *Profound Simplicity*, Will Schutz was faced with something of this dilemma when his son Caleb decided to drop out of high school. To his father's objections, Caleb challenged, "And you said people should follow their own energy. I have no energy for school. I hate to go to school. But I stay up until two in the morning working on this job I have. And I go bowling every night." Schutz realized that for all his intellectual acceptance of the benefits of following one's own energy, on the gut level he had difficulty with his son's decision. "My belief in the principles I championed extended from the top of my head down to about my throat," Schutz admitted.

Later, Schutz brought his readers up to date:

What became of Caleb? He dropped out of school, his business venture failed, and he started hanging out at bowling alleys. As a result, he became a premier bowler. Then he tired of the whole thing. On his own initiative, he began studying for the high school equivalency exam, passed it, and went to junior college a year and a half ahead of his high school class. He paid for part of his education from his winnings in bowling tournaments. He transferred to the University of California, Santa Cruz, graduated with honors, and was admitted to graduate school at UCLA.

Caleb's decision, which most certainly would be considered "wrong" by most people's Judge, worked out surprisingly well. And what if Caleb had not returned to college? Chances are that he would have been satisfied in his work or bowling venture, so where's the problem? Many young people have no commitment to college at age 18, and if they go at all, would do much better at a later date. Fortunately, society — that composite of individual opinion — has become more accepting of those who do not follow a rigid Hurry Up timetable.

Making the Commitment

After spending the entire winter going from one cold to another, and having all of my ski holidays disappear into a box of tissues, I made the decision that I did not have to kill myself through overwork. This decision was not made instantly, nor easily. Self 2 warnings like "You'll lose it all if you don't keep going" cropped up frequently. Moreover, my increased free time necessitated a new look at myself. My recognition that my body was telling me something through my constant colds, and that if I didn't listen, I would have to give myself a stronger message, led me to revise my schedule. Being self-employed, I have always had almost complete external freedom to adjust my activities. The fact that I was working more than any standard job required simply demonstrated the demands of my own Self 2 Judge.

Even when we are not free to change the actual external time structure of our positions, the level of stress can still be drastically reduced. Joyce, for example, told me that she no longer has headaches while working in her office. By turning off her incessant Be Perfect Drive, Joyce found that she was much more relaxed. Her first realization that perhaps she didn't have to Be Perfect came when she sent a letter to her sister in an envelope on which she had crossed out an error instead of rewriting the entire address again. When she cautiously commented on her mistake, her sister candidly admitted that she hadn't even noticed. "That's what convinced me," Joyce stressed, "that my perfection was not only too costly, but also unnecessary."

Only when damaging Self 2 messages have been diffused can the Intrinsic Self fully emerge. This emergence will occur automatically and naturally when there is no oppressive weight from the Self 2 Judge bearing down—constantly demanding that we strive for status, for money, for success or fame or even love.

Several weeks ago, I moved one of my plants, which had grown to near ceiling height, to a new area. Although it had not actually been touching the ceiling, it had stopped growing. Within a couple of days, this plant sent out a profusion of new shoots that were actually twice as large as those that had come before. As human organisms we are not all that different. Given room to move beyond the oppressive judgmental structure, we too send out entirely new projections. We too evidence an abundance of new energy, new ideas, and new growth.

Little wonder that many of the people I work with take drastic steps to change their living situations—move to new places, redecorate, find new working hours, new professions, new partners, new friends. The change occurring outside simply reflects an increased awareness of the inner voice. With supportive self-talk, change becomes simple, untraumatic, and constant. Appreciating and accepting the phenomenal person you are allows for a release of power, creativity, energy, and aliveness that is simply not possible when your Self 2 squashes and rallies against Self 1. Change inside, and you will create a brand new world.

For any reader who wants further information, I continue to consult and provide workshops on Talking to Yourself and other topics. Anyone desiring to contact me can write to my office at 150 Shoreline Highway, Building A, Suite 7, Mill Valley, California 94941.

Bibliography

Apfelbaum, Bernard, Martin Williams, and Susan Greene. *Expanding the Boundaries of Sex Therapy.* Berkeley, CA: Berkeley Sex Therapy Group, 1979.

Bach, George, and Peter Wyden. *The Intimate Enemy.* New York: Morrow, 1969.

Barbach, Lonnie Garfield. *For Yourself: The Fulfillment of Female Sexuality.* New York: Signet, 1976.

Beck, Aaron, John Rush, Brian Shaw, and Gary Emery. *Cognitive Therapy of Depression.* New York: The Guilford Press, 1979.

Bem, Sandra. "Androgyny vs. The Tight Little Lives of Fluffy Women and Chesty Men." *Psychology Today,* September 1975, pp. 58–62.

Berne, Eric. *What Do You Say After You Say Hello?* New York: Grove Press, 1972.

Branden, Nathaniel. *The Disowned Self.* New York: Bantam, 1973.

Bradshaw, John. *Healing the Shame that Binds You.* Deerfield Beach, FL: Health Communications, 1988.

Bukkyo Dendo Kyokai. *The Teaching of Buddha.* Tokyo: Toppan Printing, 1987.

Butler, Pamela E. *Self-Assertion for Women,* revised ed. San Francisco: HarperCollins, 1992.

Cousins, Norman. *Anatomy of an Illness.* New York: Norton, 1979.

_____. *Head First.* New York: E. P. Dutton, 1989.

Cummings, Nicholas. "Turning Bread into Stones." *American Psychologist,* December 1979, pp. 1119–29.

Donahue, Phil & Company. *Donahue: My Own Story.* New York: Simon & Schuster, 1979.

Ellis, Albert. *Reason and Emotion in Psychotherapy.* New York: Lyle Stuart, 1976.

Fasteau, M. *The Male Machine.* New York: McGraw-Hill, 1974.

Friedman, Meyer, and Ray Rosenman. *Type A Behavior and Your Heart.* New York: Fawcett Crest, 1974.

Fritz, Sara. "New Breed of Workers." *U.S. News & World Report,* September 3, 1979, pp. 35–38.

Gallwey, W. Timothy. *The Inner Game of Tennis.* New York: Random House, 1974.

Goldberg, Herb. *The Hazards of Being Male.* New York: Signet, 1977.

Gordon, Thomas. *Parent Effectiveness Training.* New York: Peter H. Wyden, Inc., 1970.

Goulding, Mary, and Bob Goulding. *Changing Lives Through Redecision Therapy.* New York: Brunner/Mazel, 1979.

Hawthorne, Nathaniel. "The Birthmark." In *Nathaniel Hawthorne's Short Stories.* New York: Knopf, 1946.

Hite, Shere. *The Hite Report.* New York: Dell Publishing Company, 1977.

Hokanson, J., and R. Edelman. "Effects of Three Social Responses on Vascular Processes." *Journal of Personality and Social Psychology* 3 (1966): 442–47.

Horney, Karen. *Neurosis and Human Growth.* New York: Norton, 1950.

Johnson, Wendell. *People in Quandaries.* New York: Harper & Row, 1946.

Kahler, Taibi. "Drivers: The Key to the Process of Scripts." *Transactional Analysis Journal* 5, no. 3 (July, 1975): 280–84.

Kamin, Ira. "Dropping the Smile for Awhile." *California Living Magazine, San Francisco Examiner and Chronicle,* January 21, 1979, pp. 6–8.

Karpman, Steven. "Fairy Tale and Script Drama Analysis," *Transactional Analysis Bulletin* 26 (April 1968): 39–43.

Keller, Suzanne. "The Female Role: Constants and Change." In *Women in Therapy,* ed. V. Franks and V. Burtle, pp. 411–34. New York: Brunner/Mazel, 1974.

Kearns, Doris. *Lyndon Johnson and the American Dream.* New York: Harper & Row, 1976.

Kinsey, A. C. et al. *Sexual Behavior in the Human Male.* Philadelphia: W. B. Saunders, 1948.

Korzybski, Alfred. *Science and Sanity,* 2d ed. Lancaster: Science Press, 1941.

Laxer, Robert M. "Relation of Real Self-Rating to Mood and Blame and Their Interaction in Depression." *Journal of Consulting Psychology* 28 (1964): 538–46.

Lazarus, Richard S. "Positive Denial: The Case for Not Facing Reality." *Psychology Today* 13, no. 6 (November 1979): 44.

Lear, Martha Weinman. *Heart Sounds.* New York: Simon & Schuster, 1980.

LeShan, Eda. "I'll Never Be Fat Again." *Woman's Day,* July 17, 1979, p. 101.

Luthman, Shirley. *Collection 1979.* San Rafael, CA: Mehetabel & Company, 1980.

Mahoney, M., and C. Thorensen. *Self-Control: Power to the Person.* Monterey, CA: Brooks/Cole, 1974.

Maslach, Christina. "Burned-Out." *Human Behavior* (September 1976): 16–22.

Masters, William, and Virginia Johnson. *Human Sexual Inadequacy.* Boston: Little, Brown, 1970.

McKuen, Rod. "I'm Strong But I Like Roses," from *Each of Us Alone.* Burbank, CA: Warner Brothers/Seven Arts Records.

Meichenbaum, Donald. *Cognitive-Behavior Modification.* New York: Plenum Press, 1977.

Melvin, Kenneth B., F. Thomas Cloar, and Lucinda S. Massingill. "Imprinting of Bob White Quail to a Hawk." *Psychological Record* 17 (1967): 235–38.

Milgram, Stanley. *Obedience to Authority.* New York: Harper & Row, 1975.

Miller, Alice. *For Your Own Good.* New York: Farrar, Straus & Giroux, 1983.

————. *Thou Shalt Not Be Aware.* New York: Farrar, Straus & Giroux, 1984.

O'Neil, Nena, and George O'Neil. *Open Marriage.* New York: Avon, 1972.

Perls, Fritz. *Gestalt Therapy Verbatim*. Lafayette, CA: Real People Press, 1969.

Pirsig, Robert M. *Zen and the Art of Motorcycle Maintenance*. New York: Bantam, 1979.

Powelson, Harvey. Personal communication.

Powys, Llewelyn. "Letter to Warner Taylor." In *The Creative Process*, ed. Brewster Ghiselin. New York: Mentor Books, 1955.

Rossman, Martin. *Healing Yourself*. New York: Pocket Books, 1989.

Rubin, Lillian. *Women of a Certain Age*. New York: Harper & Row, 1979.

Ryan, Cornelius, and Kathryn Morgan Ryan. *A Private Battle*. New York: Fawcett Popular Library, 1979.

Schutz, Will. *Profound Simplicity*. New York: Bantam, 1979.

Selye, Hans. *The Stress of Life*. Revised Edition. New York: McGraw-Hill, 1978.

Simonton, O. Carl, Stephanie Mathews-Simonton, and James Creighton. *Getting Well Again*. New York: Bantam, 1980.

Steinem, Gloria. "Erotica and Pornography: A Clear and Present Difference." *Ms. Magazine*, November 1979, p. 53.

Speer, Albert. *Inside the Third Reich*. New York: Avon, 1970.

Teale, Edwin Way. *The Wilderness World of John Muir*. Boston: Houghton Mifflin, 1954.

Tennov, Dorothy. *Super Self: A Woman's Guide to Self-Management*. New York: Jove Publications, 1977.

Weinberg, Harry. *Levels of Knowing and Existence*. New York: Harper & Row, 1976.

Woolf, Virginia. *Professions for Women*. Quoted in Tillie Olsen, *Silences*. New York: Delacorte Press, 1978.

"Your Pursuit of Happiness," *Psychology Today* (August 1976): 31.

Zilbergeld, Bernie. *Male Sexuality*. New York: Bantam, 1978.

Index

9/14/93